This book examines the relationship between the writings of Henry James and the historical formation of mass culture. Throughout his career, James was concerned with such characteristically modern cultural forms as advertising, biography and the New Journalism, forms which together constituted the 'devouring publicity' of modern life. Richard Salmon's study situates James's fiction and criticism within the context of the contemporary debates surrounding these rival discursive practices. He explores both the nature of James's contribution to the critique of mass culture and the extent of his immersion within it. James's persistent and ambivalent negotiation of the boundaries between private and public experience ranged from a defence of the artist's right to privacy, to his own counter-practice of publicity. By drawing upon contemporary critical theory, Salmon offers a reassessment of the politics of James's cultural criticism.

HENRY JAMES AND THE CULTURE OF PUBLICITY

HENRY JAMES AND THE CULTURE OF PUBLICITY

RICHARD SALMON

University of Leeds

PUBLISHED BY THE PRESS SYNDICATE OF THE UNIVERSITY OF CAMBRIDGE
The Pitt Building, Trumpington Street, Cambridge CB2 1RP, United Kingdom

CAMBRIDGE UNIVERSITY PRESS
The Edinburgh Building, Cambridge CB2 2RU, United Kingdom
40 West 20th Street, New York, NY 10011–4211, USA
10 Stamford Road, Oakleigh, Melbourne 3166, Australia

First published 1997

Printed in the United Kingdom at the University Press, Cambridge

Typeset in Baskerville no. 1 11/12½

A catalogue record for this book is available from the British Library

Library of Congress cataloguing in publication data

Salmon, Richard, 1965–
Henry James and the culture of publicity / Richard Salmon.
p. cm.
Includes bibliographical references and index.
ISBN 0 521 56249 x hardback
1. James, Henry, 1843–1916 – Political and social views.
2. Literature and society – United States – History – 19th century.
3. Literature and society – United States – History – 20th century.
4. Authorship – Social aspects – United States – History.
5. Civilization, Modern – Historiography. 6. Mass media – United States – History. 7. Publicity – United States – History.
8. Criticism – United States – History. I. Title.
PS2127.P6S25 1997
813′ 52–dc21 96–51157
CIP

ISBN 0 521 56249 x hardback

CE

Contents

Abbreviations

The following abbreviations refer to works by Henry James cited parenthetically in the text. Full references to these editions are also located in the bibliography.

A	*The Ambassadors*
AS	*The American Scene*
B	*The Bostonians*
CT	*The Complete Tales of Henry James*
L	*Henry James Letters*
LC I	*Literary Criticism* vol. I: *Essays on Literature, American Writers, English Writers*
LC II	*Literary Criticism* vol. II: *French Writers, Other European Writers, the Prefaces to the New York Edition*
NB	*The Notebooks of Henry James*
R	*The Reverberator*
TM	*The Tragic Muse*

Introduction

In an important sense, all literary texts, like all acts of criticism, are, by definition, public events. The very fact that we invariably speak of the relationship between a writer and his or her 'public' implies an understanding of the function of literary discourse which is irreducible to our simultaneous recognition of the particularity of such publics. If publics are, in fact, necessarily finite entities, the possibility of an infinite elasticity is always inscribed within the notion of 'public' circulation.[1] Since the eighteenth century, at any rate, the status of the literary text (like that of other forms of print culture) has become contingent upon its function as a commodity, capable of being disseminated throughout the various institutional and informal media of critical debate which together constitute what Jürgen Habermas has termed a 'literary public sphere'. This is true even – and perhaps especially – of those generic forms which most appear to resist or refuse the transitivity of public communication. Autobiographies or letters, for instance, are capable of attaining recognition as 'literature' only if their resistance to publicity is signalled publicly. By negotiating a passage between private and public domains, the ostensibly 'private' text draws attention to the very boundaries from which its public function emerges.[2]

From around the end of the nineteenth century, however, this Enlightenment conception of the normative function of public discourse has also co-existed with a very different understanding of the term 'publicity'. In this other, and recognizably modern, sense of the word, publicity has often been thought to mark a dissolution of the existing boundaries between private and public space, rather than simply negotiating a passage between them. Instead of occupying one side of an opposition which it otherwise preserves, modern publicity may be said to reconfigure the geography of cultural space in its entirety. In this sense, publicity may also be viewed as a symptomatic phenomenon of modern culture: one which is linked inextricably to the historical formation of mass culture and the mass media. While this historical process need not be taken to represent a catastrophic fall of 'public culture', as some critics have alleged,[3] it does, nevertheless, mark a significant shift in the public life of authors and texts. The modern writer, no less than the modern text, enters into a sphere of public circulation, and the condition of publicity alters the constitutive forms and functions of literary communication. In the process, this condition has helped to shape our own distinctively modern cultural landscape.

In the following study, my aim is to examine this cultural landscape at the turbulent moment of its formation, and to do so through a reading of the work of Henry James. Throughout his career, I argue, James was concerned with the modern phenomenon of 'publicity'. From his early book reviews of the 1860s and 1870s to his fiction and cultural criticism of the early twentieth century, references to this term recur with a remarkable frequency. The word itself appears to have borne a peculiarly intense and evocative meaning for James: although it is used to designate a wide range of cultural forms, practices and assumptions, it also seems to accrue a meaning that is singular and overbearing. With an alarming regularity, it often seems, James found the same phenomenon in very different, and sometimes unlikely, places. At the risk of schematizing such diversity of reference, however, it is possible to distinguish between three, overlapping moments in James's engagement with this phenomenon. From his earliest writings onwards, James revealed an acute concern with the cultural space of authorship, and its movement across a shifting boundary between private and public spheres. His reviews of such figures as Hawthorne, Flaubert and George Sand are full of rebukes directed towards the 'invasion of privacy' practised by biographers, journalists and the publishers of authors' private manuscripts, and these concerns were also translated into numerous, admonitory stories such as 'The Aspern Papers', 'Sir Dominick Ferrand', and 'The Real Right Thing'. With some notable exceptions, these commentaries are often sternly didactic, and might appear to represent James's cultural criticism in its most 'Victorian' guise.

During the 1880s, however, James also became aware of more organized and pervasive forms of publicity. In such novels as *The Bostonians* and *The Reverberator*, James engaged directly with the historical formation and subsequent expansion of the mass media which took place during the last two decades of the nineteenth century, and thus fulfilled the naturalistic agenda of 'sketch[ing] one's age' which he outlined in a notebook entry recorded in 1887 (*NB* 82). It was during this period, in fact, that James's critique of the 'invasion, the impudence and shamelessness, of the newspaper and the interviewer, the *devouring* publicity of life' was most explicitly and intentionally elaborated (*NB* 82). The principle of publicity, exemplified by such cultural forms as advertising and the New Journalism, was installed at the centre of modern cultural experience. In the following decade, James's career bifurcates into the apparently antithetical pursuits of popular theatrical success and an elite readership for his tales of the 'literary life'. Yet in both ventures, he was forced to confront the publicity of modern culture in equally explicit ways. The status of the 'artist' in an increasingly commodified literary culture mirrors James's personal experience of the public stage, and augments his concern with the attenuation of authorial privacy.

By the time of the so-called 'major phase', however, this programmatic engagement with publicity appears to have diminished. Conventionally, it has been argued that James's later fiction marks a retreat into the private, aesthetic world which he had so often defended in the past, and that the manifestly public concerns of his earlier, realist novels were, accordingly, abandoned.[4] In itself, this assertion is something of an oxymoron, since, for James, there is no more public concern than his concern with 'privacy'. Moreover, as a growing number of critics have begun to suggest, James's apparent withdrawal may only conceal, or indeed constitute, a deeper and more immanent form of engagement.[5] In his later fiction, I will argue, James devised new strategies of representation in order to confront an increasingly diffuse and anonymous mass media, which threatened to render his earlier censure of biographers and journalists anachronistic. In *The Ambassadors*, for instance, his treatment of the 'art of advertisement' could scarcely be described as thematic, as it is in *The Bostonians*, but the 'revelation' of its presence resonates throughout the text (*A* 341). Here, the practice of publicity is no longer confined to a readily identifiable agency, but instead saturates both the novel's representation of urban spectacle and its own formal modes of construction. If, in some ways, *The American Scene* marks a return to a more explicit mode of cultural analysis, it also continues this 'conception of publicity *as* the vital medium' of modern social exchange (*AS* 75). James's vision of the American 'hotel-spirit' instantiates publicity as a cultural condition, or form of consciousness, rather than as a purely external or mechanical force (*AS* 73).

This preliminary sketch of James's unfolding response to the modern phenomenon of publicity will give some indication of the scope of the following enquiry. While this study is both generally and specifically historical in approach, however, it does not undertake to pursue a strictly chronological reading of James's career. What is offered, rather, is a series of overlapping historical narratives which correspond, in large measure, to the narratives which James himself inscribed both within and between many of his texts. In chapters 1 and 2, for example, I begin by exploring the politics of James's response to changing conceptions of the literary public sphere and of 'the public' itself; in chapters 3 and 4, I examine the conflict between James's defence of the value of (authorial) privacy and the emergence of 'investigative' discourse in the fields of biography and journalism; and, finally, in chapter 5, I consider the development of James's later style of cultural criticism in relation to the spectacular form of modern culture. Each of these chapters represents an attempt to relocate James's writings within cultural and discursive contexts which have, to varying degrees, been neglected. While James himself is central to this enquiry, it has also been my aim to situate his texts within a much wider network of contemporaneous cultural debate than is commonly the practice. It is only by recognizing the extent of James's immersion within these debates that it becomes possible to understand the complexity of his own particular critical stance.

This, of course, is by no means an attempt to suggest that all critics have hitherto avoided the task of reading James historically. On the contrary, over the course of the past decade or so, studies by Marcia Jacobson, Anne T. Margolis and Michael Anesko have all attempted to situate James's fictional practice within the context of an expanding literary market, and have thus challenged the received myth of his self-imposed artistic isolation.[6] As a result, our understanding of James's antipathy towards the 'commercialization' of late-nineteenth-century culture has been tempered by a recognition of his own strategic exploitation of the changing relations between authors, publishers and readers. Yet the fact that James inevitably participated in the culture which he so persistently rebuked does not necessarily mean that the value of his protest is thereby diminished. One of the assumptions behind this recent body of criticism is that James's rhetorical opposition to the market simply conceals the truth of his own accommodation to it. Where this study differs, however, is in its attempt to preserve the critical character of James's response to the formation of mass culture. By entirely collapsing James's distance from the mass market, we run the risk of effacing the very sign by which the historicity of his texts may be recognized. James's cultivated aloofness from the 'vulgarities' of the literary market-place is in itself testimony to the cultural schism which, as many critics have shown, took place towards the end of the nineteenth century. As Fredric Jameson has argued, the formation of a separate entity known as 'mass culture' belongs to a wider historical process in which, simultaneously, the category of 'high culture' was generated as its mutually defining other.[7] In order to grasp the truth of this cultural schism it is necessary not only to recognize the complicity of its polarities, but also, as Theodor Adorno often insisted, their antinomy.[8] By fulfilling this dual imperative, it becomes possible to preserve both James's antagonistic relationship to mass culture and his accommodation to it. In other words, James's (apparent) distance from the arena of mass culture becomes the sign which allows us to recognize his proximity to it.

This critical strategy is, in fact, closer to the approach of a somewhat different body of recent Jamesian criticism, one which has been concerned, primarily, with examining the effects of 'commodity culture' on James's fiction. In his important essay 'The Consuming Vision of Henry James', Jean-Christophe Agnew, for example, has argued that James's 'celebrated posture of detachment . . . may have had as much to do, in the end, with the emotional and intellectual proximity he once felt to a burgeoning mass-market society as with the distance he eventually adopted'. James's withdrawal from this society coincided with an internalization of the visual and cognitive codes of consumption, which is manifested in the characteristic form of his fiction. At the same time, Agnew also recognizes James's powerful critique of the acquisitive ideology of consumerism: a critique which gains value precisely because it comes 'from within rather than from without' its object. For the purposes of this study, however, James's critique of commodity culture is not entirely equivalent to his response to the phenomenon of publicity. In Agnew's definition, James's apprehension of the 'publicity' of modern culture refers generally 'to the values and instrumentalities of a market society: the traffic in commodities, the habit of display, the inclination to theatricality, the worship of novelty and quantity'.[9] This definition aptly identifies the pervasive and informal practices of cultural representation which characterize what Guy Debord, commenting upon their later twentieth-century development, termed a 'society of the spectacle'.[10] Yet it also overlooks more formal or institutionalized media of publicity, such as the press, with which James was equally concerned. In the case of journalism, the practice of publicity must be understood not simply as a 'habit of display' or as an object of consumption, but also as its discursive ethos – as the very rationale of its social function. Likewise, James's abiding interest in the status of the writer dramatizes the conflict between publicity in its modern forms and a public sphere which is dependent upon the simultaneous preservation of authorial privacy. The point of these distinctions is to suggest that while James may certainly be read as one of the earliest and most prescient analysts of commodity culture, his analysis is also rooted within an existing lineage of cultural and political thought, from which the term 'publicity' emerges as a peculiarly contested site. In order to understand James's concern with publicity, it is important to bear in mind the cultural shift which this term was undergoing during the course of his career.

The significance of this cultural shift has, indeed, been a subject of recent debate in the field of social theory, much of it deriving from the work of Jürgen Habermas.[11] In *The Structural Transformation of the Public Sphere*, first published in 1962, Habermas charts the formation and subsequent erosion of a bourgeois conception of publicity which formed one of the central pillars of Enlightenment thought. The 'bourgeois public sphere', in this account, emerged as a site of opposition to the absolutist power of the monarchy during the seventeenth and eighteenth centuries. In order to counter the coercive exercise of public authority, alternative channels of public discourse were forged between private individuals. For Habermas, it is precisely this separation between private and public interests within the bourgeois public sphere which allowed it to assume a genuinely critical function *vis-à-vis* the public authority of the state. If, on the one hand, the autonomy of the (male) individual was grounded within an economy of private commodity exchange, on the other hand, the sphere of public debate suspended, at least in principle, the private interests of the individuals from which it was composed. Thus, the public interest was not simply defined by the quantitative aggregation of its allied or competing private interests; rather, its legitimacy rested upon a normative conception of the 'disinterested' character of public debate. Indeed, the very function of the bourgeois public sphere was to bring to light the 'secrets of state': to expose the private interests concealed behind the mask of public authority.[12]

It was during the latter half of the nineteenth century, according to Habermas, that this ideal of 'critical publicity' was challenged by a form of 'manipulative publicity' which accompanied the rise of the mass media. For Habermas, this transformation was the result of a logic that was immanent to the social structure of the bourgeois public sphere. On the one hand, the expansion of the market economy undermined the separation of private and public interests, out of which it had previously emerged as an autonomous field of social activity. On the other hand, the extension of the political franchise served only to increase the visibility of conflicts which could no longer be accommodated into the supposition of a unitary public interest, even though this process was grounded upon the supposition itself. It is the attempt to negotiate these conflicts of private interest privately, Habermas argues, which leads to a 'refeudalization' of the modern public sphere: in both economic and political domains, the boundaries which had served to demarcate civil society from the state begin to collapse. Whereas, previously, publicity had functioned as a principle of critical public scrutiny, it is now returned to something which approaches its pre-capitalist function as an asymmetrical form of social display. In the modern sense of the word, publicity is represented before a public, rather than being constituted by it: while its political legitimacy remains dependent upon the value of democratic 'openness', its own practice systematically contradicts this value since it is the product of a prior arrangement. Habermas's argument is thus more complex than the common (and usually conservative) complaint that publicity simply erodes the privacy of the bourgeois subject. While this effect is not without importance, it is also accompanied by the recognition that 'manipulative publicity' is itself the product of a 'secret politics'.[13]

Habermas's account of the transformation of the bourgeois public sphere is, of course, open to question on a number of grounds, some of which I will have reason to explore during the course of this study. For our present purposes, however, what is useful about this account is the way in which it allows James's analysis of the 'pathologies' of modern culture to be brought into a sharper historical and conceptual focus. James's cultural criticism may, indeed, be read as a prolonged experiential articulation of the historical process which Habermas externally and retrospectively reconstructs. Like Habermas, for instance, James linked the '*devouring* publicity' of modern life to 'the extinction of all sense between public and private' wrought by the 'democratization of the world' (*NB* 82). In various guises, it was this dissolution of boundaries between public and private space which he found everywhere encoded within the landscape of modern culture. James's insistence upon the necessity of maintaining these boundaries would thus appear to place him within the tradition of liberal, Enlightenment thought which insisted upon a similar separation of powers between society and state. During the nineteenth century, it was this tradition which nurtured the response of a number of prominent cultural critics to the burgeoning presence of 'mass society'. Perhaps the earliest exemplar of this liberal critique of mass culture was the French political theorist Alexis de Tocqueville, whose observations of American culture and society in the 1830s and 1840s incorporated an equally anxious recognition of the ways in which the process of 'democratization' was leading to a reconfiguration of the normative boundaries between private and public spheres. In the two volumes of his *Democracy in America* (1835, 1840), de Tocqueville had argued that the prestige attached to 'common opinion' in American society eroded the autonomy of 'private judgement', and thus collapsed the necessary lines of demarcation between the authority of the state, on the one hand, and a critical civil society on the other.[14] The fact that de Tocqueville was able to discern this process as early as the 1830s is indicative of the prototypical status of American society within contemporary discussions of the wider formation of mass culture. Throughout the course of the century, European observers viewed the United States as the paradigmatic site of a democratically expanded public sphere, and, hence, of the phenomenon of publicity in its modern sense.

During his first visit to America in 1883, for example, another renowned cultural critic – Matthew Arnold – was struck by the same phenomenon as de Tocqueville. In a letter to his sister Frances,

Arnold recorded his immediate sense of the 'blaring publicity of this place', which went 'beyond all that I had any idea of'.[15] Interestingly, in his essay 'A Word about America' (1882), written before he had actually embarked upon this visit, Arnold cited James's novel *Roderick Hudson* as an authoritative source for his prejudicial view of the homogenous Philistinism of American society. James later returned the compliment by writing a supportive essay on Arnold which was published during the course of his American lecture tour.[16] Both Arnold and James, in other words, exhibited a concern with the effects of American mass culture that was not only mutual, but also mutually admiring. This degree of proximity might again lead us to conclude that James's cultural criticism is affiliated, at least in part, to the liberal tradition of which Arnold was undoubtedly the most influential, late-nineteenth-century exemplar. One of the most obvious differences between James and his European precursors, however, is that, unlike the latter, James was also affiliated to the object of this critique. As a displaced American, James was capable, on occasions, of adopting a haughty, Arnoldian style of censure, whilst, at the same time, being saturated in the cultural forms which Arnold merely surveyed. James was both more aware of the phenomenon of publicity, and more ambivalent towards it, than Arnold ever was.

By suggesting an affinity between James and Arnold, one must, nevertheless, confront the charge of cultural conservatism which is routinely levelled against both writers. From what I have already said about the importance of James's inheritance of a particular strand of Enlightenment political thought, it should be clear that the blanket label of 'conservatism' is, at best, misleading. In his extensive reading of *The Bostonians*, Alfred Habegger, for example, has construed James's opposition to (a certain form of) publicity, and his concomitant defence of the value of privacy, as offering support to the reactionary politics of Basil Ransom. For Habegger, modern publicity is unquestionably equivalent to the democratic 'openness' which it continues to espouse, whereas privacy invariably represents an insidious occlusion of power.[17] The problem with this argument, however, is that it depends upon the very criteria of James's critique in order to attack it. It is precisely these normative assumptions of equivalence which James himself makes in the act of recognizing their absence from modern forms of publicity. In *The Bostonians*, as elsewhere in James's fiction, 'publicity' can no longer simply be opposed to 'privacy', as if this opposition represented the kind of stable ideological conflict which it did for much of the eighteenth century. Moreover, when James does invoke this opposition, the meanings attached to each term are characteristically inverted: publicity, as Habermas suggests, is itself experienced as a form of occlusion (signified, for example, by the closed site of the Boston newspaper office) whereas privacy is transfigured into an impossible state of freedom. Even these significations, however, are by no means adequate to describe the complex reconfiguration of meaning and value within the terms 'public' and 'private', which I will be attempting to trace.

In saying this, my intention is not to deny the existence of a conservative element within much of James's social and political thought, but, rather, to suggest that the question of James's politics has too often been polarized between inadequate and imprecise alternatives. Thus, while James is often viewed (negatively) as 'conservative' in his social attitudes, he is also often viewed (sympathetically) as 'radical' in his textual or aesthetic strategies. With regard to the former, it is certainly true that James's response to the emergence of mass culture suffered from the same cultural anxieties which afflicted many of his contemporaries. The very notion of a 'mass' culture was one that preoccupied James throughout his career, as his numerous critical essays on the state of contemporary literature reveal. During the late nineteenth century this notion was linked not only to questions of class distinction, but also, as Andreas Huyssen has shown, to those of gender.[18] It is not coincidental, then, that narratives of 'democratization' should so often coalesce with narratives of 'feminization' in James's criticism and fiction; nor is it inappropriate that James's response to the increasing visibility of women within the public sphere should be identified as a central aspect of his wider relationship to the mass market.[19] In this context, however, what is notable about a novel such as *The Bostonians* is the fact that James so openly confronts the question of the political legitimacy of the bourgeois public sphere. Here, as elsewhere, James does not simply invoke an idealized antithesis to the communicative practices of the mass media, and nor does he chart a straightforward narrative of cultural decline. By tracing the emergence of rival forms of public discourse in the novel, James demonstrates an awareness of the specifically gendered character of those normative assumptions upon which his own critique of modern publicity rests; and, in this respect, he offers an interpretation of the historical transformation of the public sphere which is rather more complex and conflictual than Habermas's account tends to suggest.[20]

Thus, while I have argued that James may be affiliated to a tradition of liberal cultural criticism, extending back to de Tocqueville, I will also be suggesting that James persistently questioned, and even undermined, the conceptual basis of this critique. In a general sense, the liberal conception of the public sphere was predicated upon the possibility of exercising the faculty of 'disinterested' critical or aesthetic judgement which was first systematically formulated by Kant, and which Arnold advocated in more popular terms during the 1860s.[21] As Pierre Bourdieu has observed, this notion of 'disinterested' judgement is itself dependent upon the preservation of a certain distance from its object: a distance which allows the subject to avoid the 'vulgarity' of unmediated consumption, but which also, one might add, allows for the possibility of difference between the expression of private and public interests.[22] In a similar fashion, James's concern with an impending dissolution of the boundaries between private and public spheres could be seen to convey anxiety about the attendant loss of critical distance. Publicity, particularly in James's later fiction, is a phantasmagorical condition which disorientates the process of perception and undermines the stability of perspectives. Within this spectacular world, such binary oppositions as 'subject' and 'object', and 'surface' and 'depth' undergo the same collapse as the separation between 'private' and 'public' space. This, however, is not to suggest that James's imaginative experience of the condition of publicity should be construed as entirely negative. Indeed, for a number of recent critics, it is precisely this disruption of binary or 'schismatic' modes of perception which constitutes James's most radical aesthetic and epistemological achievement.[23] While this line of argument should not lead us to discount the fact that James was also deeply disturbed by the dissolution of cultural boundaries, it is clear that his seemingly hostile apprehension of this phenomenon in many ways contradicts the 'fluidity' of his own fictional practices. Far from insisting upon rigidity, James's fiction is more notable for its relaxation or transgression of the boundaries of individual consciousness and identity. Moreover, as Ian F.A. Bell has argued, it was James's saturation in the cultural codes of publicity and performance which seems positively to have enabled his recognition of the liberating mutability of the modern self.[24]

By contrast with the Arnoldian requirement of critical distance, this aspect of James's fictional practice also challenges the assumption that it is possible to maintain a rigorous separation between private interests or desires and a disinterested public sphere. In many of his tales, James explicitly exposes the manipulative design which underlies a declaration of disinterest, and while this satirical strategy is itself directed against the exponents of journalistic or biographical publicity, it also serves to problematize his own critical stance. By questioning the objective status of biographical knowledge, for instance, James is forced to confront the possibility that all knowledge is necessarily interested, and, hence, that the borders between private and public experience are necessarily porous. It is no coincidence that James's most famous account of the process of imaginative experience bears an uncanny (and indeed scandalous) resemblance to the practice of the investigative reporter, as it appears in such texts as 'The Aspern Papers' and *The Sacred Fount.*[25] If the 'power to guess the unseen from the seen' was an important requirement for the artist, as James declared in 'The Art of Fiction', a similar capacity for transgressing the boundaries of knowledge was exemplified by the apparently antithetical figure of the journalist (*LC* I 53). In a sense, James's transitive practice of imaginative cognition is itself a 'revelatory', journalistic mode of enquiry: one that is profoundly implicated in the reconfiguration of private and public space within late-nineteenth-century investigative discourse. While James endeavoured to resist what he called the 'insurmountable desire to *know*', the very nature of his resistance was moulded by the same cultural impulse (*LC* II 297). Yet even so, the immanent character of James's response to the 'democratization' of modern culture should not be confounded with an uncritical reproduction of its characteristic tendencies. James's transgression of boundaries remained dependent upon the possibility of their existence, just as his recognition of the interested nature of knowledge was, by definition, predicated upon a regulative ideal of disinterest. To this extent, James refused to accept the reduction of all social norms to the status of manipulative fictions, and continued to practise 'the high and helpful public, and, as it were, civic use of the imagination', which he affirmed towards the end of his career (*LC* II 1230). One of the aims of this study is to suggest that these conflicting impulses, which run throughout James's fictional and critical writings, need to be examined in relation to each other. To view James's radical aesthetic and epistemological practices in isolation from the normative (or what are often thought to be the conservative) elements of his cultural and political thought is to neglect the tension which exists between the two. It is this tension or ambivalence within James's response to the culture of publicity which the following chapters seek to address.

CHAPTER ONE

Transformations of the public sphere in 'The Bostonians'

THE AGE OF PUBLICITY

On 17 November 1887, James recorded an anecdote in his notebook, from which he began to conceive the story of *The Reverberator.* The anecdote concerned an American woman – May McClellan – who had written a letter to the New York *World* in which she described in intimate detail 'the Venetian society whose hospitality she had just been enjoying' (*NB* 82). For James, this betrayal of private confidence acquires a 'strange typicality', appearing as a manifestation of 'that mania for publicity which is one of the most striking signs of our times' (*NB* 82). The culmination of his interpretation of the anecdote is an exhortation to the documentary zeal of the historical novelist:

> One sketches one's age but imperfectly if one doesn't touch on that particular matter: the invasion, the impudence and shamelessness, of the newspaper and the interviewer, the devouring *publicity* of life, the extinction of all sense between public and private. It is the highest expression of the note of 'familiarity', the sinking of *manners*, in so many ways, which the democratization of the world brings with it. (*NB* 82)

James's insistence that the novelistic task of 'sketch[ing] one's age' remained incomplete unless it took into account the 'devouring *publicity* of life' may serve as both a template and a justification for the concerns of this study. Here, James declares the urgent necessity of engaging with what he sees as a symptomatic phenomenon of modern culture.

There is perhaps no novel of which it could be more aptly said that it was written as a commentary on its age than *The Bostonians.* This, of course, is not to say that *The Bostonians* offers a more truthful account of its historical or social content than other fictional narratives by James or by anyone else. Rather, it is to suggest that, in this particular novel, the sign of the 'age' is constituted both as the object of fictional representation and as a rhetorical element in its interpretation. One of the disturbing features of James's notebook entry is, thus, the way in which it appears not simply to designate the objective content of the 'age', but also, in doing so, to perform a particular style of cultural criticism. The uncanny resemblance between the language of this passage and the invective of Basil Ransom reopens a question which has troubled many readers and critics of *The Bostonians*: the question, namely, of where (and how) to locate James's authorial voice within the evidently contested space of the novel. This question remains of importance to a reading of *The Bostonians* precisely because the fictional contest between Basil, Verena Tarrant and Olive Chancellor is itself a conflict over the appropriate form and function of public discourse, and, more particularly, over the control of a 'voice'.

In the notebook entry, James undoubtedly invokes an interpretation of the historical narrative of 'democratization', which, like that of his character Basil Ransom, owes much to the earlier (and, it should be said, somewhat diverse) formulations of de Tocqueville and Carlyle. I will be suggesting that, in a broad sense, this vein of cultural criticism issues from a particular understanding of the legitimate function of the public spheres of literature and politics, one which evidently conflicts with the formation of 'publicity' in its modern sense. Lest it be thought that James's affiliation to these exemplary models of bourgeois social theory immediately closes the question of his own authorial sympathies, however, it must also be acknowledged that the novel itself reveals the particularity of this theory. At the very least, *The Bostonians* dramatizes the emergence of rival discursive claims, from the 'counter-public sphere' of feminism to the publicity of the mass media.[1] More positively, the novel may be read as an attempt to trace the historical transformation of the public sphere in all its complex and contradictory guises: to examine a critical shift in the meaning of 'publicity' itself, to map the attendant reconfiguration of public and private space, and to inscribe these various cultural changes within an historiographical form which offers its readers an account of the rise of the mass media and of new social and political movements. Indeed, rather than presenting a singular or unified narrative of cultural decline, as the notebook entry suggests, *The Bostonians* contains a number of competing interpretive strategies, each of which attempts either to explain or to efface the origins of the modern 'age'.

To suggest that James refuses (or is unable) to provide a singular account of the historical process which he wishes to address might seem to contradict the way in which Basil's insistent evocation of the threat of 'feminization' and 'democratization' comes to inform the narrative trajectory of the novel as a whole. As Alfred Habegger has shown, this narrative of cultural decline has proved extremely persuasive with several of James's most influential twentieth-century critics. Indeed, for Habegger, James's complicity with Basil's conservative politics fundamentally authorizes such an interpretation by distorting the novel's referential claims. Whereas, in the novel, the onset of 'feminization' and 'democratization' appears to gather a sweeping historical force, in reality, Habegger points out, radical reform movements of the kind represented by James were marginalized in post-bellum American society. Yet while he recognizes the way in which the novel seems to conflate its disparate historical material, Habegger reproduces a similar elision by failing to distinguish between the oppositional status of the women's movement, on the one hand, and the increasingly powerful and institutionalized interests of the popular press on the other. Since, for Habegger, feminism and the New Journalism are equally embattled forces of radicalism, upholding the democratic value of publicity against a conservative defence of privacy, the complexity of James's negotiation of these issues is effaced.[2]

At the same time, Habegger is surely right to recognize the fraught nature of James's relationship to his protagonist. What we take to be the authoritative narratorial voice of the text often slips disconcertingly in and out of the 'voices' of its characters, resulting in an inchoate circulation of vocal registers.[3] On one occasion, for instance, the narrator appears to deliver a devastatingly ironic judgement upon the depth of Basil's political thought:

> I suppose he was very conceited, for he was much addicted to judging his age. He thought it talkative, querulous, hysterical, maudlin, full of false ideas, of unhealthy germs, of extravagant, dissipated habits, for which a great reckoning was in store. He was an immense admirer of the late Thomas Carlyle, and was very suspicious of the encroachments of modern democracy. (*B* 199)

Here, James's use of a carefully casual parataxis evidently demarcates Basil's critique of 'modern democracy' as idiosyncratic, and thus distinct from an authoritative narratorial interpretation. Elsewhere, however, the narrator adopts the very tone of epochal judgement from which he strives to remain aloof. Nowhere is this more evident than in his comments upon the self-promotional culture of advertising and the press. The 'sensational' journalist Matthias Pardon, for example, is dismissed by the narrator as an 'ingenuous son of his age', for whom 'literary enterprise' is merely a 'cultivation of the great arts of publicity' (*B* 139). As Ian Bell has noted, Pardon's quest for novelty as the principal material of publicity marks his status as a 'thoroughly modern young man': 'He regarded the mission of mankind upon earth as a perpetual evolution of telegrams; everything to him was very much the same, he had no sense of proportion or quality; but the newest thing was what came nearest exciting in his mind the sentiment of respect' (*B* 140).[4] Interestingly, one of the titles that James considered using for *The Bostonians* was *The Newness*, and another *The Revealer* (*NB* 67), both of which might be taken as referring to the figure of the journalist. The grotesque nature of this 'newness', however, is signified by Pardon's preternaturally 'hoary head' (*B* 140). The journalist's pursuit of novelty through the technologies of modern communication is so frenetic that it appears, literally, to age him. Like the degenerate democracy whose 'great reckoning' is foreseen by Basil, Pardon's modernity appears to contain the seeds of its own apocalyptic negation.

Yet while the narrator's evident antipathy towards Pardon would tend to support the view that *The Bostonians* offers only a familiar narrative of cultural decline, in which the modern is linked presumptively to the degenerate, in fact the novel also bears traces of an entirely contrary impulse, in which the novelty of publicity is unwittingly exalted above a degraded past. This conflicting narrative centres around the desire, on the part of the narrator and all the major characters in the novel, to explain the origins of Verena's talent as a public speaker. From her theatrical performances in the company of her father to the organized spectacle of her final, aborted lecture at the Boston Music Hall, Verena's career traces the emergence of the wider cultural forms with which the novel is concerned. Jennifer Wicke has indicated how such a narrative might be plotted by showing how the modern practice of advertising drew upon the existing resources of popular theatrical culture and a long tradition of itinerant self-promotional spectacles. In the late nineteenth century, these pre-capitalist forms of display were linked to wider and more organized networks of distribution.[5]

In *The Bostonians*, the locus of this historical shift in the forms of spectacular culture is the Tarrant family, and, in particular, the fraught question of Verena's relationship with her parents. Through the figure of Selah Tarrant, James refers back to an earlier moment in the self-promotional exhibition of 'miraculous' phenomena. Selah's career is satirically couched in the language of petty-commodity charlatanism: having 'begun life as an itinerant vendor of lead-pencils', he 'had afterwards been for a while a member of the celebrated Cayuga community, where there were no wives, or no husbands, or something of that sort . . . and had still later (though before the development of the healing faculty) achieved distinction in the spiritualistic world' (*B* 93). Selah's most recent discovery of his 'faculty' as a 'mesmeric' healer prompts him to assume the title of 'Doctor Tarrant', a title which further associates him with the quackery that traditionally surrounded the advertising of patent medical products.[6] The meagreness of Selah's desire for self-promotion, however, is carefully distinguished from the modern practice of publicity, exemplified by Pardon. For the journalist, Verena's father is 'quite second-rate, a votary of played-out causes' (*B* 140). Conversely, having failed in his own attempt to utilize the press as a promotional medium, Selah turns to Pardon as someone who can engineer his daughter's career on a much wider scale. He is aware that if his ambition of 'producing' Verena 'in public' is to be accomplished, she must supersede the disorganized world of publicity exemplified by her family (*B* 140).

Both Olive and Basil are also aware, ostensibly for different reasons, of the same necessity. As Bell has observed, both of these characters attempt to appropriate Verena by concealing or denying the importance of her familial origins, in much the same way that the fetishism of the commodity, according to Marx, occludes the historical nature of its production.[7] Ironically, though, their very insistence upon Verena's unique essence undermines its own ahistorical premise. When Basil persuades Verena to walk with him through Central Park, for example, he tells her: 'You stand apart, you are unique, extraordinary; you constitute a category by yourself. In you the elements have been mixed in a manner so felicitous that I regard you as quite incorruptible. I don't know where you come from nor how you come to be what you are, but you are outside and above all vulgarizing influences' (*B* 330). As a 'unique, extraordinary' spectacle, Verena's alleged distance from the 'vulgarizing influences' of her upbringing is couched in the very terms of that influence. In the same manner, Olive employs the debased language of Selah Tarrant in order to express her sense of Verena's autonomy from her parents. For Olive, the 'wonder of such people being Verena's progenitors at all' is a 'perpetual enigma', a 'mystery', which her own explanation signally fails to resolve:

> She had explained it, as we explain all exceptional things, by making the part, as the French say, of the miraculous. She had come to consider the girl as a wonder of wonders, to hold that no human origin, however congruous it might superficially appear, would sufficiently account for her; that her springing up between Selah and his wife was an exquisite whim of the creative force. (*B* 132)

Olive's admiration for Verena as a 'wonder of wonders' leaves her in the same position as an ingenuous recipient of Selah's 'healing faculty'. Her explanation of Verena's magical 'gift' of speech is unknowingly oxymoronic since the 'wonder' is not Verena's difference from her parents, but precisely the sign of her familial likeness. Like Basil, Olive wants to think of Verena as being 'like some brilliant birthday-present': an object which is (in every sense of the word) given, rather than subject to exchange as a commodity (*B* 132). Yet in order to conceive of this self-sufficient object, Olive is herself forced to initiate the novel's most graphic act of exchange by offering to buy Verena from her father.

Thus, both the language and actions of Basil and Olive are seemingly infected by the very cultural forms which they seek to repress. In what may legitimately be seen as an instance of false consciousness, Verena's apparent autonomy is conceived as a miraculous birth, an immaculate conception, which interrupts both the course of biological genealogy and the pervading narrative of cultural degeneration. On the one hand, the attempt to sever Verena's links with an earlier moment in the history of self-promotional culture constantly reminds us of the importance of these origins, and in this respect James's narrator assumes the authoritative guise of the naturalist. Implicitly rebuking the misinterpretations of his protagonists, the narrator affirms that 'whatever theory might be entertained as to the genesis of her talent and her personal nature, the blood of the lecture-going, night-walking Tarrants did distinctly flow in her veins' (*B* 292).[8] Yet on the other hand, the very desire to efface Verena's history points not to a determining instance of the past, as in naturalist historiography, but to the cultural imperatives of the present. For what induces the perceptions of Basil and Olive is precisely the promise of the 'modern' which is elsewhere seen to mark the 'age' of publicity. By reinventing Verena for their own needs, both remain firmly within a temporal horizon which consists of this same belief in the endless production of the 'new'.

THE SPECTACLE OF SPEECH

If the response which Verena induces in both Basil and Olive may be likened to a form of commodity fetishism, however, it is important to note that the object of this fetishism does not exclusively appeal to the mode of sensory perception which it might be expected to. Marx himself illustrated the 'fetishism of the commodity' by referring to the misleading 'impression made by a thing on the optic nerve'.[9] In other words, fetishism, in its Marxian sense, is often understood as a pathology which afflicts vision. Following Marx's ocular metaphor, Roland Barthes claimed that sight is the most 'magical' of the senses in his decoding of the 'mythologies' of modern advertising.[10] Likewise, recent Jamesian critics have tended to focus upon the importance of 'seeing' as a way of tracing the connections between the values of James's fiction and those of modern consumer culture.[11] Yet while I accept the view that a visual paradigm is central to this reading of James's canon (as I suggest more explicitly in chapter 5), it should also be stressed that *The Bostonians* is, above all, a text that is concerned with speech: both with the individual 'voice' and with the amplified noise of a 'talkative' age.

Hence, as we are repeatedly shown, Verena's most 'magical' attribute is, of course, her voice. At Mrs Burrage's evening lecture party, for instance, Basil is drawn towards the spectacle of Verena's performance by hearing her voice permeate through to the adjacent room where he has been detained by Mrs Luna. This example of speech being transmitted across distance is later repeated when Basil first arrives at Marmion: standing outside Olive's house, he is entranced to hear Verena's voice carried from within. If Basil and Olive invariably fetishize Verena's uniqueness, then this fetishism is as much aural and oral, as it is visual. This, of course, is not to deny the visual impact of Verena's performances. Rather, it is to suggest that, in both of these sensory modes, the formal or aesthetic properties of Verena's speech are invariably abstracted from their content. Not surprisingly, this is true primarily of Basil for whom Verena's 'nature was not to make converts to a ridiculous cause, but to emit those charming notes of her voice, to stand in those free young attitudes, to shake her braided locks like a naiad rising from the waves, to please every one who came near her, and to be happy that she pleased' (*B* 85).

Basil's theory of Verena's speech is, at the same time, both formalist and expressivist: her voice is conceived not as a medium of intersubjective communication, capable of entering into the public sphere without losing its authenticity, but as the instrument of an abstract 'personality'. Thus, while Basil appears to detach the individual form of Verena's speech from its collective content, there is also a sense in which her voice itself is rendered utterly impersonal. This understanding of Verena's voice is met with elsewhere in the novel. Before her first performance, Selah declares the 'thoroughly impersonal' nature of his daughter's talent: rather than expressing an inner self, her voice appears to come from 'some power outside – it seemed to flow through her' (*B* 79–80). Although Selah's insistence upon Verena's external inspiration is plainly intended to reveal his tawdry showmanship, his statement is also entirely accurate. Far from constituting the spontaneous expression of an organic personality, Verena's voice is often heard in situations where it is disembodied, as in the two scenes mentioned above. The voice appears as an alien object which inhabits the body: Verena is conscious of the fact that the 'voice that spoke from her lips seemed to want to take that form' (*B* 80).

One way of reading these simultaneously 'personal' and 'impersonal' aspects of Verena's voice may be gleaned from Jean-Christophe Agnew's discussion of the general disintegration of a system of fixed correspondences between commodities and their symbolic representations in modern consumer culture. According to Agnew, 'The very solidity of the commodity appears to dissolve in the presence of the newly acquired weight of the characteristics the commodity shares with other goods. These characteristics become objectified, reified.'[12] Here, Agnew is describing a process which, in Jean Baudrillard's terms, may be seen as the replacement of symbolic value by the exchange value of the sign. The material body of the commodity is no longer distinguishable from the generic symbol which represents it, but is instead assembled from a series of discrete signs, which are intended to convey its 'unique' qualities.[13] In a similar fashion, Verena succeeds in impressing upon her audience the 'personal' appeal of her performances, even though this rhetorical strategy is itself serially produced, and so undermines the very possibility of a uniquely expressive 'personality'. Basil's response to Verena's 'intensely personal exhibition' (*B* 84) again offers a particularly instructive example of this contradiction:

> The most graceful part of her was her earnestness, the way her delightful eyes, wandering over the 'fashionable audience' . . . as if she wished to resolve it into a single sentient personality, seemed to say that the only thing in life she cared for was to put the truth into a form that would render conviction irresistible. She was as simple as she was charming, and there was not a glance or motion that did not seem part of the pure, still-burning passion that animated her. She had indeed – it was manifest – reduced the company to unanimity. (*B* 265)

Here, Basil's hostility to the political content of Verena's speech is shown to be implicated within the very codes of consumption which he claims to oppose.[14] Rather than simply detaching 'form' from 'content', the latter is incorporated into the former. It is the 'earnestness', 'conviction' and 'passion' of Verena's argument which is construed as the 'most graceful' aspect of her performance. Basil's desire for Verena is thus fuelled through a determined act of resistance. Yet this act is not imposed upon Verena's performance from outside it, as he would like to think. On the contrary, Basil assumes a posture which is built into the rhetorical form of Verena's address: he believes that he alone is the privileged antagonist – the 'single sentient personality' – to whom she is appealing. Verena's attempt to forge a 'personal' relationship with her audience is couched in metaphors of oral/aural seduction. She states a desire to 'pour' her speech 'into the ears of those who still hold out, who stiffen their necks and repeat hard, empty formulas, which are as dry as a broken gourd that has been flung away in the desert . . . to press home to each of you, personally, individually . . . the vision of the world as it hangs perpetually before me, redeemed, transfigured, by a new moral tone' (*B* 267–8). But while Basil interprets Verena's invocation of a hostile, phallic figure as referring exclusively to himself, the point of this strategy is its indiscriminate appeal. Each member of Verena's audience is intended to feel that they are addressed 'personally, individually'; likewise, each member of the audience is intended to feel uniquely set apart from the rest, without recognizing the manner in which the audience as a whole is 'reduced to unanimity'.

Interestingly, Verena's oratorical technique of addressing her audience as 'a single sentient personality' bears a striking resemblance to James's comments upon Emerson's ability as a lecturer in his 1887 review of James Elliot Cabot's *A Memoir of Ralph Waldo Emerson*. While James concedes that Emerson was more a 'man of lectures' than a 'man of letters', he also argues that

> the lecture surely was never more purged of its grossness – the quality in it that suggests a strong light and a big brush – than as it issued from Emerson's lips; so far from being a vulgarisation, it was simply the esoteric made audible, and instead of treating the few as the many, after the usual fashion of gentlemen on platforms, he treated the many as the few. (*LC* I 255)

Bearing in mind Emerson's prominent position within the tradition of New England radicalism, these favourable observations on his capacity to transform the impersonal medium of public discourse into an aestheticized realm of intimacy suggest that James himself was not insusceptible to the allure of the strategy exemplified by Verena. This strategy, moreover, may be seen as symptomatic of a transformation of the function of public space which, according to several recent critics, took place during the late nineteenth century. In his book *The Fall of Public Man*, Richard Sennett, for example, has argued that nineteenth-century theatre audiences differed from their eighteenth-century predecessors in the assumptions which they held about the nature of public performance and assembly. Whereas, in the eighteenth century, theatrical performance was understood as a code of public representation that bore no intrinsic relationship to the performer's private self, in the nineteenth century, Sennett suggests, a fascination with the 'private life' of the public performer became prevalent. This latter response assumes that the public persona of the celebrated actor or actress allows an unmediated access to his or her private world. Equally, according to Sennett, members of the bourgeois public experienced the 'personality' of the performer in relation to their own situation as privatized onlookers. While Sennett's account of the privatization of public space may rely upon a somewhat idealized understanding of the universality of earlier norms of public life, as feminist critics in particular have argued, it nevertheless accords well with James's recognition (at least in *The Bostonians*, if not in the later review) of the way in which modern publicity encodes a paradoxically personalized response to the spectacle of mass consumption.[15]

If Basil's belief in the power of his solitary resistance to publicity is thus an effect of publicity itself, the apotheosis of this delusion can be seen in the concluding scene of the novel, where he enacts his fantasy of saving Verena from the fate of commodification. Waiting in the audience before Verena's scheduled lecture at the Music Hall, Basil distances himself from the vulgar 'mob':

> He was not one of the audience; he was apart, unique, and had come on a business altogether special . . . There were two or three moments during which he felt as he could imagine a young man to feel who, waiting in a public place, has made up his mind, for reasons of his own, to discharge a pistol at the king or the president. (*B* 414)

Set apart from the otherwise undifferentiated mass of the audience, Basil sees himself as the saviour of Verena's authentic self. Adopting an anarchistic posture of absolute externality to society, his 'vision of wresting her from the mighty multitude' assumes the prerogative of a 'unique' affinity with the figure of the celebrity (*B* 413). The magical charisma which has thus far been associated with Verena is now conferred upon Basil. In Max Weber's sense of the word, charisma is possessed by those individuals who experience their vocation as a 'mission', and who are able to convince others to follow them in their 'calling'.[16] In this case, however, Basil's messianic 'calling' entails the symbolic assassination of another charismatic individual. As a prototypical modern fan, he believes that only he can preserve the celebrity from harm, even at the cost of her death. Thus, in snatching Verena from the theatre, Basil only confirms the effects of publicity from which he claims to be saving her.

If this scene represents the culmination of a significant shift in the novel's distribution of charismatic powers, however, the beginnings of this process may be discerned well before this stage. While I have argued that Basil is himself deluded by the 'magic' of Verena's 'voice', this should not diminish our recognition of his desire to appropriate that voice for his own ends. Olive recognizes the violence of Basil's desire in reasoning that he 'knew that [Verena's] . . . voice had magic in it, and from the moment he caught its first note he had determined to destroy it' (*B* 369). Yet despite his ominous threat to 'strike her dumb', Basil does not simply intend to suppress or impose silence upon Verena's voice (*B* 315). Rather, silence can be seen as the first stage in his project of redeploying

Verena's voice as a normative model of female speech, and, hence, as a crucial site of cultural reproduction. It is not without significance that Basil's attempt to instil a gendered ideology of speech into Verena's voice gains its first success with the enforcement of secrecy surrounding his visit to her home in Monadnoc Place. Verena's compliance with Basil's wish that she maintain silence evidently constitutes a considerable blow against the 'talkative' world of publicity. For Verena, the visit is 'buried in unspoken, in unspeakable, considerations, the only secret she had in the world – the only thing that was all her own' (*B* 286–7). In Basil's interpretation, the installation of a 'secret' at the heart of Verena's otherwise frank relations with Olive is construed as a sign of independence: as the property of an autonomous self, which cannot be shared amongst others. From a different perspective, of course, this secret is not so much a space which is 'all her own' as one which allows Basil to gain a foothold in his endeavour to colonize Verena's voice. Once this project becomes clearer, Olive herself recognizes that the secrecy surrounding Basil's visit 'was the key of all that had happened since, that he had then obtained an irremediable hold upon her' (*B* 372). But even at this late stage in the novel, Olive fails to grasp the full import of the change which has occurred. It is not silence *per se* which marks Basil's power over Verena. When Verena finally confesses her secret to Olive, she attempts to compensate for her previous silence by an excessive volubility. Olive becomes aware that Verena's formidable eloquence is being turned against her, and used as an instrument of concealment: she acknowledges the possibility that 'Verena was attempting to smother her now in her own phrases' (*B* 371).

Whereas the imposition of silence would suggest a desire to suppress the presence of female speech altogether, Basil's ambition is more insidious. It requires both a shift in the performative space of Verena's voice and the infusion of a new content, which lead, finally, to a form of mimicry. In this respect, Brook Thomas is wrong to assume that Basil responds in a purely 'performative' or formalist manner to Verena's voice.[17] Like Olive, he wishes to appropriate her voice as a vehicle for expressing his own substantive ideas. After the acceptance of Basil's article by the *Rational Review* – an event which signals the masculinist tenor of his own discursive project – Verena offers a wholesale reproduction of his ideas to Olive, as if she were quoting from an oracular source. This final phase of Basil's counter-revolution positions Verena in the dual role of listener and responsive mimic of his speech. It is at this point in the novel, then, that we begin to notice a strange inversion taking place in the relationship between Basil as consumer and Verena as charismatic celebrity. What this inversion constitutes is nothing less than a fundamental redistribution of their access to language itself. While, for most of the novel, Verena is represented as an active producer of speech, she is eventually reduced to being a passive consumer of Basil's words. Conversely, Basil's role changes from that of listener to speaker. In persuading Verena of her 'genuine vocation . . . [Basil's] words, the most effective and penetrating he had uttered, had sunk into her soul and worked and fermented there. She had come at last to believe them, and that was the alteration, the transformation' (*B* 374). The effect of Basil's 'words' is to reconstitute an Edenic paradigm of language acquisition in which male speech impregnates its female recipient, and thus to reaffirm the symbolic function of language in its gendered form. Whereas Verena's voice is generally characterized as diffuse, enveloping, seductive and affective, Basil's words are 'penetrating', and their purpose is to 'ferment' inside Verena. At the same time, these words appear to appropriate and reproduce the very effect of oral/aural fetishism previously induced by Verena's performances. Verena, who has herself exercised a 'wizard's wand', is now placed under the 'spell' of Basil's 'magical touch' (*B* 375).

If, by the end of *The Bostonians*, Basil has effectively usurped Verena's charismatic powers of speech, and thus, symbolically at least, dispelled the threatened 'feminization' of the public sphere, this trajectory of incorporation may perhaps be read as offering some authorial support to Basil's view of the normative function of female speech. In his later years, James himself became increasingly concerned with what he saw as the declining standards of spoken English. Moreover, as Habegger has noted, James evidently saw this problem as particularly related to the social role of women: besides contributing a series of articles on 'The Speech of American Women' to *Harper's Bazar* in 1906–7, he also delivered a lecture entitled 'The Question of Our Speech' in 1905, which was actually addressed to an audience of female students at Bryn Mawr College, Pennsylvania.[18] In this lecture, James points to the degradation of what he calls the 'tone-standard' or 'vocal form' of speech. The fragmentation of spoken English into popular slang and ethnic dialects is accompanied, at the same time, by a standardization of oral forms via the medium of the mass-circulation press. In both respects, this process undermines the function of speech as a vital medium of coherent cultural values. James's plea for an authoritatively centred linguistic community, however, appears to license a requirement for invidious distinctions according to the signs of class, ethnicity and gender. While, on the one hand, he argues that speech may be broken down into 'units' of sound that possess either an 'intrinsic meanness' or an 'intrinsic sweetness', on the other hand he is forced to concede that these apparently inherent aesthetic properties can only be judged by 'the context of a given sound, and the company we perceive it to be keeping'. Vocal 'tone', James accepts, 'unites with various other personal, social signs to bear testimony' to good or bad 'breeding'.[19] James acknowledges, in other words, that speech cannot be detached from the cultural contexts which encode its status and function according to criteria other than that of the purely aesthetic.

Within circles of 'good breeding', moreover, it is women who characteristically assume the task of reproducing the cultural values inscribed within the form of speech. It is women, James informs his female audience, 'as to whom in general, and as to the impression made by whom, the question of voice ever most comes up and has most importance'. The privileged role of female speech is to represent or 'bear testimony' to the 'tone' of the community to which they belong. Thus, in a comment which illuminates the question of Verena Tarrant's voice, James argues that there is 'no such thing as a voice pure and simple: there is only, for any business of appreciation, the voice *plus* the way it is employed'. Here, James himself comes close to suggesting the need for a form of vocal training, similar to Basil's conception of Verena's voice as an empty 'vessel', lacking in content. Indeed, towards the end of 'The Question of Our Speech', James assumes a still more disquieting likeness to Basil by appearing to offer himself in an avuncular, educative role. Through his own exhortations, he hopes to induce 'the phase of awakening' in his listeners; to impregnate a knowledge 'in which you will taste all the savor of gathered fruit'. Finally, James holds out the promise to his audience that 'you may, sounding the clearer notes of intercourse as only women can, become yourselves models and missionaries, perhaps a little even martyrs, of the good cause'.[20]

This is not simply to suggest that James held the same views as those of his fictional character on the appropriate sphere of women's speech. In the first place, it would be a mistake either to assume that the complexity of *The Bostonians* is reducible to the terms of James's lecture, or to ignore the distance in time between the two texts. Second, there is ample evidence to suggest that, while James's association of women with the maintenance of aesthetic or cultural values tends to reinforce the dominant ideology of separately gendered spheres of 'influence', his own investment in this ideology was by no means unproblematic. James's later writings also reveal the extent of his identification with the 'feminine' sphere of culture in ways that both disturb the fixed polarities of (hetero)sexual difference, as in *The American Scene*, and also include positive (if still somewhat ambivalent) references to the activities of the suffragette movement, as exemplified by his essays on writers such as George Sand and Matilde Serao and his involvement in Elizabeth Robins's production of the suffragette play, *Votes for Women* (1906).[21] From the earlier perspective of the 1880s, moreover, it is clear that James was himself troubled by Basil's success in removing Verena from the public platform to the sphere of privacy, as I will be suggesting later.

Nevertheless, what is common to both *The Bostonians* and 'The Question of Our Speech' is the way in which female speech is perceived to be a crucially contested site in the conflict between rival discursive and ideological claims. The fact that Olive views Verena's voice in much the same way as Basil, suggests that the enterprise of radical feminist discourse is forced to rely upon the very models of gendered speech which it aims to subvert. Olive, too, assumes that Verena's voice is merely a manipulable 'form', and subjects it to a regime of correction, albeit to substantially different ends. While Olive wishes to 'employ' Verena's voice on the platform of public debate, her understanding of the power of this voice is implicitly derived from the settings of the domestic sphere, and their function within the circulation of feminine 'influence'.

THE PERFORMANCE OF 'PRIVACY'

The conceptions of the appropriate sphere of female speech which I have examined thus far are, of course, dependent upon a notion of 'privacy' which is equally central to *The Bostonians*. Basil's antipathy to Verena's public performance is predicated upon his belief that the aesthetic properties of her voice are best suited for the intimacy of domestic life. Yet it should also be noted that, far from preserving Verena from the fate of commodification, as he claims, the fulfilment of Basil's ambition merely institutes a different mode of commodity relations. In the final action of the novel, Basil conceals Verena in a cloak in order to make good their escape from the Music Hall. As Verena's figure is entirely effaced, the text signals her removal from the sphere of public representation and exchange which she has previously occupied. But it also signals her entry into a permanent sphere of private consumption, where, according to Marx, the commodity vanishes from circulation, leaving no trace of its passage.[22] This permanent (or at least culminating) sphere of private consumption needs to be distinguished from the innumerable occasions on which Verena's performance and image have already been consumed, not only on the platform, but also in newspapers, photographs and advertising posters. Richard Godden makes a similar distinction by opposing Basil's 'integrative' understanding of the self to the 'disintegrative' self exemplified by Verena's mass-produced image. The contradiction between these two notions of selfhood, Godden suggests, marks the contemporary historical shift from an economy based upon the accumulation of private property to one in which cycles of consumption are more rapid and cultural artefacts become disposable.[23] Thus, in the context of the novel's historical account of the formation of mass culture, Basil's desire to possess Verena as a unique and indivisible property must appear increasingly anachronistic. The violence of Basil's seizure of Verena invokes an archaic form of appropriation, similar to that which Thorstein Veblen saw as the original instance of commodity relations: the consumption of women by men in 'primitive' patriarchal societies.[24]

It is this 'primitive' mode of consumption, indeed, which is the subject of Verena's feminist critique. In one of her addresses, Verena explicitly recalls the patriarchal history of women's confinement within the private sphere: 'We require simply freedom; we require the lid to be taken off the box in which we have been kept for centuries. You say it's a very comfortable, cosy, convenient box, with nice glass sides, so that we can see out, and that all that's wanted is to give another quiet turn to the key' (*B* 268). Verena's image of a 'box' with 'nice glass sides' evokes a form of privacy which is experienced from the inside. Confinement is mitigated only to the extent of allowing a peripheral vision of the male public sphere. Significantly, though, the same image is given a different slant during the later scene in Central Park. During their walk together, Basil refers sarcastically to Verena's earlier address: 'He kept talking about the box; he seemed as if he wouldn't let go that simile. He said that he had come to look at her through the glass sides, and if he wasn't afraid of hurting her he would smash them in' (*B* 313). In Basil's version of this figure, the asymmetrical privilege of vision belongs not to the prisoner looking out, but to the spectator looking in. The 'glass sides' of the box function not so much as a concession to its occupant as the condition of her display. In this respect, Basil's use of the image of the box takes its defining characteristic from the model of the shop window: a medium in which the boundaries between private and public space, between inside and outside, are dissolved.[25] Hence, while Basil's urge to 'smash' the glass which separates him from Verena may appear as a promise of liberation – or as an impulse which seems to violate the codes of representation which his transfiguration of the image of the box invokes – this desire may also be read as a testimony to the allure of exhibition. It is precisely because Verena is framed as an object of public display that Basil wishes to possess her, and so ironically, by removing her from that frame, succeeds in destroying the very object which he desires.

In referring back to Verena's image of an archaic form of privacy, then, Basil unknowingly reveals the extent to which his own ideal of an autonomous sphere of domestic life has been undermined. His admiration for the feminine space of 'privacy' is, in fact, forged through its constant exhibition. As I have suggested, this shift in the rhetoric of the private sphere may be interpreted in relation to Veblen's celebrated (and roughly contemporary) account of the emergence of modern forms of cultural consumption in *The Theory of the Leisure Class* (1899). For Veblen, the mode of 'conspicuous consumption', exemplified by the moneyed aristocracy of modern America, is a 'derivative' practice which supplants and conceals the 'primary fact' of commodity relations. In previous eras, he claims, men of the dominant social class were content to consume women's productive labour in the household. In modern societies, by contrast, men assume for themselves the burden of production, while women of a high social status are delegated the task of consuming the fruits of their labour. Yet, in truth, the conspicuous consumption associated with women can be understood neither as a liberation from production, nor as an unmediated form of self-expression. For, according to Veblen, the real function of female consumption is secondary and emblematic: it bears witness to a higher power of male consumption, even while it occludes this primary gender division.[26]

While I would not wish to insist upon the historical or anthropological accuracy of Veblen's account, it does at least allow us to discern the contradictory dynamics behind the process by which consumption came to be construed, often invidiously, as a predominantly female activity in the late nineteenth century. In his espousal of the familiar Victorian ideology of 'separate spheres', Basil insists that the feminine domain of privacy be seen as a refuge from the world of masculine productivity.[27] His frequent visions of feminine 'interiors' invoke a world of luxurious consumption inhabited by the figure of the domestic woman. In these visions, though, it is Basil himself who consumes the image of the female consumer, exhibited amidst her tasteful possessions. To this extent, Basil maintains his privileged position within a patriarchal mode of commodity relations whilst, at the same time, confirming the dominant ideology of consumer capitalism, which situates middle-class women within an idealized sphere of 'private' consumption, rather than one of domestic labour.

It would be wrong to assume, however, that Basil's conception of the private sphere simply denotes a space of absolute domestic confinement. No overarching dichotomy between private and public spheres can offer an adequate description of the multiplicity of meanings generated by these terms in the novel. This applies not only to the way in which publicity, in its modern form, erodes such oppositions, but also to earlier notions of the public sphere. In its normative form, as Habermas reminds us, the bourgeois understanding of the public sphere was precisely that of a public sphere of private individuals: as such, 'the line between private and public sphere extended right through the home'. This definition of privacy incorporates (and distinguishes between) both the 'intimate sphere' of domesticity and the realms of civil society and commodity exchange. In these latter domains, it is the private status of the bourgeois individual which enables the constitution of an authentic public sphere, in opposition to the public authority of the state.[28] This is a conception of the public sphere to which, in many ways,

Basil would subscribe. In outlining Verena's role in their prospective domestic and social life, for example, he draws upon similar distinctions between the different forms of privacy:

> You won't sing in the Music Hall, but you will sing to me; you will sing to everyone who knows you and approaches you. Your gift is indestructible; don't talk as if I either wanted to wipe it out or should be able to make it a particle less divine. I want to give it another direction, certainly; but I don't want to stop your activity. Your gift is the gift of expression, and there is nothing I can do for you that will make you less expressive. It won't gush out at a fixed hour and on a fixed day, but it will irrigate, it will fertilize, it will brilliantly adorn your conversation. Think how delightful it will be when your influence becomes really social. Your facility, as you call it, will simply make you, in conversation, the most charming woman in America. (*B* 379–80)

If Basil's promise is to be believed, then, Verena's 'gift' for public speech will not simply be squandered in domestic intimacy with himself, but will also be allowed to 'irrigate' their private social gatherings. In this sense, the private sphere encloses a realm of 'society' in which private individuals assemble into a 'public'. Where Basil's conception of the 'really social' becomes disingenuous, however, is in its restriction of Verena's voice to an informal sphere of feminine 'influence'. Verena is not to be given access to the formal media of public debate; her speech will serve merely as a conduit in the circulation of private opinions, whereas, previously, it had served as a commodity available on the market. In this respect, Basil is again an exemplary proponent of the public sphere in its bourgeois (or 'civic republican') form.[29] For as Habermas has noted, albeit insufficiently, access to the media of public debate was, in principle, predicated upon the legal status of the bourgeois subject as property owner, and thus implicitly excluded women (as well as working-class men), in contradiction to its normative assumption of universality. These restrictions applied not only to physical sites of public assembly, but also to the medium of print through which the public sphere of private individuals was paradigmatically constituted.[30]

Thus, it is significant, as I have mentioned, that the event which enables Basil to sway Verena's allegiance to Olive is his own entry into the market-place of ideas. The acceptance of Basil's article by the portentously titled *Rational Review* lends credence to his own claim upon the public sphere of private individuals, and is evidently intended to reassert the authority of male rationality against the 'nervous, hysterical, chattering' speech of a 'womanized' age (*B* 327). Certainly, the title of this periodical is ironic, signalling as it does the self-importance of Basil's opinions and their own less than rational expression. Nevertheless, the acceptance of his article is an important juncture in the novel's engagement with the theme of publicity (in all senses of the word). Prior to this moment in the text, Basil's own public, professional status has been restricted to that of an inept and impoverished New York lawyer. To his embarrassment, Verena's commercial success as a public speaker exemplifies the virtues of the masculine 'provider' that he himself signally lacks. However illusory it may appear, the prospect of a distinguished career as author and social critic thus allows Basil the opportunity of restoring his masculine self-esteem. More importantly, Basil believes that this prospect will give him the opportunity to contribute to the 'rational' formation of the public interest: 'Should he not be able to act in that way upon the public opinion of his time, to check certain tendencies, to point out certain dangers, to indulge in much salutary criticism?' (*B* 206). Basil's ambition to be an author, who circulates his texts in order to shape the 'public opinion' of the day, can be seen as countering the insidious growth of publicity (in its modern sense) by referring back to the Enlightenment ideal of a 'critical' public sphere. In the eighteenth century, Habermas has argued, it was the establishment of a literary market which initially facilitated the formation of a critically debating public, composed of widely dispersed readers. No longer bound by aristocratic or court patronage, authors ideally embodied the individual autonomy that was seen as necessary to the separation of an authentic public sphere from the coercive authority of the state. The market established a mechanism by which the private individual was able both to contribute to the sphere of public debate and, at the same time, to remain independent of it.[31]

Yet the principle of 'critical publicity' (to use Habermas's term) becomes increasingly difficult to sustain in the face of its derivative modern forms, as Basil's own vision of authorship reveals. While Basil envisages the space of authorship as detached from the public realm through which the author's texts must circulate as commodities, James suggests that this space is itself incorporated within the process of commodification. The autonomy of the author is figured through the representation of 'privacy' as an object of consumption.

Surveying Mrs Luna's 'interior', for example, Basil briefly contemplates the beneficial consequences of marrying her:

> The lamp-light was soft, the fire crackled pleasantly, everything that surrounded him betrayed a woman's taste and touch; the place was decorated and cushioned in perfection, delightfully private and personal, the picture of a well-appointed home . . . At the end of an hour he felt, I will not say almost marriageable, but almost married. Images of leisure played before him, leisure in which he saw himself covering foolscap paper with his views on several subjects, and with favourable illustrations of Southern eloquence. It became tolerably vivid to him that if editors wouldn't print one's lucubrations, it would be a comfort to feel that one was able to publish them at one's own expense. (*B* 205)

In this scene, Basil's idealized evocation of the feminine sphere of 'privacy' gives rise to his ambition to send forth his private 'views' into the world of public opinion. Yet while these two functions of private space are gendered in different ways, they occupy the same 'delightfully private and personal' realm. Mrs Luna's interior almost literally assumes the quality of an advertisement, representing in pictorial form 'the well-appointed home'. Ironically, it is within this entirely commodified and feminized space that Basil intends to situate his rational critique of the commodification and feminization of American society. Once in possession of his wife's income, Basil dreams of pursuing his vocation as an author of 'private means'. Liberated from the competitive constraints of the contemporary literary market, authorship will be transformed into a space of freedom, disinterest and gentlemanly 'leisure'. Yet this anachronistic image of authorship may itself be seen as a product of the increasing publicity surrounding the 'private lives' of authors in the late nineteenth century. From the 1870s onwards, British and American newspapers and periodicals regularly printed illustrated articles and interviews in which famous authors were represented 'at home'. In these journalistic texts, the home of the literary celebrity was generally figured as a world of bourgeois domesticity, refined tastes and luxurious consumption, of a similar character to Basil's vision.[32] Since 'privacy' itself was capable of being incorporated into the media of publicity, it was no longer so easy for authors to maintain their position as autonomous individuals, simultaneously inside and outside the public sphere.

I will be returning to these popular representations of authorship in chapter 3, where I will consider more closely the question of

James's response to the perceived invasion of authorial 'privacy'. At present, however, it suffices to note that Basil's attempt to reclaim the public sphere as an exclusively masculine preserve of 'rational' discourse comes to resemble the journalistic strategies of Matthias Pardon. While Basil loathes the personal 'revelations' of celebrities purveyed by Pardon, his vision of authorship is clearly fuelled from similar sources. Not only does Basil desire the 'delightfully private and personal' world evoked within this form of journalistic discourse, but, in the voyeuristic intensity of his desire, he himself is figured as an intrusive interviewer. Angered by his uninvited entry into her home, Olive complains that Basil 'has stolen a march upon her privacy': a charge which was repeatedly made against the practitioners of 'investigative' journalism during the 1880s (*B* 108).[33]

More importantly, though, by presenting Basil's authorial ambitions in this manner, *The Bostonians* dramatizes a conflict between two distinct conceptions of the meaning of 'publicity'. James allows us to witness the historical process by which the previously hegemonic model of the public sphere (a public sphere of private individuals) is, on the one hand, infiltrated by the publicity of the mass media, and, on the other, challenged by the demands of those social groups who were, from its very inception, excluded from the domain of 'public opinion'. As I have already indicated, James's understanding of this historical transformation is, in part, derived from the earlier observations of Alexis de Tocqueville. In *Democracy in America*, de Tocqueville was concerned with the way in which liberal European conceptions of the relationship between the individual and the state were being undermined by the new social conditions of the United States. Whereas, according to liberal political theory, 'public opinion' emerged from the public debate of private individuals, in American society this formula appeared to have been reversed:

> In Europe we frequently introduce the ideas and habits of private life into public affairs; and as we pass at once from the domestic circle to the government of the state, we may frequently be heard to discuss the great interests of society in the same manner in which we converse with our friends. The Americans, on the other hand, transport the habits of public life into their manners in private; in their country the jury is introduced into the games of schoolboys, and parliamentary forms are observed in the order of a feast.[34]

For de Tocqueville, the authority of an expanded democratic public sphere was such that it threatened the very autonomy of those private individuals from which the category of 'the public' was constituted. Thus, he anticipates a world in which 'public opinion' stands above, rather than arising from, individual freedoms: a world in which individuals internalize public authority, rather than making the public domain into a forum for critical debate. It was this perception, as Habermas has shown, which led liberal critics such as de Tocqueville and John Stuart Mill to understand democratic public opinion as a potentially tyrannical rule of the majority, and hence, by stressing the importance of representative government by an elite minority, to negate the very assumption of universality upon which the ideology of the bourgeois public sphere was founded.[35]

Thus, while it would be unfair to conflate this liberal analysis of democracy with Basil Ransom's vaunted reactionary stance, it is appropriate that Basil should be described as an admiring reader of de Tocqueville, and that one of his rejected articles should concern the 'rights of minorities' (*B* 198).[36] Presumably, the 'minorities' with which Basil is concerned are not those social groups who have been denied access to the forum of public opinion, as a modern reader might suspect, but, rather, those individuals (such as himself) whose claims upon the public sphere are increasingly threatened by its democratization. While Basil's admiration for the likes of de Tocqueville and Carlyle is suitably distanced from any authorial perspective, it must also be remembered that James himself offered a strikingly Tocquevillean diagnosis of the 'democratization of the world' in his notebook entry of 1887. Defining the cultural experience of modern publicity as the 'extinction of all sense between public and private', James appears to concur with de Tocqueville's apprehension of the perceived loss of private autonomy, if not with the tawdry use to which Basil puts this intellectual inheritance (*NB* 82). Even if these distinctions were granted, moreover, it might still be argued that James's anxiety with publicity unwittingly reproduces a restrictive model of the public sphere: one which is inextricably bound up with a gendered ideology of separate private and public spheres. For as Nancy Fraser has cogently argued, the desire to maintain a predetermined separation between matters of 'private' and 'public' interest, whatever its intention, inevitably perpetuates the historical exclusion of the concerns of women and other minoritized social groups from public debate.[37] Accepting this possibility, however, it remains important to stress that, for James, the 'extinction of all sense between public and private' bore contradictory effects, not all of which are easily assimilable into a 'radical' (or, for that matter, 'conservative') cultural agenda. Far from simply subverting a binary construction of gender, as might be assumed, the dissolution of the boundaries between private and public spheres which the novel traces also tends to reinforce the same dichotomies. Similarly, James's narrative of 'feminization' cannot be equated indiscriminately with both the feminist demand for access to the sphere of public debate and the gendering of public space as 'feminine' within the spectacles of publicity.[38] James himself shows how these two strands of the same narrative produce the antagonistic logic upon which *The Bostonians* is founded.

In her influential book *The Feminization of American Culture*, Ann Douglas charts a similar narrative on a much wider scale. Examining the rise to prominence of female 'domestic' novelists in the middle of the nineteenth century, Douglas links the process of 'feminization' to a form of 'sentimentalism' which, as in James's text, erodes the boundaries between private and public space. According to Douglas, 'sentimentalism seeks and offers the distraction of sheer publicity'; while it is apparently concerned with representing states of 'private' emotion, in fact, the sentimental 'always attains public and conspicuous expression':

> Privacy functions in the rituals of sentimentalism only for the sake of titillation, as a convention to be violated. Involved as it is with the exhibition and commercialization of the self, sentimentalism cannot exist without an audience. It has no content but its own exposure, and it invests exposure with a kind of final significance.[39]

Yet while Douglas is rightly alert to the strategy of publicity which informs what is ostensibly a rhetoric of privacy within the domestic novel, she also assumes that this strategy represents an unambiguous occupation of the space of public discourse on the part of women writers. By offering an invidious contrast between the consumerist orientation of 'sentimental' literary culture and the strenously productive ethos of an earlier Puritan mode of reading and writing, Douglas produces a narrative of 'feminization' which is, in certain respects, not dissimilar to Basil Ransom's. The proliferation of women writers during this period is seen to represent a decisive shift in the balance of cultural (if not economic or political) power.[40] In *The Bostonians*, we witness a collapse in the ontological integrity of 'privacy' which is very similar to Douglas's discussion of the rhetoric of 'sentimentalism', but which needs to be read differently. Verena Tarrant, for example, might aptly be described as exhibiting a form of 'privacy' which 'has no content but its own exposure', and which 'invests exposure with a kind of final significance'. Verena's public persona is not differentiated from her 'private' self according to a vertical model of character, in which an authentic essence is masked by an illusory surface. On the contrary, her 'essential' self is self-negating, as it consists precisely 'of the extraordinary generosity with which she could expose herself, give herself away, turn herself inside out, for the satisfaction of a person who made demands of her' (*B* 370). Thus, Verena's 'personality' extends across a horizontal or flat plane of representation, in which her various 'private' and 'public' roles are equally (in)authentic. James's representation of Verena's enigmatic character exemplifies the strategy of 'indirect vision' which he was to justify in an explicit manner in *The Tragic Muse* (1890) (*TM* 276). It is not surprising, then, that Verena's performance as a political speaker should bear such striking similarities to the performances of the actress Miriam Rooth in the later novel. Indeed, in both texts, the performative space of the theatre may be seen as a crucial medium in the cultural transmission and public representation of femininity.[41]

As Mary Jean Corbett has recently argued, a similar reconfiguration of public and private space may be discerned in both the material construction and the dramatic productions of the late-nineteenth-century theatre. In particular, Corbett demonstrates the way in which some of the most notable actresses of the period succeeded in conveying the norms of middle-class domestic femininity whilst, at the same time, being publicly promoted as celebrities. On the one hand, the late Victorian theatre 'disseminated the signs of private domesticity in a new public forum', and thus distanced itself from the disrepute which had previously been attached to the public performance of women; yet on the other hand, the newly respectable figure of the actress was commodified on a scale which far surpassed that of the courtesan, with whose status as an object of sexual exchange actresses had previously been tainted. Hence, the actress was able to appear both familiar and remote, as Corbett suggests in her discussion of James's acquaintance, Ellen Terry. It was Terry's capacity to project a 'personality' that was 'simultaneously known and unknowable', Corbett claims, which allowed the individual spectator to experience a 'direct contact' with her. Yet this experience also concealed the cultural mediation upon which it was founded. If Terry's 'allure as a commodity' depends upon the spectator's apprehension of intimacy, 'it is also what occludes her status as commodity'.[42] In other words, the 'private', familiar self of the actress is constructed through her public status as a celebrity, even while this complicity is suppressed.

In *The Bostonians*, Basil evinces a similar confusion in believing that he is the unique recipient of Verena's public performances. Mistaking the theatrical performance of domesticity for the private sphere which it represents, he assumes that these two spaces are co-extensive. Thus, he attempts to persuade Verena that 'the dining-table itself shall be our platform, and you shall mount on top of that' (*B* 379). In supposing that the public 'platform' can be directly transposed to the private setting of the 'dining-table', Basil fails to recognize the extent to which the performative space of the former encodes his desire to reconstitute the latter. Ironically, he effaces the medium to which he is most acutely responsive. This ambivalent stance bears witness to the cultural effects of the transformation of theatrical space described by Corbett. Basil, it would seem, is torn between two appropriate, but entirely contradictory, cultural responses to the 'feminization' of public space. While he understands the public performance of women to be akin to prostitution, he is also susceptible to the new theatrical codes of domesticity, whereby the actress was domesticated for respectable bourgeois consumption. If, in his first response, Basil is especially sensitive to Verena's commodification, in his second response he completely neglects her status as an object of mass consumption. As a result, his desire to remove Verena from the public platform becomes entangled in his desire for the theatrical celebrity.

In *The Tragic Muse* James returns to the same scenario, but significantly rewrites it. As in *The Bostonians*, he depicts a man who attempts to persuade a woman to exchange the public stage for private life. In the later novel, however, James acknowledges more explicitly the contradictory and self-defeating logic of this endeavour. Echoing Basil's inducements to Verena, Peter Sherringham proposes not to constrict but to expand the scope of Miriam Rooth's performances. By promising Miriam 'a bigger theatre than any of those places in the Strand', Sherringham likewise invokes a sphere of private 'society' within which the actress can 'perform' in a manner which is analogous to, but less degraded than, her performances on stage (*TM* 466). Furthermore, this line of argument is again supported by a reading of the nature of performative art, which attempts to abstract aesthetic form from its determinate contents:

> Even if I wanted, how could I prevent a spirit like yours from expressing itself? Don't talk about my putting you in a box, for, dearest child, I'm taking you out of one. The artist is irrepressible, eternal; she'll be in everything you are and in everything you do, and you'll go about with her triumphantly, exerting your powers, charming the world, carrying everything before you. (*TM* 465)

Here, as Sherringham's metaphor of the 'box' finally confirms, James re-enacts essentially the same conflict which he had staged between Basil and Verena in the earlier novel. This conflict centres around Sherringham's desire to restore a conventional sexual division of labour within a normative conception of the public sphere. Without being prepared to give up his own career, he insists that Miriam abandon her profession and assume the private social duties that are devolved to the wife of a diplomat.

Ironically, though, it is the effect of watching Miriam perform a dramatic role that prompts Sherringham's desire to possess her privately. Whereas, in the play, Miriam is 'present essentially as the romantic heroine she represented', Sherringham responds as if he has witnessed an unmediated act of self-expression (*TM* 457). In wishing to transfer Miriam from the space of the theatre to 'the deepest domesticity of private life', he literally misplaces the object of his desire (*TM* 468). For as Sherringham himself has previously discerned, Miriam lacks any ontological core that can be deemed to be her authentic self: her 'identity resided in the continuity of her personations, so that she had no moral privacy' (*TM* 130). Here, the actress practises a form of public representation which is so voracious that it extends across the various 'private' and 'public' spaces which she may happen to occupy at any given moment. Miriam's 'self' is constituted only through the series of dramatic representations which she performs. While it is true that she continues to perform in private, as Sherringham points out, in this respect 'privacy' itself is little more than a different mode of rhetorical address.

The fact that Sherringham's endeavour to appropriate Miriam should fail so dismally, while Basil succeeds in almost exactly the same terms, suggests that James himself was uneasy with the resolution of the earlier novel. This suggestion is further supported by a letter which James wrote to Mrs Humphrey Ward in 1886, the year in which *The Bostonians* was published. In this letter, James questions the conclusion of Ward's novel, *Miss Bretherton* (1884), in which an actress sacrifices her career for marriage, by arguing that the 'egotistic' nature of the artist would forbid any such renunciation. If, as Leon Edel has argued, James unconsciously rewrote Ward's novel in order to suit his own imaginative requirements, it seems odd that James himself should have directly contradicted this advice in his most recent novel.[43] Verena's 'egotistic' nature, which lies precisely in the apparent 'generosity' of her capacity to forgo a stable ego, is as evident as Miriam's, although it lacks the institutional legitimacy of the theatre and bears the threat of political radicalism. Yet it is only with *The Tragic Muse* that James succeeded in exemplifying his own critical insight. Similarly, in the later novel, James appears to challenge the cultural association between the theatrical exhibition of the female body and the figure of the courtesan. Sherringham shares Basil's repugnance towards the bodily display of the actress, even though he is a fervent admirer of dramatic art. Yet as Miriam reminds him, the audience 'expect us to look at them too, who are not half so well worth it' (*TM* 474). By indicating that the space of the theatre does not merely construct an asymmetrical field of vision, Miriam decentres the secure assumptions of male spectatorship. It is in this respect, however, that Miriam differs markedly from Verena. While James refracts both figures through an 'indirect vision', thus rendering the 'guarded objectivity' of dramatic representation which he described in his preface to *The Awkward Age*, Miriam breaks through the medium of her objectification, and is able to exercise a subjectivity which is denied to Verena (*LC* II 1131).

In both novels, however, James is evidently concerned with a form of publicity which extends far beyond the immediate spatial confines of the theatre or public platform. In his view of Verena's prospective career as a 'distinguished actress or singer', Basil comes close to Gabriel Nash's grotesque vision of the 'machinery' of Miriam's future celebrity. For Nash, it is the 'colossal, deafening newspaperism of the period' which constitutes 'its most distinctive sign', and Miriam's success in the theatre will be accompanied, accordingly, by 'reporters and photographers, placards, and interviews and banquets, steamers, railways, dollars, diamonds, speeches and artistic ruin' (*TM* 375). Likewise, Verena's cultural visibility is not confined to the unique spatiotemporal instance of performance, but is linked to a much wider network of publicity in which different media interact. Basil is convinced that 'she could go, like that, for several years, with her portrait in the druggists' windows and her posters on the fences, and during that time would make a fortune sufficient to keep her in affluence for evermore' (*B* 314–15). Thus, even though his personalized response to Verena is channelled through the new cultural codes of commodity representation, the extension of these techniques appears to threaten this response. The display of portraits and posters signals the fact that Verena's public image is infinitely reproducible and serialized, rather than intimate and unique as it appears to be. The anxiety aroused by the mass production of Verena's image is made particularly evident when Basil notices the sale of 'Photographs of Miss Tarrant' and 'Portraits of the Speaker' prior to her anticipated performance in the Music Hall. His immediate response is to wish that he 'had money to buy up the stock' of the vendors in order to prevent their further dissemination (*B* 415). Basil evidently considers that the photographic reproduction of Verena's image multiplies and attenuates the subject which it represents, and so dilutes his own possession of her. In this view, the individual self does not bear unlimited representation: it possesses only a finite pool of resources upon which to draw, while the possibilities of mechanical reproduction are technically infinite. The mass consumption of Verena's photographic image is conceived as an erosion of the barrier which preserves the integrity of the private self from the public world. Given the reproducibility of these images, however, Basil's urge to forestall their dissemination merely by purchasing the present stock can only appear ineffectual. It is in this sense, therefore, that Ian Bell is right to observe that 'James's understanding of the renewed alterability of the world, as revealed by the spectacles of the shop-window and the advertisement, enables him to recognize a radically new liberty for the self.'[44] The dissolution of the boundaries between private and public space threatens Basil's project of ensealing Verena within a permanent sphere of private consumption. As Olive reluctantly comes to realize, it is only by accepting her fate as a commodified spectacle that Verena can hope to escape being transformed into a different form of commodity by Basil. Basil, too, understands that once Verena has become further immersed within the world of publicity, he will be unable to silence the amplification of her voice or contain the dissemination of her image.

At the same time, however, we must also recognize that it is these new forms of cultural display which incite Basil's desire to possess Verena by appearing to confirm his belief that privacy is her appropriate medium. Verena's image saturates the urban space of Boston, transforming the public realm into a feminized domain of intimacy. The effects of this 'feminization' of public space upon contemporary observers may be discerned in *The Reign of the Poster* (1895), a catalogue of advertising posters compiled by Charles Knowles Bolton and coincidentally published in Boston. Commenting upon the recent proliferation of pictorial advertisements, as opposed to purely graphic designs, Bolton acknowledged its most gratifying aspect: 'Ladies (on paper), like prospectuses, are ever attractive, and how many glad moments these poster beauties have given us as we passed from window to window!'[45] As Bolton is aware, the fixed allure of these 'poster beauties' is attributable to their function as 'prospectuses' for the commodities which they come to signify. Like Verena, the 'ladies' exist only upon a horizontal plane of representation. Yet, as Bolton's response attests, the location of such images within shop windows, or in other public sites, permeates the everyday consciousness of the urban consumer. As he strolls through the city streets, the male onlooker assumes the posture of a *flâneur*, finding casual gratification in a series of 'glad moments'.[46]

Similarly, in *The Bostonians*, James records Basil's casual observation of Verena's portrait, strategically displayed throughout the city. For much of the novel, Basil is physically detached from the scene of Verena's triumphs; yet he is rarely beyond the reach of her image. Whilst in New York, for example, he measures the extent of Verena's success by looking for her photograph in shop windows; likewise, in Boston, he searches for posters advertising her prospective performances. To a considerable extent, what Basil sees and desires in Verena is her ubiquitous representation 'on paper'. As he walks through the streets of Boston before Verena's Music Hall lecture, Basil's vision registers a world entirely saturated by such forms of display:

The shop-fronts glowed through frosty panes, the passers bustled on the pavement, the bells of the street-cars jangled in the cold air, the newsboys hawked the evening-papers, the vestibules of the theatres, illuminated and flanked with coloured posters and the photographs of actresses, exhibited seductively their swinging doors of red leather or baize, spotted with little brass nails. (*B* 412–13)

In this apocalyptic scene of the novel, forms of advertising and publicity occupy every site of the urban landscape: from shop-fronts to newsboys, from theatres to hotels, the material environment of the modern city is colonized by commodities.[47] Here, indeed, James seems to offer his most powerful critique of the appropriation of the public domain by the private interests of monopoly capitalism. If this critique may be understood as a response to the violent shock of modern publicity, it is also, as I have been suggesting, predicated upon an earlier understanding of the normative function of the public sphere. The nature of this response was, of course, not unique to James. In *The Age of Disfigurement* (1893), Richardson Evans, for example, attacked the practice of modern advertising on similar grounds. Evans – a member of the recently formed British 'National Society for Checking the Abuses of Public Advertising' – viewed the proliferation of public advertising as an insidious privatization of the public domain; rather than issuing an appeal to the 'public interest', as he claims, the advertiser is 'apparently free to inflict any discomfort or even pain upon the community, if by doing so he can secure notoriety for something in which he feels an interest'. Whereas, for Evans, public space should be used to represent 'the community' as a whole, the advertiser uses it to serve his own private 'interest'. Evans's suitably epochal critique of 'The Age of Disfigurement' bears upon James's novel in another way as well. In commenting upon the self-promotional habits of modern life, Evans points towards an understanding of how the individual self is concomitantly reshaped. If '"Cogito: Ergo Sum," was a good enough maxim once', he notes, its 'modern equivalent is "I am: therefore I announce the fact in large capital letters."'[48] What Evans humorously suggests is that the Cartesian verification of self-existence is inapplicable to modern subjects formed within a culture of publicity.

The lack of authentic interiority in James's characterization of Verena Tarrant also signals this shift in the cultural construction of the self. Verena's identity is, to the same degree, no longer authorized by an immanent *cogito*; instead, as Evans observes, the nature of the self is tied to its enunciation or performance. In *The Bostonians*, James traces the emergence of this modern performative self and explores its complex relationship to rival forms of public representation. The historical transformation of the public sphere, however, was not simply the result of changing modes of public performance. As I shall now argue, James's experience of publicity was also related to changes in the composition and, concomitantly, in the representation of 'the public' to which his own literary and theatrical performances were addressed.

CHAPTER TWO

What the public wants: criticism, theatre and the 'masses'

For the American novelist F. Marion Crawford, there were two distinct and opposing conceptions of the function of art. In his critical study *The Novel: What it Is* (1893), Crawford reacted against the contemporary vogue of 'art for art' by advocating in its place an 'art for the public'. Whereas the former, according to Crawford, was preoccupied with the value accorded to the work by its producer (or 'seller'), the latter would recognize the desire of the consumer (or 'buyer') as its determining instance. From this populist standpoint, the paying public has a right to demand 'a romance, a novel, a story of adventure', rather than 'somebody's views on socialism, religion, or the divorce laws'. It is the novel's mundane status as a commodity, subject to the regulation of 'supply and demand', which stands as its fundamental truth.[1]

Crude though it is, Crawford's proposal of an 'art for the public' serves to identify a prominent theme in the literary debates which took place in Britain and America towards the end of the nineteenth century. Observing a dramatic increase in the scale of literary production from the 1880s and 1890s onwards, contemporary critics frequently ascribed the accompanying changes in aesthetic practice to the cultural effects of an expanding readership. The belief that literary 'success' was increasingly determined by the 'demand' of a mass public powerfully reshaped existing conceptions of the relationship between authors and readers. Many critics, however, were unable to share Crawford's unabashed acceptance of the commodification of cultural products, or his willingness to be guided as a writer by the presumed 'wants' of the public. It was more often assumed that the formation of a mass reading public diminished the autonomy of authorship and eroded the aura of the book. In this vein of criticism, the growth of the public was synonymous with the narratives of cultural decline, recording the onset of 'democratization', 'feminization' and 'commercialization', which James had inscribed within *The Bostonians.*

In this chapter, I suggest that much of James's literary and cultural criticism may be understood as a prolonged reflection upon the emerging public sphere of mass culture. Recognizing James's uneasy response to the new reading 'masses' does not, however, mean viewing him, in Crawford's scheme, as an aloof votary of 'art for art'. As Michael Anesko has persuasively argued, James was himself engaged by the possibilities of popular acclaim and commercial success that were offered by an expanding literary market. The threatening spectre of the mass public was offset by the promise of a wider literary fame. Nowhere was this ambivalence more evident than in James's attempt to transform himself into a popular dramatist during the early years of the 1890s. In the theatre James's experience of the publicity of modern culture assumed its most personal and agonistic form. Yet the anxieties of exposure and fantasies of acclaim which characterized James's appeal to a mass audience cannot simply be ascribed to personal psychology, as the classic biographical accounts of his theatrical career have suggested.[2] In order to understand the intensity of his response to the theatre, and the urgency of many of his critical statements, we need to situate James's cultural thought in the context of a much wider discursive formation, in which the very nature of literary popularity was rendered problematic. James's career bears witness not only to infrastructural changes in the literary market, as critics such as Anesko and Margolis have amply shown, but also, correspondingly, to a transformation of the cultural meaning of 'the public' itself.[3]

THE LITERARY DELUGE

In a number of his critical essays and reviews, written, for the most part, during the 1890s, James directly addressed the state of contemporary literature. These texts may be read as contributions to a wider debate on the democratization of access to the formerly exclusive sphere of literary culture, and on the formation of what was subsequently termed 'mass culture'. The phenomenon with which James, like many other critics, was particularly concerned was an expansion of commercial production, which, to use the appropriate contemporary trope, assumed the proportions of a literary 'deluge'. The recurrent use of this metaphor within the sphere of literary debate does little to conceal its reference to a specifically political mode of discourse. In *The Princess Casamassima* (1887), Hyacinth Robinson had noted that the 'flood of democracy was rising over the world'.[4] In spite of Hyacinth's radical political affiliations – which are, in any case, wavering – the rhetoric of the 'flood of democracy' was clearly used to express bourgeois fears of being engulfed by the 'rising masses'. As Nigel Cross has shown, contemporary attacks upon the degradation of modern literature by members of the British cultural establishment were also couched in a language of political reaction, evoking the imminence of a biblical Flood.[5] The novelist Robert Buchanan was more explicit than most when, in *A Look round Literature* (1887), he described the growth of literary ephemera as a symptom of the 'great waters of Democracy arising to swallow up and cover the last landmarks of individualism'.[6] James deployed the same language in articulating a similar, if more nuanced, concern in his essay 'The Science of Criticism' (his contribution to a series of articles under the same title, published in *The New Review* in 1891).[7] Commenting on the proliferation of critical writing, James observed that:

> If literary criticism may be said to flourish among us at all, it certainly flourishes immensely, for it flows through the periodical press like a river that has burst its dikes. The quantity of it is prodigious, and it is a commodity of which, however the demand may be estimated, the supply will be sure to be, in any supposable extremity, the last thing to fail us. (*LC* I 95)

What is interesting about James's apprehension of the sheer quantity of ephemeral, critical texts, however, is the way in which it seems to disrupt the equilibrium of supply and demand often assumed by other critics. A more typical explanation of the literary deluge was that it merely responded to 'public demand'. This was true of both apologists and critics of the new mass market. In the latter mould, for example, Francis Whiting Halsey held the 'unguided public' responsible for having 'created' the indiscriminate flood of literary commodities: in his book *Our Literary Deluge* (1902), it is the public which, almost literally, 'demands' and determines the quantity of production.[8] In 'The Science of Criticism', on the other hand, James envisages a form of production that is autotelic, one in which supply remains in excess of an indeterminate demand.

James's perception of the disjunction between supply and demand within the current literary deluge appears to recognize the 'chronic overproduction' which, as Michael Anesko has pointed out, marked the growth pattern of the literary market towards the end of the century.[9] Within this general surplus of production, however, James also discerns a similar relationship of excess between the discourse of 'criticism' and its primary object:

> What strikes the observer above all, in such an affluence, is the unexpected proportion the discourse uttered bears to the objects discoursed of – the paucity of examples, of illustrations and productions, and the deluge of doctrine suspended in the void; the profusion of talk and the contraction of experiment, of what one may call literary conduct. (*LC* I 95)

In these terms, the phenomenon of overproduction corresponds to the excess of a signifier over its signified. The flood of ephemeral critical writing is accompanied by a dearth of authentic 'literary' texts to which, normatively, criticism refers and defers. This disturbance of the hierarchical relationship between the secondary language of criticism and the primary language of literature was a recurring theme in contemporary criticisms of the literary deluge. 'Criticism flourishes on the grave of imagination', Robert Buchanan had luridly declared.[10] The fact that critics of the literary deluge were themselves contributing considerably to the flood of ephemeral, meta-discursive commentary was an irony that few acknowledged. As Peter Keating has observed of the proliferation of literary manuals during the same period, works which thematized the professional and commercial practices of the literary industry were liable to commodification in their own right.[11]

In its own terms, however, the intensity of critical concern with the literary deluge can only be understood if it is seen as marking a profound attenuation of the cultural space and temporal horizon within which authors and books had once appeared to subsist. Francis Whiting Halsey saw the expansion of literary production as virtually synonymous with the increasing transience of the individual text. As texts and authors proliferate, so they inevitably acquire an ephemeral character, a shorter lifespan, which matches the restless attention of the reader.[12] For similar reasons, Frederic Harrison, in *The Choice of Books* (1886), figured the increasing competition between books as a 'crowded city', in which the 'aimlessly wandering' reader was 'of all men the most lonely'. Books are situated, almost literally, within an overcrowded arena, clamouring to attract the reader: like Darwinian organisms, they struggle for existence within a 'vast and teeming' jungle. For Harrison, the question of the 'choice of books' arises in response to a realization that the vast historical accumulation of texts problematizes assumptions about the self-evidence of the literary canon. In order to preserve the 'great inheritance of mankind in prose and verse' against 'the remorseless cataract of daily literature which thunders over the remnants of the past', it becomes necessary, self-consciously, to construct canons: to discriminate amongst texts which can no longer be encompassed in their totality.[13]

From a later perspective, James recorded a similar experience of the crowded field of modern literature in his autobiographical volume *Notes of a Son and Brother* (1914). Recalling his adolescent experience of perusing the first issue of the *Cornhill Magazine* in 1860, James contrasted its magnitude as an event with the satiated consumption of the present day: 'Is anything like that thrill possible to-day – for a submerged and blinded and deafened generation, a generation so smothered in quantity and number that discrimination, under the gasp, has neither air to breathe nor room to turn round?'[14] For James, the distinction of the *Cornhill* lies in its remembered singularity. Yet this singularity is marked not so much by any inherent quality which the magazine may have possessed, as by the quantitative emptiness which surrounded it. It is the magazine's freedom from the encroachment of competition that preserves its autonomous cultural space. The authoritative presence of the *Cornhill* is defined negatively by what it does not touch, what cannot contaminate it, rather than by any positive content. Clearly, this form of appreciation is shaped by James's retrospective stance; only in a seemingly replete present is it possible to know what it was that the past did not contain. It might even be argued that James's temporal distance from the event of the *Cornhill*'s first appearance is in part responsible for creating the distance which the magazine had apparently maintained in its own spatial existence. The 'aura' of an object, as Walter Benjamin suggested in his famous essay 'The Work of Art in the Age of Mechanical Reproduction' (1936), may be defined as 'the unique phenomenon of a distance'.[15] It is through this 'phenomenon' that the natural or historical object may be invested with a sanctity which is commensurate with the apparent singularity of its existence in a particular space and time. James, in fact, uses the very same word in describing the expansive horizon which magazines such as the *Cornhill* once appeared able to command. Looking back to the middle of the nineteenth century, he locates a 'time in which a given product of the press might have a situation and an aspect, a considerability, so to speak, a circumscription and an *aura*; room to breathe and to show in, a margin for the casting of its notes'.[16] Through this somewhat idealized recollection, James laments the fact that the literary text can no longer assume the same guise as an unrivalled source of cultural authority. Tracing the loss of an earlier and more spacious literary milieu, he charts the emergence of a mass culture in which publications jostle with each other for the reader's attention.

It is not difficult to see how such a narrative participates in what Pierre Bourdieu has termed the logic of cultural 'distinction'. For as Bourdieu points out, what is central to the Kantian tradition of bourgeois aesthetics is 'the distance which allows it to keep its distance': or, in Benjamin's terms, the preservation of the 'aura'. The distanced, 'discriminating' stance of aesthetic judgement is, according to Bourdieu, predicated upon an anxious refusal of the immediate sensory gratification of consumption, linked to the vulgar 'taste' of the masses. In a like manner, James's contrast between an earlier cultural scene, where there was 'room to breathe', and the present 'generation', for whom there is 'neither air to breathe nor room to turn around', reveals the nausea (or, more literally, disgust) which, for Kant, follows upon the loss of distance.[17] The metaphors of pollution and asphyxiation which are buried within this passage from the autobiography adumbrate, as did Frederic Harrison's figure of the 'crowded city', the ultimate referent which was always encoded within contemporary discussions of the 'democratization' of literature: namely, the 'masses' themselves.

On this basis, it is clear that even James's preoccupation with the literary deluge did not solely identify the problem of a surplus production. If production appeared to exceed and overwhelm consumption, as James envisaged in 'The Science of Criticism', equally the latter was already imaginatively inscribed within the former. Within the field of literary products, the figure of the 'crowd' signifies the suppressed presence of a mass readership. This transposition of the iconography of consumption into the 'deluge' of production is perhaps most visible in James's 1899 essay 'The Future of the Novel'. Here, James switches his concern from the 'river' of criticism to the still greater 'flood' of fiction. The preponderance of fiction within the total output of literary production does not, however, yield the forms of 'literary conduct' to which James gave primacy in the earlier essay. Indeed, the charge of ephemeral productivity is levelled against fiction, as it had been against criticism. In this degraded form, the production of fiction, one might say, is virtually synonymous with the act of being consumed. The metaphor of the 'flood' indicates a facility of production that registers its orientation towards a similarly rapid, disposable and visceral consumption. In this respect, James differed from his contemporary Walter Besant who, in his *Autobiography* (1902), attempted to distinguish between the 'flood' of fictional 'trash' and the character of the reading public. While Besant acknowledged that 'Thousands of bad books may be produced', he also claimed that 'they never get circulated; nobody buys them; they drop still-born from the press; they swell the statistics alone'.[18] Since the 'flood' of fiction refers only to the moment of production, it cannot be used as a means of drawing invidious inferences about public taste. Besant's interest in fostering 'a love and appreciation of Art . . . among the masses of the People' (the title of an address which he delivered to the Social Science Congress in September 1884) suggests a paternalistic liberal faith in 'popular' education which James did not share.[19]

In 'The Future of the Novel', in fact, James alludes sceptically to recent attempts to educate the reading public. It is the increase in the number of 'common schools', he argues, that largely accounts for the growth of the public by 'making readers of women and of the very young' (*LC* I 100). James was not unique in linking the phenomenon of the literary deluge to the widening access to public education which, in Britain, followed in the wake of Forster's Education Act of 1870 and subsequent legislation. Once again, Robert Buchanan offered a suitably apocalyptic judgement: 'After the School Board has come the Deluge.'[20] James, however, offers a more explicitly gendered account of the same equation. The 'contemporary deluge' of fiction, he insists, is predicated on 'the making itself supremely felt, as it were, of the presence of the ladies and children – by whom I mean, in other words, the reader irreflective and uncritical' (*LC* I 103). In this reading, it is the prior 'presence' of the public which comes to infuse the flood of literary production, thus reinscribing the notion that 'public demand' actively determines the degraded products of mass culture. At the same time, this public is explicitly defined by its juvenility and femininity: by a mode of consumption that is 'irreflective and uncritical'. There is an interesting contradiction, here, since James appears to conceive of this expanding readership as both active and passive, demanding and facile. This duality is also adumbrated in the language with which he describes the process of consumption in 'The Future of the Novel':

> The flood at present swells and swells, threatening the whole field of letters, as would often seem, with submersion. It plays, in what may be called the passive consciousness of many persons, a part that directly marches with the rapid increase of the multitude able to possess itself in one way or another of the book. The book, in the Anglo-Saxon world, is almost everywhere, and it is in the form of the voluminous prose fable that we see it penetrate easiest and furthest. Penetration appears really to be directly aided by mere mass and bulk. There is an immense public, if public be the name, inarticulate, but abysmally absorbent, for which, at its hours of ease, the printed volume has no other association. (*LC* I 100)

In this passage, James articulates a number of assumptions about mass culture and the nature of a 'mass' public, which subsequently became embedded within the dominant mode of early twentieth-century cultural criticism. The idea that mass consumption is merely unconscious, passive and 'inarticulate', while, conversely, the forces of production are purely instrumental is clearly evoked in the essay.[21] This distribution of active and passive functions also connotes a gendered distinction between 'masculine' production and 'feminine' consumption. James's sense of the 'passive consciousness' to which the 'flood' of fiction appeals is implicitly related to his belief in the predominance of women readers.

As Andreas Huyssen has recently argued, the insistent feminization of consumption during the late nineteenth century may be seen as a constitutive moment in the emergence of the subsequent division between high modernism and mass culture. While modernist writing is itself often claimed to be a 'feminine' form, from Flaubert onwards, Huyssen alerts us to the way in which many modernists, in fact, privileged an austere 'masculine' ethos of production over the facilities of a feminized consumer culture. In this respect, at least, James may be seen as an exemplar of the founding rhetoric of modernist high culture. By inverting the accepted gender determinations of high culture and mass culture, however, Huyssen is unable to account fully for the marked instability of these formulations. In James's case, consumption is not simply understood as passive: much of his concern with the reading 'masses' arises precisely from a sense of their active voracity. This characterization of the nature of the public is, of course, no less gendered than the other. Yet it reveals an ambivalent mixing of metaphors: the feminine public is not only 'absorbent', but also signified by the engulfing 'flood'. By the same token, what appears as a masculine 'penetration' of the public, in the passage quoted above, is none other than the 'flood' of fiction itself. To this extent, the active and passive functions of production and consumption are always unstable and reversible. It would be wrong to assume that James firmly identified his authorial and critical position as 'masculine' in the way that Huyssen's account might suggest: disturbed by the aggressive instrumentality of the mass market, James himself often assumed the role of a passive, victimized author.[22]

It is clear, nevertheless, that through the metaphor of the 'literary deluge' contemporary critics found a means of encoding not only their concern with the onset of 'democratization', but also with a perceived process of 'feminization'. Indeed, these two narratives were often so conflated as to be practically interchangeable: 'The fear of the masses', as Huyssen has rightly observed, was 'always also a fear of woman'.[23] The surplus character of the 'literary deluge' – which Frederic Harrison likened to a 'sewage outfall' – was not merely a symptom encoded as 'feminine', but was also directly ascribed to women writers.[24] James himself never tired of insisting upon the excessive 'fluency' and 'fluidity', which he saw as characteristic of both the form and output of female novelists, even if, as has recently been suggested, he expended a similarly excessive energy in his own writings.[25] His essays on George Sand, in particular, may be read as a prolonged metaphorical elaboration upon the discourse of the 'literary deluge'. Sand's 'work', James wrote in 1902, was 'so beautiful, plentiful and fluid' that it 'has floated itself out to sea even as the melting snows' (*LC* II 759). For James, she appears to have stood as an individual representative of the cultural phenomenon which characterized the modern literary market as a whole.[26]

From as early as the 1860s, as both Habegger and Margolis have shown, James had an acute sense of the extent to which his own professional arena was shaped by the presence of women writers and readers.[27] What I particularly wish to note, however, is the way in which this awareness came increasingly to define his understanding of the nature of 'the public' as such. In a notebook entry written in

1895, for example, James responded to his reading of a book by 'Brada' (the pseudonym of Henriette Consuelo), entitled *Notes Sur Londre*, by recording the cultural significance of 'the *avènement* of the women'. In particular, James was struck by 'the fact that, in many departments and directions, the cheap work they can easily do is more and more all the "public wants". The "public wants" nothing, in short, today, that they *can't* do' (*NB* 196). Within his own 'department' of literature, James's concern assumes that there is an affinity, or even identity, between the facility of women writers and the 'wants' of the reading public. As literary producers, women are characterized by their intuitive capacity to understand the patterns of consumption, and are thus placed in an exemplary position to act as purveyors of 'art for the public'.[28] By contrast, the quotation marks which James places around the phrase 'public wants' suggest both an uncomfortable and an ironic sense of distance from the public. On the one hand, James ruefully (or perhaps strategically) accepts his own inability to fulfil the 'wants' of a wider readership; on the other hand, he conveys a certain scepticism as to what this term means. In the latter sense, James's quotation marks acknowledge what is already a prior quotation: the phrase 'what the public wants' is not so much a spontaneous expression of collective subjectivity, as, to quote Theodor Adorno's words, a 'reified object of calculation', drawn from the pre-existing rhetoric of marketing.[29] This distinction is an important one because it suggests that, while James (rather like Adorno) was himself prone to offering a totalizing account of the formation of mass culture, it was also the very homogeneity ascribed to 'the masses' which he wished to prise apart.

'THE QUESTION OF THE OPPORTUNITIES'

Thus far, I have stressed only one of these aspects of James's critical thought. As a critic of the literary deluge, James envisaged the growth of the mass market as an indefinite extension of the phenomenon of 'mere mass and bulk' (*LC* I 100). Moreover, since, in common with other critics, James projected both an apocalyptic vision of the absolute extension of quantity and its always existing saturation of cultural space, his account of the formation of mass culture appears curiously static, and even monolithic. In this respect, the discourse on the literary deluge is indeed theological, as it assumes that the temporality of the present is at once endlessly unfolding and yet already consummated. Yet it must also be stressed that James did not entirely or uncritically accept this pessimistic and largely conservative response to the democratization of culture. The 'question of numbers' was, for James, also a 'question of the opportunities', as he argued in his essay of that title, published in 1898 (*LC* I 651).

In 'The Question of the Opportunities', James considered the implications of a mass readership for the future of American literature in particular. Casting 'a slightly affrighted look at the mere numbers of the huge, homogenous and fast-growing population from which the flood of books issues and to which it returns', he perceives that new forms of literary 'expression' must be understood in terms of the demographic transformation of the American public (*LC* I 651). In this instance, however, James carefully distances himself from a too 'precipitate and premature' judgement of the 'hitherto almost unobserved' conditions of the mass market (*LC* I 653, 651). While he recognizes that the existence of a reading public on the sheer scale of that of the United States marks a decisive historical break with all previous literary cultures, the past is not thereby idealized:

> It is assuredly true that literature for the billion will not be literature as we have hitherto known it at its best. But if the billion give the pitch of production and circulation, they do something else beside; they hang before us a wide picture of opportunities – opportunities that would be opportunities still even if, reduced to the *minimum*, they should be only those offered by the vastness of the implied habitat and the complexity of the implied history. It is impossible not to entertain with patience and curiosity the presumption that life so colossal must break into expression at points of proportionate frequency. These places, these moments will be the chances. (*LC* I 653)

This is certainly an unusual statement when read in the context of essays such as 'The Future of the Novel' and 'The Science of Criticism'. Nevertheless, it is one that deserves to be taken seriously. The possibility which James considers here is that the quantitative expansion of the mass market may generate qualitatively new forms of literary 'expression' through the unfolding of its own immanent logic. This possibility is not merely an arbitrary wish on James's part: rather, he suggests that the social and economic forces which determine the creation of a mass market may, in turn, produce an internal fragmentation that would challenge the very notion of a unitary, 'mass' public. Unable to sustain its cohesion on such a vast scale, the massification of the public contains the structural conditions of its own collapse. Hence, James anticipates the emergence of heterogeneous publics, for which it is possible to envisage correspondingly differentiated forms of literary practice. It is at this moment that a 'break into expression' occurs, thus averting what James sees as the danger of cultural homogeneity: 'the grossness of any view, any taste or tone, in danger of becoming so extravagantly general as to efface the really interesting thing, the traceability of the individual' (*LC* I 654). In short, James attempts to trace the dialectical logic of 'mere numbers', from their pure accumulation within the form of the mass to their dispersion into newly defined reading and writing communities.

In this respect, it might be argued that the logic of James's essay is not dissimilar to that of Matthew Arnold's more familiar celebration of the elite cultural 'remnant' within American democratic society. In his 1884 essay 'Numbers; or The Majority and the Remnant', Arnold also salvaged a positive moment from the quantitative expansion of the public. Only in the enlarged civic society of the modern democratic state, Arnold argued, is it possible for a sufficiently numerous cultural elite, or 'remnant', to contest and shape the opinions of the uncultivated 'majority'. Thus, like James, Arnold conceives of a reaction to the force of 'numbers' which arises from, and works through, the same cultural process. Paradoxically, Arnold implies, it is the minority 'remnant' which gains most from its numerical expansion. It is Arnold's quantification of this minority, however, which reveals the precariousness of his argument. For in this reckoning, the cultural distinction between the majority and the minority threatens to become almost entirely nominal. On the one hand, Arnold proclaims the universal principle that 'in the present actual stage of the world, as in all the stages through which the world has passed hitherto, the majority is and must be in general unsound everywhere'. On the other hand, he frames this judgement within a millennial scenario of conversion in which, finally, the 'remnant' will 'recover the unsound majority'.[30] Thus, if the 'remnant' is to exercise its proselytizing function, it risks accumulating the very 'numbers' which would undermine the basis of its validity. By defining the strength of his elite in quantitative terms, Arnold jeopardizes the cultural prestige which it derives precisely from its exclusiveness.

It is possible that James's positive projection of the fragmentation of the mass reading public may also have in mind the formation of a strengthened 'remnant', albeit in a different sense. As the work of Peter Keating has shown, the massification of the literary market in the late nineteenth century was indeed accompanied by a simultaneous process of product diversification, which led both to an increasingly sharp division between 'high' and 'low' cultural forms and also, within the field of popular culture itself, to a proliferation of distinct fictional genres with their own relatively autonomous readerships.[31] It was this process of differentiation, as Anne Margolis has observed, which enabled James to address (if not always wholeheartedly) a cultural elite which was becoming economically viable as a 'niche' market. The bifurcation of high culture and mass culture into separate and apparently antithetical spheres opened up new cultural spaces within which authors such as James could situate their work.[32] Indeed, James's account of the disintegration of the public in 'The Question of the Opportunities' strongly suggests his awareness of these possibilities:

> the public we somewhat loosely talk of as for literature or for anything else is really as subdivided as a chess-board, with each little square confessing only to its own *kind* of accessibility. The comparison too much sharpens and equalizes; but there are certainly, as on a map of countries, divisions and boundaries; and if these varieties become, to assist individual genius or save individual life, accentuated in American letters, we shall immediately to that tune be rewarded for our faith. (*LC* I 653–4)

James recognizes that a literary market composed of heterogeneous readerships must also allow a differential access for authors. The forms of address appropriate to one sphere of literary discourse are not universally applicable. To this extent, James's dialectic of 'numbers' reproduces the economic and cultural logic of the market itself. It traces the relationship between the formation of a mass readership, on the one hand, and its incipient subdivision into 'target' groupings, on the other.

On this point, however, James interestingly departs from the Arnoldian critique of mass culture. Whereas James suggests that the dissolution of cultural homogeneity may forge new conditions in which 'individual genius' can flourish, Arnold views the strengthening of the minority as a means of securing or re-establishing its threatened cultural centrality. While James identifies the massification of the public as the primary danger to literary 'expression',

Arnold pits one monolithic body against another in a Manichaean struggle between the 'majority' and the 'remnant'. Thus, for Arnoldian critics such as the Leavises, the emergence of mass culture charts an archetypal fall from cultural homogeneity. In *Fiction and the Reading Public* (1932), for example, Q.D. Leavis traced the decline and fragmentation of the supposedly stable, integrated readership of the mid-Victorian circulating libraries. For Leavis, the expansion of the reading public towards the end of the nineteenth century undermined a prevailing consensus concerning literary and cultural values. What precipitated the disintegration of this homogenous readership was a failure to assimilate the 'ranks of the half-educated' whose admittance to the official public sphere of literature was accelerated by the educational reforms of the 1870s.[33]

James's criticism suggests a more complex understanding of the formation of mass culture than that offered by either Arnold or Leavis. Certainly, James too was concerned by the perceived loss of an endogamic cultural community, as may be seen from his autobiographical recollections of the *Cornhill Magazine*. At the same time, he clearly lacked Arnold's secure assumptions as to where this stable community might be found. Nowhere is this contrast more apparent than in their very different responses to the burgeoning ethnic heterogeneity of the American public. Arnold's faith in the American 'remnant' was founded not only upon a supposition of its increasing numerical strength, but also upon its core of 'excellent Germanic stock'. Like other contemporary English writers, he contemplated the possibility of forging a single, transatlantic 'Race Union'.[34] By contrast, in 'The Question of the Opportunities', James makes a clear distinction between the growing Anglophone public and the ethnic diversity of its composition. His characterization of the American public as 'homogenous' is deliberately and paradoxically formulated in the knowledge that, at the same time, precisely the opposite is true:

> Homogenous I call the huge American public, with a due sense of the variety of races and idioms that are more and more under contribution to build it up, for it is precisely in the great mill of the language, our predominant and triumphant English, taking so much, suffering perhaps even so much, in the process, but giving so much more, on the whole, than it has to 'put up' with, that the elements are ground into unity. (*LC* 1 652)

James was thus convinced of the homogeneity of the American public, even though he was clearly aware of the phenomenon of mass immigration well before his return to the United States in 1904. Yet unlike Arnold, it is this process of standardization, by which the diverse constituents of the American public are assimilated into the dominant ethnic culture via the medium of language, to which James objects. While there is certainly an ambivalence in James's characterization of English as a language which is both 'suffering' and 'triumphant', it is the latter of these two concerns which bears the main burden of his argument. In this sense, as Ross Posnock has argued persuasively in his reading of *The American Scene*, James valorizes cultural difference as a residual site of otherness.[35] Indeed, in 'The Question of the Opportunities', it is cultural difference which offers the most solid empirical basis for the possibility of differentiation in literary expression which James so desires.

In the same way that James offers a more nuanced account of the opposing tendencies of mass culture in 'The Question of the Opportunities', so too he strikes a balance between the 'promise' and the 'threat' posed by the 'feminization' of the public. By pursuing this process to its full extension, he locates a positive, if somewhat ambiguous, outcome. As elsewhere, James equates the massification of the public with its feminization: the 'mass' is figured as a collective feminine body. Of the 'extraordinary dimensions of the public', he claims, 'nothing is more unmistakable than the sex of some of the largest masses. The longest lines are feminine – feminine, it may almost be said the principal front' (*LC* I 656). James's choice of metaphor, here, gives some indication of the threat of violence which was commonly evoked by the analogy between literary and political 'democracy'. What is, after all, a reading public is imaginatively transfigured into a military formation. Moreover, as in his notebook entry of 1895, James links the feminization of the public to a monopolization of 'public taste' on the part of women writers:

> The public taste, as our fathers used to say, has become so largely *their* taste, their tone, their experiment, that nothing is at last more apparent than that the public cares little for anything that they cannot do. And what, after all, may the very finest opportunity of American literature be but just to show that they can do what the peoples will have ended as regarding as everything? (*LC* I 656)

Here, the positive turn in James's reading of the growth of the mass public seems less convincing and more arbitrary than in other respects. While he again wishes to proclaim the possibility of a dialectical 'break into expression', it is not difficult to discern a latent unease behind such confidence. By invoking the patriarchal lineage of 'public opinion', James emphatically announces its appropriation by women writers, and perhaps records his own sense of dispossession. Moreover, the 'opportunity' which he holds out with one hand can be ironically deflated with the other: the capacity of achieving 'what the peoples will have ended as regarding as everything' is evidently not quite the same thing as achieving everything. This, of course, was a lesson which James had already drawn from his experience earlier in the 1890s.

APPEALING TO THE CROWD

When we turn to look at the body of imaginative writing which James produced during this decade, what is so remarkable are the contradictory imperatives which it managed to sustain. Throughout the first half of the 1890s, at least, this contradiction was expressed through what Anne Margolis has termed a 'schizophrenic' self-division in James's authorial ambitions. On the one hand, he writes a series of fictional tales which consecrate, however ironically, the distance between the solitary artist and the 'vulgar' public, and addresses them to the elite readership of avant-garde periodicals such as *The Yellow Book*; on the other hand, he is actively engaged in cultivating a popular audience within the theatre.[36] While these projects run parallel to each other, each postulates a radically different conception of the relationship between artist and public. Other writers, it is true, also attempted to appeal to the mass audience of the theatre, while maintaining their status within the apparently autonomous sphere of 'aesthetic' culture: Oscar Wilde being the most notable and successful example, as Regenia Gagnier has shown.[37] Yet perhaps no other writer of the period went to such lengths to achieve popular success while, at the same time, maintaining the very cultural division which ensured that it would remain inimical or suspect. It is James's internalization of this division which makes any attempt to view him either as an aloof aesthete or as an aspiring popular writer both equally inadequate and equally compelling. While his tales of distinguished 'artists' cannot be detached from his pursuit of popular acclaim, neither can they be assumed to cohere within a unitary form of cultural expression. In this respect, the contradictory dynamics of James's career both exemplify and resist the contemporary bifurcation of high culture and mass culture, and in doing so reveal, in the words of Adorno and Horkheimer, that 'division itself is the truth' of modern culture.[38]

It is for these generally unacknowledged cultural reasons, I would suggest, that James's unsuccessful attempt to transform himself into a popular dramatist has exerted such a fascination upon biographers and critics alike. Since Leon Edel's classic biographical account of the 'dramatic years', the agonistic form of James's response to the theatre has become familiar enough. More recently, Michael Anesko has challenged Edel's somewhat defensive interpretation of the motivation of James's theatrical venture by revealing the extent to which he actively desired popular success, rather than merely hoped for financial gain, from the theatre. While offering a valuable corrective to Edel's overly mythopoeic account, however, Anesko's desire to recover a more worldly, pragmatic James risks effacing the constitutive ambivalence which is attached to this episode in his career. What is missing from both these accounts, moreover, is any attempt to explain the significance of James's theatrical ambition in terms of a general cultural anxiety, rather than a merely idiosyncratic personal psychology.[39] One thing that seems clear is that James ascribed wildly fluctuating motives to this ambition. In the first place, as Edel has stressed, he justified his appeal to a more 'popular' audience on the grounds of financial necessity, insisting that his motives were 'exclusively mercenary' (*L* III 306). In a letter to his brother William, dated 23 July 1890, James denied any real desire for popular acclaim by pronouncing that 'One has always a "public" enough if one has an audible vibration – even if it should only come from one's self' (*L* III 300). Throughout his involvement in the production of *The American* (1890–1), James attempted to enforce this minimal definition of a 'public' by preserving an authorial space of privacy. When raising the prospects of the play with his closest correspondents, he constantly enjoined them to secrecy and silence: 'publicity', he remarked in a letter to William, 'blows on such matters in an injurious and deflowering way'; to speak of the play at all was 'the real giving one's self away'.[40] Even in the midst of his pursuit of public acclaim, then, James attempted to buttress his private 'self' against the threat of dispersal. The performance of the play was envisaged as the ultimate alienation, or 'sacrifice', of the author's creative product.[41]

Yet while James was prone to imagining himself as the victim of a degraded theatrical public, he was also capable of assuming a posture that was its direct antithesis. In a letter to William, written soon after the first performance of *The American* in 1891, he positively accepted the 'practical odiousness' of the material conditions of dramatic production, insisting that 'one isn't at all, needfully, their victim, but is, from the moment one *is* anything, one's self, worth speaking of, their *master*; and may use them, command them, squeeze them, lift them up and better them' (*L* III 329; italics in the original). Such comments reveal an inherently unstable duality in the violent fantasies which underscored James's ambivalence towards the theatre and, more particularly, towards the 'masses' of the theatrical public. If James conceived of the theatre as an arena in which the ontological integrity of the private self was subject to violation, equally he projected a scenario in which, by inverting this relationship, he could attain a supreme 'mastery' over its conditions. Within this field of polarities, however, there appears to be no intermediate position: the role of 'victim' can be exchanged for the role of 'master', but without otherwise disturbing the sacrificial logic which governs both possibilities. The desire for 'mastery' over the theatre is, indeed, predicated upon an initial assumption of martyrdom to it. In a different temporal sequence, James's dramatic career affords instances of both these extremes, as his responses to the respective opening nights of *The American* and *Guy Domville* testify. After the first of these events, James recalled how the audience had vociferously called for the 'author, *author*, AUTHOR!' to receive his customary plaudits on stage; the appreciative applause of the audience had, he felt, been 'really *beautiful*' (*L* III 320). Evidently, in this instance, the heightened public exposure which James faced in the theatre was a source of gratification. Theatrical performance allowed for a coincidence between the production and consumption of the author's work, and, hence, for an immediate acclamation of authorship with which James the novelist was unfamiliar. The scene of popular acclaim which James proudly recounted in 1891, however, is uncannily polarized by the scene of public humiliation which he was to evoke four years later. Writing to William on 9 January 1895, four days after the premiere of *Guy Domville*, James again recorded the public reaction to his play and to the appearance of its author. On this occasion, however, the tumultuous uproar which ensued is figured as a Manichaean struggle between the applauding 'forces of civilization', on one side, and 'the hoots and jeers and catcalls of the roughs', likened to 'a cage of beasts at some infernal "zoo"', on the other (*L* III 508). Here, the audience appears to divide along the lines of class which were inscribed within the physical separation between gallery and box, and James's response to this uproar invokes visions of an Arnoldian conflict between culture and anarchy: a conflict in which the cultivated author is threatened, almost bodily, by the insurrection of the 'mass'.

This, of course, is not to say that James was, in actual fact, faced with the disapproval of a mass audience. Indeed, according to Edel, several contemporary witnesses claimed that the number of jeering spectactors was only a small minority.[42] My immediate concern, however, is not with establishing the veracity of James's response to this famous incident; rather, it is the nature of the response itself which is of interest here. In this respect, it is important to note that what is evoked in James's account of this episode amounts to a scene of crowd violence. This is also the iconographical resonance which subsequent biographical narratives have extracted from the episode without it being explicitly acknowledged. In the most influential of these accounts, Leon Edel, for example, endorsed James's sense of having been in the presence of a 'howling mob', in spite of his own evidence to the contrary (*L* III 510). In his foreword to *Guy Domville*, written in 1949, Edel censured the behaviour of the 'unruly' section of the audience as an improperly active form of spectatorship. 'The audience', he explained, 'was now participating in the play, reaching across the footlights to the actors instead of being reached by them – and with the childish cruelty that mass hostility frequently assumes.'[43] Edel's reading of the events of the night of 5 January 1895 may certainly be questioned on the grounds of its unquestioned assumptions about the asymmetrical nature of dramatic communication. Yet his translation of James's experience into the terms of twentieth-century 'mass psychology', which gives rise to these assumptions, was not an entirely unwarranted interpretive strategy. For in attempting to ascribe James's dramatic failure to the irrational nature of the 'masses' upon whom popular success depends, Edel was merely following a motif that was already present both within James's private correspondence and fiction, and, more generally, within late-nineteenth-century culture.

It was during this earlier period, in fact, that the 'masses' were first constituted as an object of scientific discourse. With the emergence of social psychology on the one hand and strategies of market research on the other, the very existence of a collective nature was attributed to the modern phenomenon of the 'mass'. As Habermas has shown, it was through techniques such as these that the category of 'public opinion' was rendered accessible to an objectivating mode of analysis, and thus underwent a significant conceptual change.[44] Edel's psychologizing of James's theatrical experience thus echoes an earlier form of psychological interpretation that was applied in remarkably similar contexts. This similarity is particularly evident in the case of 'crowd psychology', a pseudo-scientific discipline that first came to prominence during the 1890s. The most influential theorist of the crowd was Gustave Le Bon, whose seminal work *La Psychologie des foules* was published in 1895 and translated into English as *The Crowd: A Study of the Popular Mind* in the following year. While Le Bon was concerned primarily with the political organization of the crowd, and thus with a formation of the 'masses' that might seem alien to James's understanding of this term, what is interesting is the extent to which his psychological theory draws upon the same metaphors and examples which James invoked in both his literary criticism and his private writings on the theatre. According to Le Bon, the homogeneity of the crowd marks an atavistic instinct within the otherwise evolutionary trajectory of the progressive differentiation of organisms: its 'special characteristics' include 'impulsiveness, irritability, incapacity to reason, the absence of judgement and of the critical spirit, the exaggeration of the sentiments, and others besides'. Moreover, since these traits were to be found primarily in those social groups which Le Bon classified as 'inferior forms of evolution – in women, savages, and children', the supposedly increasing power of the 'masses' within modern urban society was figured as a disturbing process of feminization and ethnic contamination. On the first of these points, Le Bon is categorical: 'Crowds', he insists, 'are everywhere distinguished by feminine characteristics.' If, initially, it may appear somewhat surprising that Le Bon should ascribe 'feminine characteristics' to what he also sees as the agent of violent political disturbance, the reason for this characterization lies in his understanding of the 'suggestibility' of the crowd, which renders it open to the manipulative influence of external stimuli, whether in the form of political leaders or through the appeal of advertising.[45] It is on this account that Andreas Huyssen cites Le Bon as an exemplar of the pervasive gendering of mass culture during the late nineteenth century: a strategy in which popular cultural forms are equated with a peculiarly passive, 'feminine' mode of consumption.[46] Yet as in the case of James's conception of the reading public, Le Bon's theory of the crowd must also be understood as contradictory and overdetermined in its character. If, on the one hand, the crowd is defined as being essentially passive and manipulable in its nature, on the other hand it is feared as the site of a revolutionary impulse that erupts uncontrollably, bringing with it the spectre of an insatiable 'public demand'. In this latter form, Le Bon entirely reverses the relationship between the crowd and its leaders. 'A curious symptom of the present time', he remarks, 'is to observe popes, kings and emperors consenting to be interviewed as a means of submitting their views on a given subject to the judgement of crowds.' Taking as his example the recent journalistic innovation of the interview (a phenomenon which James also noted with horror), Le Bon assumes that the products of mass culture belong, in a wholly unmediated fashion, to the spontaneous collective experience of the 'masses'.[47] Throughout *The Crowd*, one finds the same oscillation between active and passive versions of the crowd, without any apparent recognition of contradiction between the two. Thus, while Le Bon ostensibly warned of the dangers of the susceptibility of the crowd to authoritarian control, he tacitly (and, later, with increasing openness, as Robert A. Nye has shown) advocated the necessity for such control.[48]

The theory of the crowd offers its most uncanny resemblance to James's experience of the nature of the public, however, when Le Bon turns towards the theatre as a specific example of the threatening energies of 'mass' consumption. The application of crowd psychology to the question of literary popularity locates similar contradictory pressures within the relationship between authors and their publics. If, according to Le Bon's theory, the author might be thought to occupy the role of the charismatic leader, capable of commanding popular assent, conversely it is the irrational whim of the crowd which issues the verdict of 'success' or 'failure'. To the extent that a fear of the latter prevails, the aspiring popular author is forced to adapt himself to the demands of the public in such a way that he risks immersion within the very body of the crowd:

> The art of appealing to crowds is no doubt of an inferior order, but it demands quite special aptitudes. It is often impossible on reading plays to explain their success. Managers of theatres when accepting pieces are

themselves, as a rule, very uncertain of their success, because to judge the matter, it would be necessary that they should be able to transform themselves into a crowd.[49]

For Le Bon, therefore, the pursuit of popular success involves a precarious and debilitating act of self-annihilation. Its attainment requires an abandonment of the individual self in order to inhabit the mind of the collective. If it can be assumed that these imperatives apply as much to the dramatist as they do to the manager of the theatre, their resemblance to the anxieties which dogged James's quest for popular acclaim become apparent. From his correspondence of the time, it is clear that James, too, understood his ordeal in the theatre as entailing both a descent into the 'popular mind' and an attempt to master the 'art of appealing to crowds'. His alternating fantasies of sacrifice and control correspond to the violent polarities of Le Bon's psychology, in which the crowd assumes a character that is at once absolutely demanding and absolutely compliant.

In suggesting that the theatre may be viewed as a site in which anxieties linked to the formation of mass culture were crystallized during the late nineteenth century, it must again be stressed that my argument does not immediately concern the empirical composition of the theatrical public. To object that the theatre is, by definition, a space of direct public assembly, and thus incommensurate with the mediated construction of the public that is constitutive of modern forms of mass culture would be to take the analogy too literally, and so neglect the processes of imaginative abstraction and substitution which typify contemporary representations of the 'masses'. John Carey expresses this point well when, referring to similar representations of the period, he observes that the 'mass' is not a real entity but a 'metaphysical' body 'that can take on conceptual form only as metaphor'.[50] Once this process is taken into account, it is not difficult to see how the theatre came to offer the most concrete – and yet for that very reason the most strictly inappropriate – embodiment of 'mass' culture. Alongside more traditional anxieties which continued to surround the question of dramatic representation, it was the perceived presence of the 'masses' which aroused concern amongst commentators on the theatre. In his attacks upon the elaborate spectacle of Wagnerian opera, Nietzsche, for example, gave vent to the most virulent strain of contemporary mimophobia. 'In the theater', Nietzsche wrote in *The Gay Science* (1887), 'one is honest only in the mass; as an individual one lies, one lies to oneself

. . . No one brings along the finest senses of his art to the theater, nor does the artist who works for the theater.' As with Le Bon, the theatre is viewed as a site in which the individual (male) artist is subsumed within a feminized mass; where 'even the most personal conscience is vanquished by the levelling magic of the great number'.[51] The extraordinary intensity of Nietzsche's counter-reaction against his own earlier admiration for Wagner offers an interesting case for comparison with the fluctuating course of James's attraction and repulsion to and from the theatre. In particular, Nietzsche's comments may be read as an extreme version of the self-dramatizing mythology which James derived from his own experience as a dramatist. James was likewise convinced that the integrity of the artist was sapped within the theatre, and while this belief was no doubt justified by the extent of the concessions that he was forced to make in the way of cutting his own texts, it was also fostered within a more general climate of cultural anxiety.[52]

Arguably, James came closest to expressing the visceral repugnance which characterizes Nietzsche's commentaries upon the 'mass' in the novel which he published immediately prior to his theatrical venture in 1890. In *The Tragic Muse*, the Wildean aesthete Gabriel Nash speaks in a Nietzschean manner when he denounces the bondage of dramatic art to the heteronomous conditions of theatrical production. The dramatist, he argues, is forced to yield the integral nature of his art in order to cater for

> the *omnium gatherum* of the population of a big commercial city, at the hour of the day when their taste is at its lowest, flocking out of hideous hotels and restaurants, gorged with food, stultified with buying and selling and with all the other sordid speculations of the day, squeezed together into a sweltering mass, disappointed in their seats, timing the actor, wishing to get their money back on the spot before eleven o'clock. (*TM* 50)

If, elsewhere in the novel, Nash's aestheticism is carefully distinguished from any authorial perspective, on this particular matter he anticipates James's private response to the failure of *Guy Domville*. More generally, Nash's remarks suggest the extent to which James saw the consuming public of the theatre as emblematic of the wider formation of urban mass culture. It is not without significance that this vision of the theatre-going public also alludes to the new 'scientific' epistemologies through which the figure of the crowd became subject to objectifying analysis. The degraded conditions of the theatre will be more widely recognized, Nash asserts, 'when the essentially brutal nature of the modern audience is still more widely perceived, when it has been properly analysed' (*TM* 50). Here, the complicity between Nash's aestheticist disdain for the vulgarity of the public and the seemingly quite different posture of scientific or market analysis of mass consumption becomes clear. If the former recoils from the instrumentality of the mass market, it also participates in the objectification which is made possible by the latter.

The concerns articulated in *The Tragic Muse*, however, were not simply restricted to statements made about the theatre in other media. There is reason to suggest that the anxiety which surrounded the formation of a mass-consuming public shaped the self-reflexive content of contemporary drama itself. James, for instance, would have found the Nietzschean conflict between the individual and the mass, as well as the social-psychological notion of the contagious 'suggestibility' of the crowd, explored in Ibsen's *An Enemy of the People* (1882): a play to which he refers in his 1891 essay 'On the Occasion of *Hedda Gabler*'.[53] In *Guy Domville* itself, moreover, James dramatized the strangely unmotivated vacillation of a man caught between the radically polarized attractions of monastic solitude and worldly indulgence. What is so fascinating about *Guy Domville* is precisely what contemporary critics perceived to be its weakness: namely, the way in which Guy is seemingly propelled from one extreme to the other without the assistance of plausible mediation.[54] Whereas, in Acts 1 and 2 of the play, Guy is presented in his two antithetical guises, Act 3 fails to deliver the expected moment of dialectical synthesis. The problem is not simply that these oppositions are irreconcilable in principle, but, rather, that they are not even sufficiently contiguous to establish the basis of a choice. Hence, Guy's eventual decision to enter the priesthood appears as an arbitrary, if predictable, selection from two equally compelling possibilities. Edel is right, moreover, to suggest that Guy's dilemma may be read in an allegorical manner, even though this results in an uncritical perpetuation of James's mythopoeic drama.[55] Guy's vocation for the priesthood is evoked in language which James often used to describe his own artistic self-absorption: initially, he appears destined for the 'cold cloister', surrounded at Porches by a 'little cluster of the faithful'. This vision of solipsistic withdrawal, however, is disturbed when Lord Devenish arrives to open up the alluring horizon of the 'world': 'It only lies with yourself', he promises Guy, 'to be surrounded with the homage of multitudes!'[56] It would not be entirely far-fetched, then, to suggest that, in postulating such a conflict, James was himself dramatizing the contradictory ambitions and anguished alternatives which he experienced in his role as dramatist. In this reading, *Guy Domville* would itself contain an ironic anticipation of its own fate on the stage. James's desire for 'the homage of multitudes' would end, like that of his character, in retreat.

By projecting the conclusion of *Guy Domville* on to James's career as dramatist, there is, of course, a danger of succumbing entirely to the allure of such teleological anticipations. To assume that the alternatives which James confronted in the theatre can be decided either in favour of private retreat or of worldly engagement is simply to repeat the logic of which *Guy Domville* itself reveals the impossibility. This, however, was the logic which James himself employed in the immediate aftermath of the failure of the play. Adopting the terms of his dramatic protagonist, James took pains to announce that he had relinquished his ambition for popular acclaim. Significantly, in recounting the scene which followed the first performance of *Guy Domville*, James expressed particular annoyance at the way in which his leading actor, George Alexander, had appeared to accommodate the hostility of one section of the audience by 'deferring to the rumpus as to the "opinion of the public"' (*L* III 508). Against Alexander's assumption as to what constituted 'public opinion', James was keen to inform William James of the favourable expressions of '*private* opinion' which he had subsequently received (*L* III 508; italics in the original). Private opinion, through its cumulative expression, appears to have offered some compensation for 'public' failure. Indeed, James's repeated emphasis on this term suggests that it be viewed as the authentic medium of public opinion:

> As for the play, in three words, it has been, I think I may say, a rare and distinguished private success and scarcely anything at all of a public one. By a private success, I mean with the even moderately cultivated, civilized and intelligent *individual*, with 'people of taste' in short, of almost any kind, as distinguished from the vast English Philistine mob – the regular 'theatrical public' of London, which, of all the vulgar publics London contains, is the most brutishly and densely vulgar. (*L* III 515)

By insisting upon a distinction between 'private' and 'public' expressions of acclaim, James recapitulates the theological dualism of the pure and the impure which he had invoked, more appropriately, in *Guy Domville*. 'The stupid public is the big public, and the perceptive one the small', he observed in the same letter to William (*L* III 515). Such dualistic formulations, of which James's correspondence during this period is full, also mark a return to what might be termed an Emersonian definition of 'success'. In his essay of that title, published in *Society and Solitude* (1870), Emerson offered a similar means of distinguishing between an authentic meaning of 'success' and its popular, worldly value: 'One adores public opinion, the other private opinion; one fame, the other desert; one feats, the other humility; one lucre, the other love; one monopoly, and the other hospitality of mind.'[57] The measure of true success, Emerson suggests, lies immanently within the achievement of the solitary individual, which cannot be judged according to extrinsic criteria. Nietzsche – himself a student of Emerson – recognized the same equation: '*Success* in the theater', he acidly remarked, 'with that one drops in my respect forever; *failure* – I prick up my ears and begin to respect.'[58] By these means, both Emerson and Nietzsche anticipated James's strategy of turning to advantage his 'failure' as a popular dramatist; for, judged in these terms, 'failure' can be seen as the very mark of 'success'.

In 'The Next Time' (1895) – the tale which he began to write immediately after the failure of *Guy Domville*, and which was clearly modelled upon this experience – James offers a parodically inflated version of the logic behind this strategy. Echoing Nietzsche's remark, the story is centred around an ironically inverted calculus of 'success' and 'failure'. The case of the distinguished but unpopular novelist Ray Limbert is symmetrically opposed to the case of Jane Highmore, whose novels are popular and hence presumptively lacking in distinction. Whereas Limbert needs to achieve commercial success for financial reasons, Highmore envies the cultural prestige that is accrued by 'failure in the market' (*CT* IX 186). Both writers strive to achieve their opposing definitions of 'success' (or 'failure'), and both fail (or perversely succeed), but to opposite effects. Thus, despite all attempts to be 'subtle', Highmore is unable to prevent the spontaneous consumption of her fiction: the public 'straightway rose on the contrary to the morsel she had hoped to hold too high, and making but a big cheerful bite of it, wagged their great collective tail artlessly for more' (*CT* IX 187). In this respect, Highmore exemplifies the intuitive knowledge of 'public wants' which James enviously, but invidiously, characterized as the particular facility of women writers. For the male 'artist', by contrast, popularity is only to be achieved through an arduously self-conscious attempt to construct an instrumental relationship between author and public. Limbert comes to recognize that he 'must cultivate the market', and 'go in for an infernal cunning' (*CT* IX 208). Yet while the two novelists assume antithetical positions in relation to the mutually exclusive spheres of art and the market, their difference is marked by an underlying likeness. Just as Highmore cannot avoid a degrading popularity, so Limbert cannot avoid producing a succession of unsaleable masterpieces. In their absolute alterity to the other, each is trapped within the absolute self-identity of an inherent predisposition. Thus, in their different ways, both Limbert and Highmore demonstrate the proverbial wisdom which James took as the moral of his story, as well as of his own experience in the theatre: 'you can't make a sow's ear out of a silk purse'.[59] Limbert, indeed, stands in the same relationship to Highmore as James himself did to his more successful competitor, Oscar Wilde. On the opening night of *Guy Domville*, James had been to see Wilde's play *An Ideal Husband* and, in a subsequent letter, claimed to have asked himself the question: 'How *can* my piece do anything with a public with whom *that* is a success?' (*L* III 514). The logic of this question points to the same ineluctable incapacity for self-difference which is posited in the scenario of 'The Next Time'.

What is interesting about this scenario, however, is that while James wishes to suggest that both Limbert and Highmore are incapable of rationalizing their different forms of 'success', he does so in a manner that parodically instantiates the process of market rationalization. If Limbert's attempt to study the 'science' of the market is constantly foiled by the 'law of one's talent', the perversity of this law is as predictable as that which it appears to elude (*CT* IX 208). The pathos of Limbert's fate offers a mirror-image of the successful commodity which he cannot produce: his next novel will be just the same as the last – 'and then the next and the next and the next!' (*CT* IX 220). Likewise, in outlining the opposite dilemma of Jane Highmore, James presupposes a form of rational understanding that masquerades as an elective affinity. The idea that literary popularity cannot be rationalized – that it is simply a matter of innate disposition – is itself a product of the kind of 'scientific' enquiry which Limbert endeavours to pursue. In his recognition that Highmore's success is 'all intuition; her processes are obscure', Limbert recalls the irrational nature of the public as it was defined within the formulas of crowd psychology (*CT* IX 208). For Gustave Le Bon, as I have suggested, popular acclaim is unpredictable because it is contingent upon an ability to fathom the depths of the collective mind. Yet, at the same time, it is this unpredictability which crowd psychology claims to predict. To this extent, Limbert's scientific study of the market attains significance precisely *because* it is destined to fail.

It is worth noting that James himself adopted a similar posture of authorial enquiry in his preface to 'The Next Time'. In defining the object of his own fictional study, James acknowledged that 'The Next Time' was 'in essence a "story about the public", only wearing a little the reduced face by reason of the too huge scale, for direct portrayal, of the monstrous countenance itself' (*LC* II 1233–4). The interest of the tale, he suggests, is derived from the light which it sheds upon the collective character of the public, rather than upon any individual fictional character deployed in the process of illustration. Thus, in accounting for his motives in writing 'The Next Time', James reproduces Limbert's motivation within the story itself. He had proposed to himself a 'study of just where and when, just how and why recognition denies itself to the appeal at all artfully, and responds largely to the appeal coarsely enough, commingled': a 'study' which was to be undertaken, moreover, in 'the light of "comparative science"' (*LC* II 1233). James's invocation of the rhetoric of scientific enquiry is, of course, as ironic in the preface as it is in the tale. This is no reason, however, for diminishing its significance. The point is not that James succeeded in exercising an 'infernal cunning' in his dealings with the market, but that, through his comic confessions of defeat, he achieved an indirect mastery over the inscrutable public. What matters for this project is not so much its success in rendering transparent the inarticulate wants of the public, but, rather, its very ascription of opacity, which, while appearing to signal the public's resistance to appropriation, only confirms its manipulable character.

James was certainly not the only contemporary novelist to show an interest in determining the 'character' of the new mass reading public. By the turn of the century, as Keating has shown, the question of literary popularity attracted increasing attention from authors and publishers, as was manifested by such commercial practices as the publication of 'best-seller' lists.[60] Popularity on the scale of a mass readership was perceived to be a distinctively modern cultural phenomenon, calling for equally new techniques of analysis. In his study *Fame and Fiction: An Enquiry into Certain Popularities* (1901), Arnold Bennett, for instance, adopted a stance that was broadly sympathetic towards popular fiction, and aimed specifically against those 'literary reactionaries' who decried the 'democratization' of literature. Instead of disparaging popular novelists such as Ouida and Mary Braddon, he set out to understand the reasons for their success. Like James, however, Bennett believed that the vexed question of just how and why certain authors and novels achieve popularity could be answered through a scientific study of the nature of the public. The 'secret of popularity in an art', he observed, posed a 'particular problem in the "psychology of crowds"'. Thus, despite their differences, Bennett's descriptions of the reading public accord very much with James's. While Bennett rebukes the elitism of those critics who look with disdain at the formation of a democratically expanded readership, he himself characterizes the public in terms which likewise reduce it to an irrational entity. The 'great public', he declared, is 'huge and simple and slow in mental processes, like a good-humoured giant, easy to please and grateful for diversion'; its 'predilections' are 'subtly and mysteriously instinctive'.[61] In short, Bennett's public is as monstrous and monolithic a figure as James's in the preface to 'The Next Time'. His explicit reliance upon the 'insights' of crowd psychology renders his avowedly democratic stance towards popular literature more questionable, certainly, than Carey has recently claimed.[62] By assuming that the process of mass consumption is largely unconscious and instinctual, Bennett concedes that popularity is merely an object to be gained, or an accolade to be conferred. Accordingly, the public is reduced to an esoteric object of knowledge, subject to the probing of the market analyst.

In the year that Bennett made his enquiry into the 'secret of popularity', however, James offered a rather different analysis of the same question. In an essay on the French dramatist Edmond Rostand, James returned again to the subject of the theatre, and revealed his continuing attraction to the idea of popular success. Like Bennett, James argues that in modern societies the sheer 'scale on which a work of imagination, so called, may, in especial, see itself multiplied, advertised, acclaimed, diffused, makes the mystery of popularity more than ever difficult to analyse'. Yet whilst this phenomenon ensures that there can be no immediate assumption of equivalence between popularity and artistic distinction, neither does it entail their mutual exclusion. James confesses that he is 'unable altogether to dissociate the idea of acclamation from the idea of distinction', thus calling into question the ironically predictable calculus of 'success' and 'failure' which he had constructed in 'The Next Time'. The author of *Cyrano de Bergerac* offers him an example of a writer who has effectively disproved the 'simple law' by which art and commerce constitute entirely separate spheres of value. It is Rostand's ability to combine both commercial and artistic 'success' – achieved, ironically, in the same year that *Guy Domville* had failed – which demonstrates the continuing allure of popular acclaim even within an age of mass culture: 'what is universal recognition', James asks in the essay, 'but glory, and what is behind glory, by the ancient rule, in these fields, but somebody's achievement of something supreme?'[63] James's association of 'glory' with popular 'acclamation' does not, of course, escape the fantasy of domination which persisted alongside his antithetical myth of martyrdom. It was within an encompassing ideal of 'glory', as James recounted in *A Small Boy and Others* (1913), that the worlds of 'beauty and art' were capable of being reconciled with those of 'history and fame and power'.[64] To this extent, James's desire for popular acclaim, just as much as his rejection of it, remained distant from its object.

Nevertheless, James's essay on Rostand suggests that his immediate response to the failure of *Guy Domville* could offer only a temporary and unstable solution to the 'mystery of popularity'. It was during this period of reaction that James embraced, in its starkest form, the bifurcation of the 'big public' and the 'small'. Yet, as I have attempted to suggest, the course of James's career also resists the cultural logic in which it participates. By adopting both sides of this historical separation, James allows us to witness the truth of division itself. The idea that James finally retreated into a private domain of art after the abrupt termination of his theatrical aspirations is one that has been rightly questioned by recent critics.[65] While James himself did much to perpetuate this idea, his drama and fiction constantly remind us of the impossibility of reaching a state of irreducible externality to the public domain. On the other hand, James's ideal of authorial privacy should not simply be dismissed as an ideological illusion, to which the pragmatic imperatives of his own literary career give the lie. If James refused to sever his links with the mass market, equally he wished to maintain his distance from it.

CHAPTER THREE

'The insurmountable desire to know': privacy, biography and 'The Aspern Papers'

Just as James insisted upon the value of 'private', as opposed to 'public', opinion in the immediate aftermath of the failure of *Guy Domville*, so, on an earlier occasion, he had followed the same impulse. After the stress of seeing *The American* through production in 1890, James expressed relief at being able to re-enter his private study: 'Meanwhile the soothing, the healing, the sacred and salutary refuge from all these vulgarities and pains is simply to lose myself in this quiet, this blessed and uninvaded workroom in the inestimable effort and refreshment of art, in resolute and beneficent production' (*NB* 111). Remarks such as this are often used to confirm the idea that, in departing the public arena of the theatre, James returned to his proper sphere: an autonomous and sanctified realm of art. His invocation of a 'sacred and salutary refuge' appears to suggest a state of privacy which exists both apart from and prior to the author's entry into the sphere of public circulation, either as dramatist or novelist.

A closer reading, however, suggests that, far from merely celebrating the sanctity of an autonomous space of creative labour, James persistently questioned both its utility and its possibility. In the first place, James was sceptical of the kind of solipsistic aesthetic practice which he associated with the example of Gustave Flaubert, as a number of his critical essays and fictional tales demonstrate.[1] By detaching himself entirely from the realm of social experience, James perceived that the solitary artist would undermine the grounds of his own art. Hence, in recording his experience of the theatre in the same passage from the notebooks, he is forced to accept 'the terrible law of the artist – the law of fructification, of fertilization, the law by which everything is grist to his mill – the law, in short, of the acceptance of all experience, of all suffering, of *all* life, of *all* suggestion and sensation and illumination' (*NB* 111). According to this 'law', the internal functioning of the artist's 'blessed and uninvaded workroom' is, of necessity, contingent upon the importation of matter from outside. The border which separates James's private retreat from the public domain must remain permeable, since it constitutes the point of exchange at which the raw material of life is converted into aesthetic experience, or is, as James puts it, '[p]urchased by disgusts' (*NB* 111). In this sense, the private sphere of art is required to incorporate the external social pressures which it is formed to resist, and thus cannot be considered as logically or temporally prior to the public world.

Even if it had been desirable to retreat into an autonomous domain of authorial privacy, however, James was manifestly aware of the difficulties of doing so. The possibility of preserving an 'uninvaded workroom' is precisely what is at issue in many of his most celebrated tales of the 'literary life', as well as in numerous critical commentaries on contemporary authors. In these texts, James attempted to defend the author's 'right to privacy' against the encroachment of publicity, even though his aesthetic theory questions the efficacy of an absolute separation between the two spheres. His critique of the publicity of modern culture was thus not confined to the public spaces of the theatre and the political platform, which I have examined so far; it also incorporated the domain of privacy from which it was issued. It was because the private sphere of art could no longer safely be assumed to be a 'refuge' from the sphere of public circulation that James's concern with publicity took on its most urgent form. As he was only too aware, authors themselves were often the subjects of publicity: far from escaping its glare, the author's private 'workroom' became one of the most conspicuous objects of public knowledge towards the end of the nineteenth century. In retreating from the theatre, then, James was forced to confront the problem which he had sought to avoid, all the more directly.

THE RIGHT TO PRIVACY

From as early as the 1870s, James had recognized that the cultural situation of the modern author was changing. Whereas, formerly, authorship had occupied a space between private and public spheres, in the latter half of the nineteenth century it was increasingly subsumed into the latter. From its inception, of course, the literary market had enhanced the public circulation of private subjectivities: as a commodity, the literary text functioned as an exemplary medium of 'intimate' communication within the public sphere. Yet the public function of the print medium was also predicated upon the assumption that authors themselves simultaneously inhabited the sphere of private individuals.[2] By contrast, during the course of his own career, James witnessed the emergence of new practices of biographical and journalistic representation in which both the 'personality' of the author and the material site of artistic labour were systematically exhibited as objects of public consumption. The author's 'life' became a site of publicity as much as, if not more than, his or her 'work'. For James, such investigative practices were symptomatic of a cultural impulse which threatened to erode all distinctions between private and public spheres, even those which remained open to the necessity of productive interchange. The privacy of the artist was threatened by what he termed an 'insurmountable desire to *know*' (*LC* II 297).

In his early reviews of Hawthorne's *French and Italian Journals* (1872) and the *Correspondence* of William Ellery Channing (1875), James had already begun to formulate his apprehension of a conflict between the claims of privacy and knowledge. Here, the posthumous publication of 'private' writings is an occasion which prompts as much reflection as the content of the texts themselves, as it was to do throughout his later criticism. While acknowledging the 'merits' of Channing's correspondence, for example, James asks his readers to consider 'what degree of merit it is that would make it right we should read them at all' (*LC* I 212). Rather than accepting the text as natural or given, he is characteristically alert to the material event of publication itself, and to the ethical and epistemological questions that it raises. The fact that Channing's authorial intentions – he had requested that the letters be either returned to him or destroyed – had been so signally disregarded leads James to speculate upon a phenomenon of wider cultural significance:

> We touch upon this point because the case seems to us a rather striking concession to the pestilent modern fashion of publicity. A man has certainly a right to determine, in so far as he can, what the world shall know of him and what it shall not; the world's natural curiosity to the contrary notwithstanding. A while ago we should have been tolerably lenient to non-compliance on the world's part; have been tempted to say that privacy was respectable, but that the future was for knowledge, precious knowledge, at

any cost. But now that knowledge (of an unsavoury kind, especially) is pouring in upon us like a torrent, we maintain that, beyond question, the more precious law is that there should be a certain sanctity in all appeals to the generosity and forbearance of posterity, and that a man's table-drawers and pockets should not be turned inside out. (*LC* I 212)

What is important about James's reading of the publication of Channing's *Correspondence* is the way in which he locates this event within a particular historical moment: a moment in which the existing equilibrium between the rival claims of knowledge and privacy becomes unbalanced. At this juncture, he is able to recall a defence of the 'sanctity' of privacy which is merely 'respectable', and which pales beside the promise of a future in which the horizons of 'knowledge, precious knowledge' are constantly expanding. This retrospective vision of the unfolding parameters of knowledge, however, is already exceeded by the present 'torrent'. The Enlightenment ideal of the critical function of 'natural curiosity' is transformed into 'the pestilent modern fashion of publicity'.[3]

James's historiography is, no doubt, open to question on empirical grounds. Similar complaints concerning the intrusive character of biographical knowledge had been articulated from the beginning of the nineteenth century at least.[4] None the less, the review marks an important conceptual shift in the relationship between knowledge and privacy, and hence in the understanding of the principle of publicity itself. As Habermas has shown, in the bourgeois political theory of the eighteenth century, publicity was considered necessary to the formation of a critically debating public. Against the traditional defence of monarchical and aristocratic private privilege, the bourgeois public exercised a legitimate or quasi-juridical 'right to know'. Thus, the pursuit of knowledge as a means of bringing matters into the light of public reason assumed a radical political function: that of unveiling the occluded sites of private interest and power.[5] During the nineteenth century, however, this positive meaning of publicity came under increasing strain. While liberal critics continued to accept the principle of the public's 'right to know', they often experienced difficulty in reconciling this regulative ideal with the emerging practices of the mass media, and hence with the phenomenon of publicity in its recognizably modern sense. The result of this discrepancy was an ambivalence towards the antagonistic claims of knowledge and privacy, revealed with particular clarity in contemporary criticism of investigative journalism and biography. An instructive example of this criticism may be found in an article on the recently instituted practice of journalistic interviewing, published in *The New Princeton Review* in 1887. The article begins with an attempt to rationalize this practice by claiming that it provides 'about the only means by which the public can learn some things which it has a distinct right to know and which it is the interest of designing persons to conceal'. According to this exemplary statement of the ethos of 'critical publicity', it is legitimate for journalists to publicize matters of private interest in so far as these impinge upon, or positively obstruct, the interests of the public. This initial conceptual justification of the interview, however, is immediately contradicted by the evidence of its practical application. Whereas, ideally, the 'business of the newspaper is to furnish private people with the public news', in its present form the press endeavours 'to furnish the public with the news of private people'.[6] Thus, in fact, the new 'sensational' journalism, exemplified by such techniques as the interview, inverts the normative function of publicity which it nevertheless continues to espouse. Rather than being exposed to critical debate amongst a public of private individuals, 'privacy' is exhibited as an object of consumption before a mass public.

It is for this reason that privacy itself comes to be seen as in need of protection. In response to this manifestation of a thoroughly instrumentalized 'right to know', the anonymous contributor to *The New Princeton Review* calls for a corresponding re-evaluation of what James termed the 'right to determine, in so far as he can, what the world shall know of him and what it shall not'. Drawing up an ethical code for the observance of this right, he or she insists that '[a] private conversation is as sacred as private correspondence . . . An interlocutor has no more right to publish my private correspondence than to ransack my drawers for private papers.'[7] Formulated against the increasingly intrusive practices of the popular press, this declaration of the sanctity of privacy bears an obvious resemblance to James's earlier observations on the publication of Channing's private correspondence. In both instances, we are able to witness a shift in the axis of the competing claims of knowledge and privacy. If, previously, the ethical and juridical claim of the public's 'right to know' had been of paramount importance, both writers now insist upon the need to balance this claim by affirming a corresponding, or even countervailing, 'right to privacy'. What is more, James shares with this anonymous critic a common language in which 'privacy' and the threat to its sanctity is encoded. The assumption of a proprietorial 'right' to what is, by definition, an abstract and intangible cultural space is consecrated and consolidated by a metaphorical analogy to the theft of private property: to the 'ransack' of 'a man's table-drawers' and the physical appropriation of his 'private papers'.

The first serious attempt to construct a legal basis for these informal assertions, however, was the work of two American lawyers, Samuel D. Warren and Louis D. Brandeis. In their seminal article, 'The Right to Privacy', published in the *Harvard Law Review* in 1890, Warren and Brandeis responded to the same concerns as previous commentators, but they also recognized the difficulty of grounding their defence upon the existing protection of private property rights. In the first case, the need for establishing a right to privacy was demonstrated by the quotidian experience of modern culture:

> The press is overstepping in every direction the obvious bounds of propriety and decency. Gossip is no longer the resource of the idle and of the vicious, but has become a trade, which is pursued with industry as well as effrontery. To satisfy a prurient taste the details of sexual relations are spread broadcast in the columns of the daily papers. To occupy the indolent, column upon column is filled with idle gossip, which can only be procured by intrusion upon the domestic circle. The intensity and complexity of life, attendant upon advancing civilization, have rendered necessary some retreat from the world, and man, under the refining influence of culture, has become more sensitive to publicity, so that solitude and privacy have become more essential to the individual; but modern enterprise and invention have, through invasions upon his privacy, subjected him to mental pain and distress, far greater than could be inflicted by mere bodily injury.[8]

Within this scenario, modern culture gives rise to a traumatic contradiction. On the one hand, the desire for privacy arises in direct proportion to the increasing 'intensity and complexity' of life; on the other hand, it is the condition of modernity which threatens to erode the possibility of any such 'retreat from the world'. Thus, modern man finds publicity intolerable at the very moment when it is rendered inevitable. It is because publicity is experienced as an affliction of consciousness – as a cause of 'mental pain and distress' greater than that of 'mere bodily injury' – however, that Warren and Brandeis are forced to relinquish the analogy between the right to privacy and private property rights. What is significant about their attempt to construct a legally enforceable right to privacy is the recognition that publicity cannot be understood as a form of either theft or defamation, against both of which legal protection already existed. Instead, they argue, privacy may best be defended through the common law right to 'intellectual and artistic property'. Whereas a charge of theft or defamation seeks to establish the material loss – of property or reputation – suffered by the victim, only the right to intellectual property sufficiently respects the immaterial nature of privacy. In their recourse to such a right, Warren and Brandeis have in mind the same instance of publicity with which James was preoccupied: the unauthorized publication of 'private' texts. Prior to all subsequent measures to control the production and distribution of texts, including copyright legislation, the author possesses an inherent and inalienable right to the products of his or her creative labour. Hence, Warren and Brandeis conclude that 'The principle which protects personal writings and all other personal productions, not against theft and physical appropriation, but against publication in any form, is in reality not the principle of private property, but that of an inviolate personality.'[9] According to this formulation, the text exists in a state of originary privacy, in which it forms an extension of the 'personality' of its author. By definition, the text cannot be alienated from the author because it does not belong to the common order of private property. It remains possible to speak of the author's 'ownership' of the text only to the extent that the author is also conceived as the owner of his or her own private experience. Privacy is thus the deepest, most integral form of property conceivable: it constitutes a state of self-possession which unites proprietor and property within the same body.

In this respect, Warren and Brandeis's understanding of the condition of privacy resonates strongly with James's writings on the same theme. If James often envisaged the invasion of authorial privacy as an act of theft, what is 'stolen' in these instances is not simply the dead body of the text, but also the living 'personality' of which it forms a material trace. In his review of Hawthorne's *French and Italian Journals*, for instance, James raised the 'general question of the proper limits of curiosity as to that passive personality of an artist of which the elements are scattered in portfolios and table-drawers' (*LC* I 307). Commenting upon the increasing publication of authors' 'literary remains', he foresaw that 'Artists, of course, as time goes on, will be likely to take the alarm, empty their table-drawers, and level the approaches to their privacy' (*LC* I 307). In a very real sense, then, James considered the publication of private texts to be a violation of the author himself. The literary text, and its physical containers, retain the capacity to exude the 'personality' of the artist, even after death. It is this organic relationship between author and text which is specified by the term 'literary remains': the textual corpus is conceived as a residual extension of the authorial body. For James, however, organicism is used not to license the anthropocentric assumptions which fuel the desire for biographical knowledge, but to resist them. That the private text functions as a material trace of the authorial 'personality' is not to suggest that this presence can or, indeed, should be known, although, as I shall argue, it may also serve to incite just such a belief.

The ethical imperative which James formulated in his response to contemporary biographical and journalistic invasions of privacy is most forcibly illustrated in his later fiction. In 'Sir Dominick Ferrand' (1892), for example, he reasserts his defence of the author's 'right to privacy', even though the story's eponymous English statesman might initially be construed as a legitimate subject of knowledge under the terms of a 'critical publicity'. The story concerns a struggling journalist, Peter Baron, who unexpectedly discovers a bundle of letters hidden in the secret compartment of a second-hand davenport which he has recently purchased. This discovery threatens to tarnish the posthumous reputation of Sir Dominick Ferrand by implicating him in an illicit sexual relationship. Working against the temptation to disclose his findings, however, is Baron's fixation with the gothic motif of the secret compartment, which tangibly circumscribes the sanctity of Ferrand's private correspondence. A residual trace of the author's physical presence in the act of composition seems to emanate from the material location of the letters, thus allowing Baron to experience a direct proximity to this absent figure. It is Baron's sense of intimacy with Sir Dominick which finally prevents him from selling the letters to an interested magazine. Tempted by financial necessity, he is at first able to justify the ensuing prospect of a scandal by virtue of the high public office formerly occupied by Sir Dominick. The magazine editor, Mr Locket (the name is ironically inappropriate), argues that the revelation of Ferrand's private conduct would constitute a 'service rendered to historical truth' (*CT* VIII 395). Publication of the letters would expose the hypocrisy of the statesman's claim to moral rectitude, and so inform a misled public. Behind such rhetoric, though, Baron recognizes nothing but 'interested palaver, the false voice of commerce and of cant' (*CT* VIII 395). The editor violates his notion of a disinterested 'historical truth' by introducing into this public realm the concealed private motive of profit. In this sense, Locket is the object of James's satire not because he is an agent of publicity as such, but because he negates the very principle of publicity which he espouses.

It is for this reason, moreover, that Baron's refusal to comply with Locket's 'interested' designs should not be dismissed as a mere obfuscation or repression of the demands of biographical 'truth'. For what James challenges in this and other tales is precisely the assumption of a straightforward opposition between revelation and concealment. The desire to unveil the 'truth' – to exhibit the privacy of the biographical subject in the light of the public domain – is not in itself a purely transparent gesture: in the case of Mr Locket, revelation is as much a form of concealment, just as publicity is the manifestation of a private impulse. By contrast, Baron's act of concealment is at least consistent. In refusing to sanction the disclosure of Sir Dominick's private correspondence, he recognizes an ethical commitment to the continuing presence of the author in his texts: 'It didn't matter that the individual was dead; it didn't matter that he was dishonest. Peter felt him sufficiently alive to suffer' (*CT* VIII 398). This sense of responsibility towards the subject of posthumous biographical knowledge was not, of course, unique to James. Late-nineteenth-century debates on biography often centred around the same moral dilemma. In 'The Ethics of Biography' (1883), the novelist Margaret Oliphant voiced similar alarm at 'that prying curiosity which loves to investigate circumstances, and thrust itself into the sanctuaries of individual feeling'.[10] This suspiciously phallocentric urge to 'investigate', which characterizes modern biographical practice, is silently charged with a form of necrophilia. Like James, then, Oliphant insists upon the biographer's responsibility towards the dead:

To bring a great man, who has lived in the common daylight without reproach during his life, to the bar of this world's opinion after his death, is in itself a painful act. The defendant is, in all cases, silenced by English law; but, at least, he has the privilege of communicating all the facts in his favour to his advocate, and furnishing explanations of his conduct for counsel's use. But the dead have no such safeguard; they have no longer any privacy; their very hearts, like their desks and private drawers and cabinets, can be ransacked for evidence to their disadvantage. Is it in any conceivable case a biographer's duty to do this?[11]

Here, it would seem as if the 'prying' biographer is engaged in a simultaneous exhumation, anatomization and legal interrogation of his subject. The public's 'right to know' is transfigured into an act of judicial torture. In response to the question which Oliphant poses at the end of this passage, James, we may assume, would have answered in the negative. We 'know' from his own biography that James enacted in real life Baron's concluding action in 'Sir Dominick Ferrand': 'he burned the collection with infinite method' (*CT* VIII 399). His eminently self-conscious desire to prevent future biographers from making public use of his private papers extended to the burning of numerous manuscripts and letters, as well as to the issuing of private injunctions to his literary executor. Towards the end of his life, as Ian Hamilton has recently noted, James categorically expressed his 'utter and absolute abhorrence of any attempted biography or the giving to the world by "the family", or by any person for whom my disapproval has any sanctity, of any part or parts of my private correspondence'. While recognizing that the endeavour to prevent biographical investigation was only 'imperfectly possible', his 'sole wish' was 'to frustrate as utterly as possible the post-mortem exploiter' (*L* IV 806).[12]

What is striking about James's desire to 'frustrate' future biographers, however, is the way in which it actively incites the hermeneutic impulse which it aims to resist. The analogy between biography and the investigative sciences, which, as Richard Altick has observed, became prevalent during the nineteenth century, defined a process of acquiring knowledge in which the biographer not only expected to meet resistance, but was vindicated in doing so.[13] It was through the resistance of his material that the biographer was able to gauge the measure of his own search for 'truth', since knowledge was always presumed to lie within a penetrable, interior, psychologized space. Within Victorian biographical practice, as Altick notes, it was held as 'axiomatic that the letters of a man *contained* his life': it was assumed, in other words, that the private texts of the biographical subject would somehow reveal a 'deeper' truth than his or her public works.[14] By actively resisting biographical investigation, then, James only confirms the privileged status of privacy as a domain of revelatory signs, and intensifies the hermeneutic desire which is directed towards it. The complicity of this resistance, however, should not be read simply as a sign of its incorporation into a dominant epistemological structure. James's vision of the frictional struggle between the biographer and his subject also recalls the positive side of Michel Foucault's account of the relationship between power and pleasure within modern discourses of sexuality. In the first volume of *The History of Sexuality*, Foucault (echoing Nietzsche) sets out not 'to determine whether these discursive productions and these effects of power lead one to formulate the truth about sex, or on the contrary falsehoods designed to conceal that truth, but rather to bring out the "will to knowledge" that serves as both their support and their instrument'.[15] Much the same could be said about James's understanding of the way in which biographical knowledge is produced. In resisting the pursuit of biographical 'revelations', James is unable to stand outside its regime of knowledge: he does not offer a 'contrary falsehood designed to conceal that truth'. It is for this reason, though, that he is able to avoid the mistake of assuming that resistance simply negates the desire for truth. By recognizing the mutually inciting forces of desire and resistance, James reveals the structure of the 'will to knowledge' itself.

This insight is exemplified in the most remarkable manner in James's essay on George Sand's correspondence with Alfred de Musset, published under the title *Elle et lui* in 1896. Unlike the earlier cases of Hawthorne and Channing, in which James could argue that authorial privacy had been violated from the outside, Sand offers the disturbing example of a writer whose autobiographical documents positively pre-empted the pursuit of biographical 'revelations'. Yet if the self-revelatory character of these texts might be thought to disarm the impulse of external investigation, it also represents a surrender of the sovereign 'secrets' of privacy. For James, the conflict between the 'reporter' and the 'reported' is not to be averted either by the latter's prior accommodation or by an opposing gesture of absolute refusal. Only 'in a regular organization of the struggle' is it possible for the author to ground an immanent resistance to enquiry (*LC* II 742): 'Then the cunning of the inquirer, envenomed with resistance, will exceed in subtlety and ferocity anything we to-day conceive, and the pale forewarned victim, with every track covered, every paper burnt and every letter unanswered, will, in the tower of art, the invulnerable granite, stand, without a sally, the siege of all the years' (*LC* II 743). In this scenario, James gives a striking exposition of the nexus of power and pleasure which, according to Foucault, constitutes the production of knowledge in general. Biographical investigation is understood as a form of power which takes pleasure, not merely in the pursuit of 'knowledge', but in the resistance which this pursuit engenders; just as, conversely, such resistance take pleasure, in Foucault's words, 'at having to evade this power, flee from it, or travesty it'.[16] James is evidently well aware that resistance will only serve to inflame, rather than to curtail, the impulse of enquiry, but it is from this knowledge that his own pleasure is derived. In a calculated act of retaliation, the author infects the 'inquirer' with a venom which intensifies the desire to know by systematically erasing its object. If the 'victim' cannot escape the compulsive process of biographical interpretation, neither, James ensures, can the 'inquirer'.

In this respect, James suggests an understanding of the nature of biographical 'truth' which differs from the majority of recent historical accounts. For most modern historians of biography, there is a clear distinction between the characteristic 'reticence' or reverence shown towards their subjects by Victorian biographers and the more 'candid', investigative mode of biography which emerged towards the end of the nineteenth century. Richard Altick, for example, dismisses the Victorian concern with privacy as a mark of repression from which later biographers were thankfully liberated. By contrast, the pioneering works of J.A. Froude in the 1880s, and later of Lytton Strachey, are seen as heralding a return to the proper pursuit of truth in biography.[17] It was Strachey who offered the most incisive definition of the aims of the 'New Biography' when he wrote in his Preface to *Eminent Victorians* (1918): 'Je n'impose rien; je ne propose rien: j'expose.'[18] Yet to assume, as Altick does, that the impulse to 'expose' represents a pure antithesis of the impulse to conceal is to neglect the fact that each impulse requires the other. Just as the desire to unveil the privacy of the biographical subject is already inscribed within the desire to conceal it, so the rhetoric of openness and transparency which sustains investigative biography is reliant upon the very cultural prohibitions which it claims to have broken. In the often vehement debates which surrounded the question of the appropriate limits of biographical knowledge in the late nineteenth century, this unspoken unanimity becomes clear. Regardless of whether the intention was to reveal or to conceal the privacy of the subject, privacy itself was invariably construed as the site in which truth was necessarily contained. It was for this reason, of course, that the private texts of authors aroused both such curiosity and such anxiety. For if the private text was assumed to contain the interior essence of the authorial 'personality', then its capacity to reveal truth was already presupposed. Within contemporary theories of autobiography, this presupposition led to the fear of an involuntary self-disclosure, in which the 'secrets' of the author would be 'revealed' by the evidence of his own writing. 'As a matter of fact', wrote one commentator in 1891, 'the secrets of personality cannot be kept, and a man's nature betrays itself without his knowledge of the betrayal. The truth is suggested by words from which truth is absent; the writer, though consciously false, reveals himself unconsciously; and if we lose the real man at one point we catch him at another.'[19] No matter how much the autobiographer attempts to suppress or manipulate the record which he presents as truth, autobiographical writing is, by its nature, self-revelatory, since there is nothing more revealing than concealment. This conception of autobiography could be applied equally to the 'autobiographical' documents sought by biographers.

If James's recognition of the complicity between revelation and concealment challenges the conventional opposition of these impulses within historical accounts of biography, it also suggests an important difference between his own formulation of a 'right to privacy' and that of most other contemporary commentators. Whereas Warren and Brandeis, for example, are forced to postulate a state of privacy which exists in irreducible externality to the public sphere, James is more knowingly aware that privacy is always already subject to 'knowledge'. The attempt to ground a legal definition of the right to privacy on the basis of an 'inviolate personality' assumes that such a right can exist prior to its transgression. But the very fact that this right was first formulated in response to the historically specific practices of the popular press suggests otherwise. The need to preserve an autonomous space of privacy arose only in relation to modern forms of publicity. To this extent, privacy can only be deemed 'inviolate' once it is already subject to violation.

This is a paradox which James revealed with particular clarity in his fabulistic tale, 'The Private Life' (1892). According to the narrator's initial hypothesis, privacy is the essential site of Clare Vawdrey's artistic self, whereas his public persona presents merely a puzzling façade. The image of the novelist writing in a darkened room recalls James's invocation of his own private 'workroom', recorded shortly before the writing of the tale, and appears to suggest a conventional topography of social space in which privacy exists before or behind the process of public self-representation. In support of this reading, Blanche Adney remarks that 'if Clare Vawdrey is double', Lord Mellifont 'has the opposite complaint: he isn't even whole' (*CT* VIII 211). While it is possible for Vawdrey to maintain a phenomenal existence within 'two quite distinct and "water-tight" compartments', as James declared in his preface to the tale, Lord Mellifont's condition does not allow for a similar duality (*LC* II 1254). Since the latter's 'real' self lies, conversely, in his public performance, privacy is relegated to the status of the inessential, and loses phenomenal existence altogether. Privacy is literally unimaginable as anything other than a realm of authenticity. Thus, unlike Vawdrey's successful projection of a public façade, Lord Mellifont's corresponding lack of privacy can only be envisaged as a deficiency.

At the same time, James problematizes this parabolic reading of the story by ironically undermining the interpretive procedures of the narrator and his confidante. It is because Vawdrey's 'private life' is capable of phenomenal existence that it is accessible to the narrator's observation, and, hence, violation. The narrator's entry into the novelist's private room provokes Blanche Adney's 'insane desire to see the author', and recalls more explicit scenes of biographical or journalistic intrusion in James's fiction (*CT* VIII 216). As a result, Vawdrey's 'privacy' is incorporated into an order of visual signs which negates his ostensibly solipsistic self-absorption.[20] Curiously, it is Lord Mellifont's (lack of) privacy which approximates more closely to 'the withdrawn, the sequestered, the unobserved and unhonoured position' which James ascribed to Vawdrey in his preface to 'The Private Life' (*LC* II 1255). Behind Lord Mellifont's 'door', there lies 'inveterately nothing': his private self literally *cannot* be witnessed (*LC* II 1255). The implications of this unrepresentable state of privacy are also adumbrated in the tale itself. Although Lord Mellifont's public manner is seemingly designed to be reported in 'the morning papers, with a leader', the narrator deduces 'something that wouldn't be, that never could be, though any enterprising journal would give one a fortune for it' (*CT* VIII 214). Unlike Vawdrey, then, Lord Mellifont is freed from the anxiety of investigative exposure, if only because (rather like George Sand) his prior publicity already precludes it. As I have suggested, this was not a form of freedom to which James himself subscribed. My purpose, here, is not to claim that Lord Mellifont offers a viable alternative model of authorial privacy. By way of opposition, however, he reveals the fragility of Clare Vawdrey's ostensibly 'inviolate personality'. James was aware that the 'private life' of the artist was not as easily defended as Warren and Brandeis had supposed.

'THE ASPERN PAPERS'

James's recognition of the difficulty of defending an authorial 'right to privacy' against the voracious pursuit of biographical knowledge was given its most complex and ironic expression in 'The Aspern Papers' (1888). It is in this tale that we can see most clearly the extent of James's ambivalence towards the investigative 'curiosity' of modern culture: an ambivalence which confounds (even while maintaining) constitutive oppositions between revelation and concealment, publicity and privacy. To acknowledge the complexity of 'The Aspern Papers' should not be taken as a means of diminishing the force of James's critique of biographical representation. But, equally, I wish to argue against a reading of the story which simply stresses James's hostility towards his scheming, investigative narrator. 'The Aspern Papers' is an interesting tale because it lacks the obtrusive didacticism of otherwise similar stories such as 'Sir Dominick Ferrand' and 'The Real Right Thing' (1899). Whereas, in these two later texts, James signals his opposition to the invasion of authorial privacy by means of a strategic 'supernatural' intervention, in which the potential publicist is warned against the dangers of further intrusion, in 'The Aspern Papers' he offers a more searching exploration of the psychology of the 'will to knowledge'. The results of this exploration, moreover, do not leave James's own authorial epistemology untouched.

In some respects, of course, James's satire in 'The Aspern Papers' bears notable similarities to his method in 'Sir Dominick Ferrand'. One way of reading the story is to see it as a sustained ironic exposition of the subjective motivations which underpin the narrator's supposedly disinterested pursuit of knowledge. The narrator is constantly insisting upon the impersonal nature of his desire to possess the Aspern papers: 'It isn't for myself', he informs Miss Tita, 'there is no personal avidity in my desire. It is simply that they would be of such immense interest to the public, such immeasurable importance as a contribution to Jeffrey Aspern's history' (*CT* VI 335). Thus, like the editor in 'Sir Dominick Ferrand', the narrator disavows his own private interest in revealing 'private' papers to the public by appealing to 'historical truth' as the legitimate ground of publicity. This assertion of disinterest is entirely characteristic of the way in which the narrator endeavours to efface himself from the investigative project which he has instigated. What this project requires, however, is a separation of private and public roles which the evidence of the narrative itself undermines. Rather than maintaining a rigorously professional interest in the Aspern papers, the narrator unwittingly reveals the presence of the 'personal avidity' which he wishes to suppress. His initial success in entering Juliana Bordereau's Venetian *palazzo*, for instance, is judged as a 'triumph, but only for the editor (in the last analysis), not for the man, who had not the tradition of personal conquest' (*CT* VI 290). As Susanne Kappeler has observed, such statements demonstrate a logic of 'metonymic displacement' by which the narrator habitually forges a relationship of equivalence between objects of sexual desire and objects of textual enquiry. By coyly claiming a lack of success in the 'tradition of personal conquest', the narrator merely confirms the reader's suspicion that the 'obsessionality with which he pursues the literary documents has all the characteristics of sexual desire', and that it is this desire which lies behind his disinterested pursuit of 'knowledge'.[21] This is not to say that the Aspern papers are merely surrogate or derivative objects of desire. In fact, the distinction between textual and sexual enquiry is conflated, since the narrator's desire to possess Aspern's letters to Juliana is itself predicated upon his supposition that they will offer further evidence of the poet's legendary sexual charisma. The promise of sexual knowledge, in other words, is inscribed within the texts themselves.

What the objects of this sexual knowledge might be, however, is by no means as transparent as Kappeler assumes. If, on an immediate level, the narrator couches his siege of the Bordereaus in terms of a violent heterosexual conquest, structurally both Juliana and Miss Tita serve as conduits, or instrumentalized objects, within a process of hermeneutic desire which is ultimately fixated upon the figure of Aspern himself. It is not insignificant, then, that the narrator should evoke Aspern's heterosexual prowess by casting the poet's relationship to his female admirers in terms of the fable of 'Orpheus and the

Maenads'. 'Almost all the Maenads were unreasonable', he proclaims, 'and many of them insupportable; it struck me in short that he was kinder, more considerate than, in his place (if I could imagine myself in such a place!) I should have been' (*CT* VI 278). Besides revealing a pervasive misogyny, as Kappeler notes, the narrator's mythical reconstruction of Aspern's life indicates the way in which he simultaneously positions himself both as an authoritative subject of biographical interpretation and as its surrogate object.[22] In the first instance, the narrator sees himself as protecting and reclaiming Aspern's reputation from the threatening embrace of the 'Maenads', and their surviving counterparts, Juliana and Miss Tita. Thus, he is anxious to distinguish between the austerity of his own masculine enthusiasm for the poet and the merely 'personal' interest shown by his female readers. Aspern, he stresses, 'was not a woman's poet': or at least not 'in the modern phase of his reputation', although 'the situation had been different when the man's own voice was mingled with his song' (*CT* VI 278). At the same time, the narrator's desire to reclaim custody of Aspern's reputation contains a moment of imaginary identification in which he himself takes the place of the beleaguered poet. The ambiguity of this substitution resides in the force which is to be attached to the narrator's parenthetic 'if': while this conditional clause allows him to 'imagine' himself vicariously as an object of female desire, and so to assume the complacent pose of sexual mastery which he deploys in his relationship with Miss Tita, conversely it can also be taken to refer to what is precisely *unimaginable* about this scenario. The narrator cannot sufficiently adopt Aspern's position as an object of female desire in so far as Aspern is the object of his own desire.

In this respect, the narrator reaches an epistemological impasse similar to that which has been described by Eve Kosofsky Sedgwick in her important reading of 'The Beast in the Jungle'. Like John Marcher, one might argue, the narrator is caught within a double bind which simultaneously compels and prohibits the recognition of a 'homosexual secret' of desire. In its inscription of this 'secret', 'The Aspern Papers' shares many of the features which Sedgwick ascribes to the later tale.[23] Most importantly, as I have already suggested, the narrator's desire to reveal the 'secrets' of Aspern's sexual 'knowledge' can only be mediated through the female figures of Juliana and Miss Tita. It is because he is unable to participate in this 'knowledge' that his quest is ultimately frustrated: by refusing Miss Tita's offer of marriage at the end of the tale, all hope of possessing the papers is also lost. The narrator's dilemma thus derives from the fact that, in order to attain knowledge through a homo-social exchange with Aspern, he is forced to enter into a state of heterosexual congress. This scenario anticipates a similar, if more ironic, stricture upon the pursuit of textual 'knowledge' in 'The Figure in the Carpet' (1896). Here, too, the narrator's attempt to reveal a male author's literary 'secrets' is apparently subject to the condition of heterosexual transmission. In much the same way that Gwendolen Erme is seen (mistakenly or not) as the repository of Hugh Vereker's sexually contagious 'secret', so, by virtue of her relationship with Aspern, Juliana is construed as a conduit of the knowledge sought by the narrator of 'The Aspern Papers'.[24] Through her possession of the papers, as well as through the intimate 'knowledge' which this possession is taken to represent, Juliana bears the aura of the great poet from the past down to the present: the narrator is aware that, before seeing her, he 'had not been able to look into a single pair of eyes into which his [i.e. Aspern's] had looked or to feel a transmitted contact in any aged hand that his had touched' (*CT* VI 279). Yet if, in this sense, Juliana brings the narrator closer to Aspern, she is also the bearer of an inheritance which, on account of its exogamous transmission, he can only usurp. In planning for the eventuality of Juliana's death, and the subsequent ransacking of her table-drawers, the narrator is prepared to destroy his most immediate link to Aspern in order to take her place in proximity to the poet.

The violence with which the narrator's desire for knowledge is both pursued and frustrated is thus indicative of the disturbing sexual charge encoded within late-nineteenth-century biographical discourse. If, as Sedgwick has argued, 'epistemological pressure of any sort seems a force increasingly saturated with sexual impulsion' during this period, the practice of investigative biography may be seen as one of the primary vehicles of this 'impulsion'.[25] The simultaneous urge towards incitement and resistance which can be observed in James's comments upon the invasion of authorial privacy bears evident similarities to the contradictory epistemological injunctions involved in the recognition of 'homosexual' identity. By unmasking the 'private interests' which impel his narrator's pursuit of knowledge, James himself unavoidably reinforces these injunctions. His satirical strategy in the tale is marked by a desire to expose the rhetoric of 'exposure', and so reproduces (by inverting) the very impulse of which the narrator is his degraded exemplar. 'The Aspern Papers', indeed, offers only one example of the cultural anxieties surrounding this moment of impossible revelation. In 'The Real Right Thing', the male biographer's attachment to his dead male subject is similarly, but more explicitly, figured. George Withermore anticipates his evening research sessions in the 'personal presence' of Ashton Doyne, 'very much as one of a pair of lovers might wait for the hour of their appointment' (*CT* x 477). Not surprisingly, Withermore arrives one day to find the admonitory presence of Doyne's ghost forbidding entry to his study. In this instance, the ghostly admonition does not simply represent James's formal defence of the author's right to privacy, but also appears to prohibit a particular content of (self-)knowledge. More generally, it might be argued that James's persistent concern with the pursuit of biographical 'exposure' was intrinsically bound up with the homophobic mechanisms of compulsion so evident in the contemporary discourse of 'scandal'.[26]

It was James's internalization of this 'epistemological pressure', however, which allowed him to question the objectivism of prevailing forms of biographical interpretation. In 'The Aspern Papers', the narrator's identification with the figure of the poet collapses the dichotomy between subject and object upon which his assumption of scholarly disinterest rests. If the aim of the narrator's project is the recovery of a prior biographical 'truth', the object of investigation must be insulated from the force of the subject's desire. James, however, anticipates Freud in suggesting the impossibility of this task. In his biographical sketch, 'Leonardo da Vinci and a Memory of his Childhood' (1910), Freud criticized the customary tendency of biographers to present an idealized image of their subjects. Out of a desire to protect 'their hero', he observed, biographers often 'smooth over the traces of his life's struggles with internal and external resistances, and . . . tolerate in him no vestige of human weakness or imperfection'. Rather than offering a neutral assessment of the subject's achievement, biographers are actively engaged in the work of transference, 'aimed at enrolling the great man among the class of their infantile models'. While Freud's characterization of biography as a form of hero-worship would seem to refer primarily to the Victorian hagiographical tradition, he also recognized similar dangers of subjective investment in the apparently more objective methods of investigative or 'scientific' biography (including his own pyschoanalytic method of 'pathography'). Indeed, in a strange act of displacement, Freud examined the posture of the 'scientific' investigator in the figure of his own biographical subject: Leonardo da Vinci is himself seen as an archetypal instance of the sublimation of sexual drives into a consummate 'urge to know'.[27]

In both of these aspects, Freud's awareness of the inevitable 'distortions' of biographical representation is remarkably close to James's position in 'The Aspern Papers'. James's narrator, we might say, combines the reverence of the traditional Victorian biographer with the investigative passion of a Leonardo (which Freud famously, and perhaps not coincidentally, saw as evidence of a latent 'homosexual attitude').[28] On the one hand, his attempt to vindicate Aspern's conduct in relation to his female admirers offers a graphic example of what Freud saw as the biographer's desire to erase the uncomfortably physical 'struggles' of his subject's life: his research, he insists, has 'never failed to acquit [Aspern] conscientiously of shabby behaviour' (*CT* vi 278). On the other hand, the narrator evidently regards this reverential biographical approach in the light of an objective excavation of knowledge. As a professional literary editor or scholar, he is, as he informs Miss Tita, 'looking for more material' on the poet (*CT* vi 323). The fallacy of the narrator's mode of interpretation lies not only in the fact that he reads Aspern's 'work' as if it were merely a transparent expression of his 'life', but also in his assumption that the 'life' is itself nothing more than an accumulation of textual traces. If James himself made similar assumptions about the inherent revelatory capacity of an author's 'literary remains', the narrator's quest for private documents reduces the status of the public work to that of a verifiable hypothesis. Research into the lives of 'great philosophers and poets' is necessary, he argues, because the work is 'all vain words if there is nothing to measure it by' (*CT* vi 341). Juliana's riposte to this calibration of the 'work' with the 'life' clarifies the assumptions behind it: 'You talk as if you were a tailor', she remarks (*CT* vi 341). It is the narrator's positivistic enquiry, rather than his reverence for Aspern, which is at issue here. For whereas the latter represents the necessarily subjective investment to which he is blind, the former presumes that 'knowledge' is entirely detached from its knower. Truth, according to the narrator's mode of scholarly investigation, lies waiting to be discovered.

As J. Hillis Miller has recently suggested, it is this belief in the transparency of hermeneutic 'penetration' and 'revelation' which forms the central target of James's criticism in 'The Aspern Papers'. The narrator's assertion that critics possess the power to 'lay bare the truth' about writers of the past aspires to a state of absolute knowledge which exceeds the contingency of all interpretations. In this sense, as Juliana observes, 'The truth is God's, it isn't man's: we had better leave it alone' (*CT* VI 341): only from a transcendent interpretive position is it possible to know the whole truth of a life. This does not mean, however, that biographical truth is simply unknowable, as Hillis Miller wishes to argue. In Miller's view, the narrator can only come to know the truth of Aspern's life through 'knowledge' of a 'bodily, material kind': through a repetition, in other words, of Aspern's sexual knowledge. Yet it is precisely this form of 'knowledge', Hillis Miller claims, which cannot and, indeed, should not be 'narrated in a cognizable historical text'.[29] Not only does the ethical injunction of this argument imply that the narrator *ought* to participate in the particular form of 'knowledge' acquired by Aspern, but it also reinforces the cultural assumption that such knowledge belongs to a sphere of experience which is and should remain prohibitively private. By reading 'The Aspern Papers' solely as a critique of its manipulative narrator, Hillis Miller offers a one-sided account of James's authorial stance in the tale. While it is true that James wishes to mount an ethical defence of the author's right to privacy, the text itself reveals the difficulty of maintaining such a stance. James's understanding of the necessarily subjective and interested nature of knowing points to a deep-seated ambivalence in his response to the practices of biographical investigation. For if, on the one hand, he insists upon the separation of private and public spheres as a means of obstructing the insatiable 'urge to know', on the other hand he is aware that the boundaries between these spheres are always provisional and unstable. In fact, it is only upon this shifting foundation that James is able to base his critique of the biographical invasion of privacy. The narrator, we should remember, is not simply the representative of a form of publicity which stands opposed to the realm of privacy; in bringing Aspern's 'secrets' to light, he also carries his own private desires into the public realm of historical truth. By undermining the narrator's assumption of disinterest, however, James also unavoidably questions the principle upon which his own opposition to biographical investigation is grounded. This opposition cannot remain outside the conflict of interested forces of which it is itself an element.

This ambivalence in James's thought may again be illustrated (this time more directly) by the 'concept' of the 'will to knowledge' which Nietzsche began to formulate during the 1880s. For Nietzsche, the possibility of attaining an 'unconditioned' knowledge – a knowledge which lies beyond and apart from its knower – is an illusion that is produced by the will to power itself. 'Coming to know', he writes in a note dated 1885–6, 'is always "placing oneself in a conditional relation to something" – one who seeks to know the unconditioned desires that it should not concern him, and that this same something should be of no concern to anyone.' This posture of disinterested enquiry, however, 'involves a contradiction, first, between *wanting* to know and the desire that it not concern us (but why know at all then?) and, secondly, because something that is of no concern to anyone *is* not at all, and thus cannot be known at all'.[30] Nietzsche's 'demystification' of the rhetoric of Kantian epistemology thus aims to demonstrate the extent to which 'knowledge' is produced through the very impulse of wanting to know. The subject's desire to maintain a separation from the object of knowledge is seen as a strategy by which he or she attempts to deny or conceal an interest in the outcome of the enquiry. This strategy can be refuted, however, since, were this separation to be fully upheld, the object could not possibly be an object of *knowledge*; even if 'knowledge' was understood as radically unknowable, as it is in Hillis Miller's alternative sense of the word, the same criticism would apply.[31] Nietzsche's analysis of the manipulative strategies involved in the apparently disinterested pursuit of philosophical and scientific knowledge also offers an incisive commentary upon the self-effacing investigative procedure of James's narrator in 'The Aspern Papers'. The narrator, as we have seen, is anxious to deny his personal interest in Jeffrey Aspern in order to assert the disinterested nature of his enquiry and the objective character of its findings. In ironizing this interpretive stance, however, James would probably have agreed with his brother William, who, in his essay 'The Will to Believe' (1896), wrote that the 'most useful investigator, because the most sensitive observer, is always he whose eager interest in one side of the question is balanced by an equally keen nervousness lest he become deceived'.[32] For William James, as for Nietzsche, the desire to know is not driven by 'a disinterested love of information' but, rather, by a form of 'aesthetic interest', as he had written on an earlier occasion.[33] Properly speaking, this 'interest' cannot even be described as 'subjective', since it is through the impulse of knowing that the categories of subject and object are themselves generated.[34]

Where Nietzsche's critique of the 'will to knowledge' most closely resembles James's authorial stance, however, is in its confessed inability to stand outside the phenomenon which it seeks to diagnose. Nietzsche's critique must remain immanent since it is of the very nature of its object to undermine the possibility of an external act of ethical judgement. At the same time, it is precisely this form of judgement which Nietzsche's demystification of knowledge as a form of power appears to wish to maintain. This ambivalence is expressed in a notation recorded in 1888: 'The "will to truth"', Nietzsche writes, 'would then have to be investigated psychologically: it is not a moral force, but a form of the will to power. This would have to be proved by showing that it employs every *immoral* means.'[35] Here, 'psychological' enquiry is upheld as a means of refuting the moral basis of the desire for knowledge. The 'will to truth' is nothing more than a concealed manifestation of a fundamental 'will to power'. In exposing this strategy of dissimulation, however, Nietzsche himself reintroduces the language of ethical judgement, if only to reveal its divergence from its own criteria. The conflicting impulses contained within this proposal may also be read as a remarkably precise description of James's critical project in 'The Aspern Papers'. In this tale, James, too, offers a 'psychological' (rather than a crudely didactic) exposition of the desire for knowledge, thereby undermining the ethical ground of his critique. At the same time, he is also clearly concerned to reveal the violent and '*immoral* means' which his narrator employs in the service of this desire.

It is this ambivalence which raises the disturbing question of how James's authorial stance may be distinguished from the blatantly self-deluded interpretive procedures of his narrator. If James reveals the perilously subjective impulses which lie behind his narrator's posture of disinterest, this gesture of ironic detachment should not disguise the fact that similar perils are also contained within James's understanding of the constructive nature of all imaginative experience, including his own. A particularly striking example of this complicity between author and narrator occurs in chapter 4 of 'The Aspern Papers'. Here, the narrator is sitting in Juliana's garden, gazing at the inscrutable façade of the *palazzo*, behind which the object of his quest is apparently contained:

It was as if at such a moment as that, in the stillness, after the long contradiction of the day, Miss Bordereau's secrets were in the air, the wonder of her survival more palpable. These were the acute impressions. I had them in another form, with more of a certain sort of reciprocity, during the hours that I sat in the garden looking up over the top of my book at the closed windows of my hostess. In these windows no sign of life ever appeared; it was as if, for fear of my catching a glimpse of them, the two ladies passed their days in the dark. But this only proved to me that they had something to conceal; which was what I had wished to demonstrate. Their motionless shutters became as expressive as eyes consciously closed, and I took comfort in thinking that at all events though invisible themselves they saw me between the lashes. (*CT* VI 306)

This passage is of interest, first, for the way in which it exemplifies the manipulative, and entirely circular, hermeneutic procedure by which the narrator comes to 'know'. His triumphant demonstration of the existence of Juliana's 'secrets' involves a blatant fabrication of evidence. Although, from all the available information, there is no positively ascertainable response to his observation, the narrator forces this very absence of signification to confirm a 'certain sort of reciprocity' between himself and the Bordereaus. By figuring the blank exterior of the *palazzo* as a human face, he is able to interpret its 'motionless shutters' and 'closed windows' as eyes that are 'consciously closed'. Hence, the manifestly tranquil existence of the Bordereaus is charged with the furtive design of concealment, and, still further, with a surreptitious surveillance of the narrator himself. With this last inductive manoeuvre, the narrator succeeds in erasing his own agency from the elaborate fiction of 'reciprocity' which he has just constructed. He positions himself as the passive recipient of the object's meaning, rather than its active creator. The purpose behind this vertiginous flight of logic is not hard to fathom. In order to restrain the spectre of a monstrous subjectivity, unleashed from all moorings in the objective world, the narrator needs to believe that the Bordereaus are active participants in his investigative pursuit, even if their function is one of resistance to it. The importance which the narrator attaches to Juliana's green shade is symptomatic of this need: the 'mystifying bandage', which constantly screens Juliana's eyes from view, literally and symbolically prevents the narrator from objectifying himself in her gaze, and so from authenticating his interpretive design by proving her knowledge of his knowledge (*CT* VI 324). Again, the only way in which this blank surface can be made to serve the narrator's purpose is by his reading it as a sign of conscious concealment. Significantly, however, his sole glimpse of Juliana's eyes comes in the climactic scene of the story when he is caught ransacking her apartment. There, the narrator's attempt to reveal Aspern's 'secrets' is matched by his own exposure as a 'publishing scoundrel' (*CT* VI 363).

In his later preface to 'The Aspern Papers', James tacitly acknowledged the extent of his narrator's self-delusion by commenting upon the generally precarious process by which 'one must induce almost any "Italian" subject to *make believe* it gives up its secret, in order to keep at all on working – or call them perhaps rather playing – terms with the general impression' (*LC* II 1173). Here, the interpretive procedure followed by the narrator is reduced to little more than a 'convention of the real revelations and surrenders on one side and the real immersions and appreciations on the other': to a dangerous hermeneutic fiction, from which 'we exaggerate our gathered values only if we are eminently witless' (*LC* II 1174). Yet while these deprecatory remarks may be read as a stinging rebuke of the narrator's investigative practice, they are also explicitly offered as a series of observations on the perils of the artistic imagination. In this respect, the preface reads very much like a recantation of James's celebrated argument in 'The Art of Fiction' (1884). In the earlier essay, James had strongly affirmed the process of imaginative induction, and its capacity to deliver the phenomenal truth of experience. The artist's 'power to guess the unseen from the seen, to trace the implication of things, to judge the whole piece by the pattern', he had declared, 'may almost be said to constitute experience' (*LC* I 53). Commenting upon this passage, Paul B. Armstrong has suggested that James was already aware of the 'risk of solipsistic delusion' inherent within his account of the imagination: as a theory of knowledge, James's phenomenological notion of the 'impression' does not claim to uncover the truth of objects in themselves, even if it cannot conversely be charged with licensing a pure subjectivism.[36] Nevertheless, 'The Art of Fiction' offers a remarkably positive reading of the revelatory capacity of the creative imagination, especially when set beside the evident fallibility of this same process in 'The Aspern Papers'. The similarity between the language of James's characterization of imaginative experience in the essay and his ironic exposition of the narrator's hermenutic enquiry in the tale thus appears as something of a shock. Just as James himself had compared the creative consciousness to 'a kind of huge spider-web' which 'takes to itself the faintest hints of life' and 'converts the very pulses of the air into revelations' (*LC* I 52), so the narrator acquires 'knowledge' (in the passage quoted above) by sensing that 'in the stillness, after the long contradiction of the day, Miss Bordereau's secrets were in the air' (*CT* VI 306). The verbal resemblance between these two passages suggests that James's authorial stance cannot be as comfortably detached from his narrator's more overtly fantastic flights of imagination as would at first appear. Indeed, in some respects, the narrator may be seen as an exemplary practitioner of Jamesian imagination, as it is conceived in 'The Art of Fiction'. His ability to discern 'secrets' behind the blank surface of objects cannot easily be distinguished from James's paramount artistic virtue of 'guess[ing] the unseen from the seen'.

It is this complicity between the hermeneutic strategies of author and narrator which James's preface to 'The Aspern Papers' both acknowledges and attempts to conceal. The acknowledgement, as I have suggested, occurs in the form of an analogy between James's self-deprecating remarks upon the imaginative 'observer' of Italy and the figure of the narrator. Yet while James tends to downplay the status of imaginative experience in the preface, he also wishes to maintain its superiority over a positivistic acquisition of knowledge. In this regard, the preface strives to reinforce the distinction which it has already served to collapse by comparing the interpretive method of the 'historian' with that of the 'dramatist' or 'man of imagination'. Unlike the historian, James argues, the dramatist does not seek 'knowledge' through empirical investigation: whereas the former 'wants more documents than he can really use', the latter 'only wants more liberties than he can really take' (*LC* II 1175). The dramatist's imaginative cognition, he suggests, is at least as true as the historian's assumption that 'truth' resides in an accumulation of documents. By taking liberties with one form of truth, the dramatist avoids 'the undue simplicity of pretending to read meaning into things absolutely sealed and beyond test or proof' (*LC* II 1175). James's opposition between historical and dramatic truth is evidently intended to disassociate his own epistemological practice from that of the narrator. By restricting the narrator to the role of empiricist historian, however, James strategically diminishes the disturbingly imaginative side of his desire to know, which emerges in the story itself. Both the preface and the story reveal the difficulty of maintaining a rigorous separation between these two modes of truth.

This difficulty becomes especially apparent when, as in 'The Aspern Papers', the dramatist himself assumes the task of representing an historian's search for documents. In the preface, James's account of his own imaginative process re-enacts the enquiry of the real historian upon whom the figure of the narrator was modelled. Recounting the *donnée* of the story, in which a certain Captain Edward Silsbee had approached Jane Clairmont, an 'intimate friend' of Byron's, with the aim of possessing her collection of Shelley's private papers, James reveals that he too 'had passed again and again, all unknowing, the door of her house, where she sat above, within call and in her habit as she lived' (*LC* II 1175).[37] At the time, James had been unaware that Clairmont's residence in Venice had 'overlapped' with his own. It was this lack of knowledge, he claims, which subsequently allowed him to reconstruct the actual intrusion of the historian. Had he himself attained a 'nearer view of the case', he would have been unable to write a fictional story dramatizing the effects of precisely that 'nearer view' (*LC* II 1175–6). By insisting upon the artist's necessary abstention from action in the field of historical events, however, James distinguishes his practice from that of the historian in order to create the basis of an imaginary identification. The artist's imaginative truth does not belong to the same order of knowledge as the historian's pursuit of documentary evidence, but neither is the former simply opposed to the latter. Thus, the 'curiosity' which impels many of James's imaginative observers is invariably susceptible to the charge of vulgar 'detection', which he himself levelled against the practitioners of investigative biography and journalism. In *The Sacred Fount* (1901), for example, Ford Obert's similar attempt to discriminate between an 'ignoble' application of 'the detective and the keyhole' and an 'honourable' reliance 'on psychologic signs alone' evidently fails to reassure the narrator of his own purity of motive.[38] As in 'The Aspern Papers', what emerges from this later novel is not so much a clear distinction between the 'detective' and the 'man of imagination', as a compromising resemblance.

This resemblance is perhaps indicative of James's recognition of his own fascination with the 'revelations' of biographical enquiry. As Ian Hamilton has recently observed, James's hostility towards biographical intrusion was contradicted by his own practice, both as a biographer and as a keen reader and reviewer of biographical texts.[39] In his reviews of George Sand, for example, resistance to biographical enquiry co-exists with an evident curiosity towards the 'scandalous' material which is being unveiled. James declares his opposition to the revelation of Sand's 'private' affairs before proceeding to recount details of her relationship with Alfred de Musset with positive relish.[40] 'The Aspern Papers' is marked by a similar ambivalence. As Gary Scharnhorst has convincingly argued, James's troubled relationship to his narrator may well have been derived from a sense of guilt at his own pursuit of biographical knowledge concerning a figure who, in many respects, resembles that of Jeffrey Aspern. James's study of Hawthorne, published in Macmillan's 'English Men of Letters' series in 1879, may not represent a revelatory biographical enquiry of the kind criticized in his reviews, but it did provoke a scandalized response on other grounds.[41] On this reading of the tale, James can be identified both with Juliana's attempt to frustrate the narrator's pursuit of knowledge and in the pursuit itself. James's fascination with narratives of biographical enquiry, however, should not be used as a means of reinscribing the hermeneutic assumptions of biography, as some critics appear to suggest.[42] On the contrary, it is by taking both sides of the conflict between the inquirer and his subject that James is able to reveal the structure of biographical knowledge itself.

In this regard, there is another and, to my knowledge, unrecognized 'source' upon which James may well have drawn in writing 'The Aspern Papers'. In an essay entitled 'The Interpretation of Literature', published in *The Contemporary Review* in May 1886, Edward Dowden outlined a theory of the relationship between author and reader/critic which strikingly anticipates both the language and the form of James's story. For Dowden, the interpretation of the literary text also involves a violent, antagonistic struggle between the critical inquirer and his subject. The purpose of studying a critical model such as Sainte-Beuve, he suggests, is to discover 'how he made his advances; how he invested and beleaguered his author; how he sapped up to him, and drew his parallels and zigzags of approach; how he stormed the breach and made the very citadel his own'. As in 'The Aspern Papers', such critical violence requires the resistance of its subject in order to validate the truth of its hermeneutic assumptions. Thus, Dowden claims that 'Every great writer has his secret, and there are some writers who seem to cherish their secret and constantly to elude us, just at the moment of capture; and these, perhaps, are the most fascinating of all, endlessly to be pursued.'[43] Here, the manipulative incorporation of resistance as a strategic moment within the dialectical process of textual interpretation is revealed with particular clarity: the elusive nature of the author's 'secret' does little to interrupt (and much to sustain) the subsequent critical pursuit. This scenario is familiar, of course, not only from 'The Aspern Papers' but also from 'The Figure in the Carpet', as well as from James's remarks in his review of George Sand's *Elle et lui*. Reading these texts alongside Dowden's essay, however, reveals the extent to which James was consciously parodying the beliefs of contemporary biographical critics. By reproducing the apparently insoluble conflict between critic and author, James recognizes that this very conflict is itself inscribed within the rhetoric of investigative discourse. At the same time, James radicalizes this conflict in such a way that resistance threatens to lose its operative status, and to function as an absolute barrier to biographical 'knowledge'. Although the desire for knowledge is not curtailed by resistance in 'The Aspern Papers', all possibility of its realization is demonstrably removed.

Whether or not James had actually read Dowden's essay before writing 'The Aspern Papers', its connection with the story goes still further. In the same year that 'The Interpretation of Literature' was written, Dowden also published his influential biography of Shelley which contributed to a renewed flurry of interest in the 'lives' of the Romantic poets during this period. By recurring to the same moment of literary history, it is clear that James conceived 'The Aspern Papers' as a satirical response to the reverential and mythologizing stance of biographers and critics such as Dowden.[44] In particular, James was reacting against the conception of the author as a unique 'personality' that was propagated by such publications. Dowden's theory of critical interpretation is itself biographical in approach: it relies upon a 'psychological method of study' (which should not be confused with the Nietzschean 'psychology' of 'The Aspern Papers') in which the 'personality' of the author is understood to be the generative source of the text. Hence, biographical criticism is essentially retroactive in its procedure: 'From each single work of a great author', Dowden wrote, 'we advance to his total work, and thence to the man himself – to the heart and brain from which all this manifold world of wisdom and wit and passion and beauty has proceeded.'[45] The author is hypostatized as the final goal of textual interpretation; the 'work' is of interest only in so far as it 'manifests' the presence of the 'life'. In these assumptions, Dowden exemplifies a predominant strain of late-nineteenth-century critical discourse: one which offered theoretical legitimacy to similar, but more popular, biographical and journalistic strategies. As I have already noted, James himself believed that the private text was capable of retaining traces of authorial personality, and so may appear to license similar hermeneutic assumptions. For James, however, the status of the private text is quite different from that of the public 'work', and in many of his later tales this distinction forms the basis of a more radical critique of the claims of biographical knowledge.

THE AUTHOR AT HOME

As Tzvetan Todorov has suggested, James countered the practice of 'psychological criticism' by inverting its procedure. Whereas in the form of biographical interpretation advocated by Dowden, it is the work which is reduced to an epiphenomenon of the life, in many of James's tales the reverse holds true: the life, rather than the work, assumes the status of what Todorov terms an 'unessential presence'.[46] James's insistence upon the necessity of maintaining an interpretive separation between the 'life' and the 'work' is, of course, a familiar enough motif of the proto-modernist aesthetic which he derived from Flaubert. What is insufficiently recognized, though, is the extent to which James's aesthetic theory was formulated in direct response to the threat of publicity. In an 1882 review of Ernest Daudet's *Mon frère et moi*, for example, James declared that 'In our opinion, the life and the work are two very different matters, and an intimate knowledge of the one is not at all necessary for a genial enjoyment of the other.' The immediate context of this statement, however, is his concern with 'the growing taste of the age for revelations about the private life of the persons in whose works it is good enough to be interested': a phenomenon which is again manifested in the publication under review (*LC* II 214–15). James's adoption of a stance similar to Flaubert's doctrine of the 'impersonality' of the artist was thus inextricably bound up with the formation of an opposing object of critical discourse, namely the construction of the author as 'personality'.[47]

This conflict between 'personal' and 'impersonal' forms of critical discourse is evidently central to the tales of the 'literary life' which

James began to write during the 1890s. In 'The Death of the Lion' (1894), most notably, it is mapped on to a whole series of analagous binary terms, through which the narrator of the tale articulates his opposition to the lionization of the novelist, Neil Paraday. 'Let whoever would represent the interest in his presence', the narrator declares, 'I should represent the interest in his work – in other words, in his absence. These two interests were in their essence opposed' (*CT* IX 95). The terms of this essential opposition are clear enough: whereas biographical interest in the 'life' or 'personality' of the author is predicated upon the desire to witness his unmediated presence, the theory of artistic impersonality claims that the author is irretrievably absent from his work, and so reveals the lacuna which exists at the centre of all biographical interpretation. It is from passages such as this that Todorov derives his analysis of the formal structure of James's 'quest' narratives. If, on the one hand, these narratives (which include most of the tales which I have been discussing in this chapter) are motivated entirely by the desire to uncover an '*absolute and absent cause*', on the other hand an opposing impulse constantly frustrates and resists this investigative movement, and so condemns the quest to remain absorbed in its own self-referential presence. The fact that several of these narratives are directed towards the discovery of a textual 'secret' is significant, moreover, because the work of art, according to Todorov, is 'the most present absence of all'.[48] Biographical enquiry founders upon the 'work' since the very object of the quest is, by definition, absent from it: far from revealing the personality of its author, as many contemporary critics assumed, the work is a site from which all trace of personal identity has been erased. To Todorov's account of James's resistance to 'psychological criticism', however, we must add two qualifications. First, this reading assumes that narratorial statements, such as the passage from 'The Death of the Lion' quoted above, correspond transparently to James's own authorial position. This neglects the possibility that James is also ironizing the complacency of his narrator's declaration of artistic impersonality, as I suggest later. Second, Todorov's schematic analysis abstracts such terms as 'absence' and 'presence' from the specific cultural context of James's tales.

In 'The Death of the Lion', James is concerned with a shift in contemporary journalistic practice which corresponds to the changes which I have already discussed in relation to biography. The narrator of the story is himself a journalist who resigns his post in protest at the more 'personal' methods being introduced by a new editor, Mr Pinhorn. The nature of these methods is indicated by the narrator's characterization of Pinhorn as a man whose 'sincerity took the form of ringing door-bells and whose definition of genius was the art of finding people at home' (*CT* IX 78). Here, James is alluding specifically to the technique of the interview which was one of the most innovative strategies of the so-called New Journalism which emerged in the 1880s and 1890s. This journalistic innovation quite literally demanded the 'presence' of the journalist as a witness to the authenticity and intimacy of his encounter with the celebrity. By writing a critical appreciation of Paraday's work, rather than offering an 'intimate' glimpse into his life, the narrator is thus open to the charge of being 'deucedly distant' from his subject (*CT* IX 81). Later in the story, however, the narrator is given a lesson in how this new, 'personal' journalism should be conducted. Paraday is approached by a journalist named Mr Morrow who attempts to conduct an interview in the home of the celebrated novelist. The interviewer's desire to record the interior space of authorship encompasses the minutiae of Paraday's domestic surroundings, as he reveals with comic gusto:

> I was shown into the drawing-room, but there must be more to see – his study, his literary sanctum, the little things he has about, or other domestic objects or features. He wouldn't be lying down on his study table? There's a great interest always felt in the scene of an author's labours. Sometimes we're favoured with very delightful peeps. Dora Forbes showed me all his table-drawers, and almost jammed my hand into one into which I made a dash! (*CT* IX 90–1)

Morrow's intervention illustrates the way in which Paraday's new-found status as a public figure generates interest in his privacy. As a celebrity, the author is known not only by his success in 'society', but also, paradoxically, by his apparent detachment from the public sphere. In this respect, James's parody of the New Journalistic rhetoric is more accurate than might be supposed.

Like the somewhat later phenomenon of the New Biography, the New Journalism was understood by its practitioners as a form of investigative discourse which aimed to disclose the private domain of its subjects.[49] Moreover, as in the case of the former, authors were often the subjects of this new mode of enquiry. From as early as the 1840s, as Richard Altick has noted, the home of the author had been an object of interest to both literary critics and tourists.[50] It was only much later in the century, however, that journalists began to conduct interviews with literary celebrities in their homes. One of the earliest exponents of this genre was the journalist Edmund Yates whose series *Celebrities at Home* was published in his weekly newspaper *The World* during the late 1870s and early 1880s. In Yates's hands, the home of the celebrity was not merely a convenient site in which to conduct interviews; rather, it offered an objective correlative to the rhetorical strategy of the interview itself. The home functioned as a signifying space in which it became possible to represent public figures as creatures of privacy. Yates pursued this strategy with remarkable vigour: in each article he proceeded to describe the home of the celebrity in minute detail, systematically exploring and documenting the interior domain of the subject. The aim of these enquiries, however, was not merely to confirm the exalted social status of the celebrity, but, rather, to suggest that material possessions were capable of offering a privileged insight into a unique 'personality'. The physical exploration of the home was mapped on to a narrative of biographical revelation. Describing Mark Twain's home in Connecticut, for example, Yates insisted that its architectural style and rich ornamentation were 'no mere extraneous accumulations such as any man of wealth might create, but a gradual and organic outgrowth of the owner's mind which gives you a delightful peep into the inner recesses of his character'.[51] Like many biographers of the period, Yates was also fascinated by the hermeneutic significance of the author's 'literary workshop': with the locked drawers and concealed manuscripts which were taken to represent the innermost sanctum of authorial creativity.[52] The popularity of *Celebrities at Home* is indicated by the fact that it ran continuously in *The World* for over six years, and totalled more than 300 separate articles.[53] Although Yates himself did not use the term, the series pioneered many of the characteristic narrative strategies and rhetorical tropes of the celebrity 'interview', as it was later developed. By the 1890s, interviews with literary celebrities were beginning to appear in a wide range of newspapers and periodicals. In new monthly magazines, such as *The Idler* and *The Strand* for example, these texts were often accompanied by photographic illustrations of the 'celebrity at home'.[54]

James's parodic rendition of the rhetoric of the interview thus refers to a form of journalistic discourse which had become generically recognizable at the time that he was writing. In his preliminary notebook sketch for 'The Death of the Lion', James adverts apocalyptically to this 'age of advertisement and newspaperism, this age of interviewing' in which the author is simultaneously 'made up to, *fêted*, written to for his autograph, portrait, etc., and yet with whose work . . . not one of the persons concerned has the smallest acquaintance' (*NB* 148). It would be easy to assume that this vision of a degraded mass culture is merely a further example of the distorted and self-valorizing mythology of artistic martyrdom to which I refer in the previous chapter. Yet while it is true that tales such as 'The Death of the Lion' and 'The Next Time' are self-consciously fabulistic in form, what should not be forgotten is the precision of James's cultural references. The 'scene of an author's labours' did indeed come to represent one of the most visible cultural signs by which the public status of the literary celebrity was ratified. Yet James was also aware of the contradictory cultural injunctions which this new iconography of authorship tended to conceal. Journalists such as Yates attempted to invoke the 'sanctity' of the private sphere whilst, at the very same time, systematically exhibiting it. By representing the celebrity in solitary or familial domesticity, the figure of the author was seemingly detached from the world of publicity into which it was, in fact, utterly incorporated. Privacy itself was thus reduced to a strategy of publicity; rather than offering a refuge from the public domain, the 'private life' of the author became the very sign of celebrity.

It was for this reason, moreover, that James was forced to problematize his satire of literary publicity. In 'The Death of the Lion', James characteristically undermines the security of the satirical position which he appears to be adopting through the figure of the narrator. As in 'The Aspern Papers', suspicion is cast upon the narrator's assertion of critical disinterest, and hence upon the very possibility of cultural resistance. On the surface, the narrator's response to the intrusive designs of Mr Morrow would appear to represent an exemplary affirmation of the religious aestheticism to which journalistic irreverence is often opposed in the story: 'I entertained an insurmountable, an almost superstitious objection to his crossing the threshold of my friend's little lonely, shabby, consecrated workshop', he confides to the reader (*CT* IX 91). By invoking the sanctity of Paraday's 'workroom', however, the narrator simply reflects the terms in which interviewers themselves approached the home of the great author. It was this very attribution of sanctity to the home of the literary celebrity which incited the transgressive desire for intimacy. In contemporary journalistic texts, the home was often seen as a 'literary shrine', just as the pastime of visiting the 'homes and haunts' of authors, living or dead, was described as an act of 'pilgrimage'.[55] While opponents of these practices dismissed them as intrusive, journalists themselves presented their activity as a form of homage. Paradoxically, the strategy of the interview was not to dispel the aura that was attached to 'privacy', but to reinforce it. By attempting to protect Paraday from the attentions of others, therefore, the narrator seems only to be reserving for himself the pleasure of an intimate revelation. While claiming to be the guardian of 'the interest in his work', the narrator frequently betrays the same veneration of the personality which he insistently rebukes. His Flaubertian theory of artistic impersonality is used to manipulative effect, for example, when he attempts to steer Fanny Hurter away from personal contact with Paraday only to assume an eroticized relationship to the 'master' himself. As the privileged recipient of a private reading of Paraday's latest work, the narrator enthuses that he has 'never been so throbbingly present at such an unveiling' (*CT* IX 83), thereby anticipating the ingenuous conflation of sexual and textual knowledge assumed by the narrator of 'The Figure in the Carpet'. In this instance, moreover, the narrator replicates the very language of the interviewer's desire to witness the disclosure of authorial presence.

In his later tale, 'John Delavoy' (1898), James constructs a similar scenario in which the possibility of eluding the investigative narratives of publicity is ironically undermined. The story begins with a scene in the theatre during which the narrator observes the sister (initially thought to be the daughter) of the recently deceased novelist, John Delavoy. The narrator's response to this vision, however, is ambiguous:

> She was the image of a nearer approach, of a personal view: I mean in respect to my great artist, on whose consistent aloofness from the crowd I needn't touch, any more than on his patience in going his way and attending to his work, the most unadvertised, unreported, uninterviewed, unphotographed, uncriticised of all originals. Was he not the man of the time about whose private life we delightfully knew least? The young lady in the balcony, with the stamp of her close relation to him in her very dress, was a sudden opening into that region. (*CT* IX 405)

From these initial reflections, the narrator proceeds on two parallel courses of action. On the one hand, he attempts to prevent the exploitative publicity which surrounds Delavoy's posthumous reputation, thus offering a further sardonic commentary upon the journalistic promotion of literary 'personalities'. The editor Mr Beston, he recognizes, is interested only in 'anecdotes, glimpses, gossip, chat; a picture of his "home life", domestic habits, diet, dress, arrangements – all his little ways and little secrets' (*CT* IX 428). On the other hand, the narrator is himself enticed by the opportunity of a 'personal view' of the novelist represented by his sister. By aligning himself with Miss Delavoy's desire to honour the work, rather than the life, of her brother, the narrator eventually succeeds in marrying her, and so ironically achieves the 'nearer approach' to the artist which his own critical stance disavows. As in 'The Death of the Lion', then, the narrator's attention to the artist's work sits uneasily with his unacknowledged (and here impossible) desire to be in the physical presence of the author. In this regard, the name 'Delavoy' is wryly significant: both the narrator and Mr Beston wish to return to the oracular, and supposedly authentic, source of literary expression, the voice of the author himself. For Beston, Delavoy's interest as a subject of publicity derives from the very fact that little is known about his private life. He wishes to acquire Miss Delavoy's portrait of her brother simply because it bears witness to this absence of knowledge. Being the only visual image of the artist in existence, the portrait 'tells nothing in the world but that he never sat for another' (*CT* IX 415), but therein lies its value. It is Delavoy's avoidance of publicity which becomes the editor's selling point. Despite his opposition to such journalistic strategies, however, the narrator is entranced by a similar logic. The obscurity of Delavoy's private life is what compels him to pursue a 'sudden opening into that region', and so to negate the authenticity of privacy in the very gesture of upholding it.

This irony is characteristic of the way in which James disarmingly denies any secure foundation to the ostensibly one-sided satire of his tales. In both 'John Delavoy' and 'The Death of the Lion', the self-proclaimed defenders of art are as implicated as any journalist in the values and practices of the mass media. Indeed, James suggests that the very act of narrating these stories is inevitably entangled with the cultural forms which it wishes to oppose. The 'literary' text is forced to confront the issue of its own publicity, as the fragmented narrative form of the tales self-consciously concedes. In 'The Death of the

Lion', for instance, the narrator prefaces his story by insisting that 'These meagre notes are essentially private, so that if they see the light the insidious forces that, as my story itself shows, make at present for publicity will simply have overmastered my precautions' (*CT* IX 80). There is a similar moment in 'John Delavoy' where the narrator offers the cryptic but deliberate declaration that his own text is merely a 'private record', not intended for public consumption. These apparently casual extradiegetic remarks are telling reminders of the way in which James questions not only the efficacy of his 'cultured' narrators, but also the status of his own narrative texts. In the first example, the narrator's assertion of the intended privacy of his text seems designed to signal his resistance to the 'insidious forces' of publicity which the story takes as its theme. By way of refusal, the declaration appears to hold out the possibility of an alternative mode of textual and authorial circulation to that which has been witnessed in the case of Neil Paraday. Yet this possibility is immediately withdrawn in the second half of the narrator's statement. The initial assertion of privacy seems redundant since the very fact that we read it confirms the narrator's suspicion that the form of the text has indeed been 'overmastered' by the logic of its content. The redundancy of this gesture, however, is also its point: what the 'story itself shows' is equivalent to the fact of its being shown at all. Through the voice of his narrator, then, James registers a protest against the forces of publicity, whilst, at the same time, recognizing that the dissemination of his own text cannot avoid participating in the same phenomenon. James's strategy of defamiliarizing the communicative function of fiction is further illustrated by an inconsistency between the different narrative forms of which the narrator's text is comprised. Towards the end of 'The Death of the Lion', the narrator switches from a direct, first-person narration to an epistolary form consisting of the transcription of his letters to Fanny Hurter, before reverting back to his initial method. The first shift involves the introduction of a more intimate mode of communication into the narrative, to such an extent that the narrator is keen to stress that he has obtained the permission of his addressee before transcribing the letters. The narrator's anxious profession of respect for the privacy of his correspondent, however, sits oddly with his earlier statement: if the text is already intended to be 'essentially private', it is hardly necessary for the narrator to obtain Fanny's permission before reproducing private documents within it. Once again, this contradiction should not be read simply as a lapse of naturalistic consistency within the fictional world of the tale, but, rather, as part of a self-conscious endeavour to address the question of publicity at the level of textual communication itself. James does not attempt to conceal such elaborate inconsistencies beneath the surface of a smoothly realistic fiction; instead, he concedes the improbability of the narrative as a way of registering the cultural pressures to which it is subject.

It was through this reflexive strategy that James was able to mount a more cogent and complex critique of the commercial practices of modern literary culture than is often assumed. In the tales of the literary life, James himself constructed a series of 'biographical' narratives recording the experience of his fictive authors. Yet he also attempted to write the 'life' of the author in such a way that he would avoid simply reinscribing the contemporary biographical and journalistic fascination with literary 'personalities'. In these tales, the figure of the artist is often presented in an oblique fashion, not only in the case of 'John Delavoy' where he is literally absent from the text, but also in 'The Death of the Lion' and 'The Next Time' where the artist is conspicuously distanced from the narratorial consciousness. In 'The Death of the Lion', for example, the narrator indicates his opposition to the investigative narratives of journalism by self-consciously refusing to recount his 'introduction to Mr. Paraday or of certain proximate steps and stages' (*CT* IX 80); he is evidently aware that the meeting of the journalist and his subject was often dramatized as a revelatory moment in contemporary celebrity interviews.[56] Characteristically, though, James also demonstrates his narrator's unwitting collusion with the cultural forms which he claims to oppose. Not only does the narrator himself evince a 'personal interest' in Neil Paraday, as I have observed, but the very form of his narrative acknowledges an inability to preserve the private sphere of authorship. The form of the text threatens to repeat its content, exemplifying, rather than resisting, the cultural phenomenon which it seeks to address. This recurrent narratorial anxiety is indicative of James's understanding of the problematic relationship between cultural criticism and its object. Throughout his many reflections on the subject of biographical and journalistic 'intrusion', James was aware of the difficulty of grounding his own critical response within an autonomous and anterior domain of privacy. Within these new forms of investigative discourse, 'privacy', it seems, was already subject to a knowledge that claimed not to know it. In 'The Death of the Lion', one might argue, James acknowledges the extent to which the 'insidious forces' of publicity inhabit his own private space of authorship. This is an insight which I explore further, and on a larger scale, in my final chapter on *The Ambassadors*; before doing so, however, it remains important to offer a more extended consideration of James's response to the emergence of investigative discourse as it came to occupy the institutionalized medium of the press.

CHAPTER FOUR

The power of the press: from scandal to hunger

In 1888 James published two major works of fiction: 'The Aspern Papers' and *The Reverberator.*[1] If the former exemplifies his concern with the prevailing pursuit of biographical 'revelations', the latter takes as its theme the analagous phenomenon of 'investigative' journalism. Indeed, despite exhibiting very different aspects of James's stylistic practice, these two texts reveal a number of similarities. The narrator of 'The Aspern Papers', for example, likens himself to 'the reporter of a newspaper who forces his way into a house of mourning' (*CT* VI 336), while, conversely, the activities of the journalist George M. Flack recall the manipulative strategies of the literary biographer. In many respects, the object of James's satire is essentially the same in both texts. At the same time, James's concern with the cultural effects of modern journalism cannot simply be reduced to the anxieties of biographical 'exposure' which I examined in the previous chapter. The figure of the journalist is one that recurs frequently in James's fiction (from *The Portrait of a Lady* (1880–1) to *The Wings of the Dove* (1902), not to mention the other novels and tales to which I have already referred), and it is often assumed that 'journalism' is subjected to his most savage criticism. For earlier critics, this alleged antipathy was attributed either to personal resentment caused by James's unhappy association with the New York *Tribune* in the 1870s, or simply to a constitutional sensitivity towards the 'vulgarities' of the popular press.[2] More recently, Alfred Habegger has argued that James's satire of the press was a product of ignorance, and that his fictional journalists bear 'only a superficial connection with their times', unlike the more informed criticism of his friend and compatriot William Dean Howells.[3] None of these critics, however, has attempted to assess either the extent and purpose of James's critique, or its intimate relationship to the historical formation of the mass media.

It is no coincidence, for example, that *The Reverberator* was conceived in the same year that Matthew Arnold noted the appearance of a 'new journalism', and thus coined a phrase which gained wide currency in subsequent debates upon the changing form of the popular press.[4] Arnold's disparaging remarks, which were aimed specifically at W.T. Stead's editorship of the *Pall-Mall Gazette*, were published in May 1887; in November of that year James was recording in his notebook the 'queer incident' of May McClellan, to which I referred in chapter 1. It is in the course of this sketch, it will be recalled, that James goes on to express his sense of 'the devouring *publicity* of life', and to argue the necessity of taking account of 'the invasion, the impudence and shamelessness, of the newspaper and the interviewer' in any attempt at 'sketch[ing] one's age' (*NB* 82). In the novel itself, moreover, James engages directly with many of the issues that occupied the attention both of critics such as Arnold and of journalists themselves. Before I consider how *The Reverberator* might be situated within the context of these debates, however, it is first necessary to give a fuller account of what was meant by the term 'New Journalism'.

Two years after Arnold's initial identification of a 'new journalism', T.P. O'Connor, the editor of the recently founded London *Star*, responded by offering a clarification and systematic defence of the same phenomenon. In an article entitled 'The New Journalism', published in the *The New Review* in 1889, O'Connor noted that the 'main point of difference' between the old and the new journalism was 'the more personal tone of the more modern methods'. Whereas formerly, for example, journalists had been content merely to report the spoken words of statesmen, the New Journalism attempted to reproduce a 'photograph of the outward man'. Instead of transposing speech into the neutrality of print, O'Connor's aim is to reveal the 'personality' of the speaker, and thus to scrutinize 'the man – a weak man or a strong man, high or low, generous in purpose or base in intrigue'.[5] By embodying speech in this manner, O'Connor hopes to restore the evidential truth of oral communication to the impersonal medium of the press: only by observing the character of the speaker is it possible to exercise the critical function which behoves a politically active readership.

O'Connor's belief that the 'more personal tones' of the New Journalism would reveal a form of truth which had been veiled by the impersonality of existing journalistic practice was also shared by contemporary opponents of journalistic anonymity – a convention which still persisted in much of the newspaper press. If the New Journalism was noted for its concern with revealing the 'personality' of its subjects, equally, during the same period, attempts were made to acknowledge the personal identity of the journalist.[6] Writing in the same year and journal as O'Connor, Tighe Hopkins, for example, similarly contrasted the transparency of personal journalism with the cultivation of an oracular impersonality. Arguing in favour of signed articles, Hopkins endeavoured to demystify the habit of employing a plural, collective subject of editorial address:

> The 'We' is not really 'We'; it is 'I'. If this be so, what or whose interest is served by the maintenance of the incognito? Not the interest of the writer, assuredly; and not, I think, the interest of the public. The writer suffers in his proper dignity by being compelled to withhold his name from his work in obedience to a custom which has its chief sanction in the credulity of *le gros public*; and in what other respects he suffers I have already shown. As for the public, it ought to be a sufficient objection to the anonymous system that, whilst this system does not and cannot give any *real* force to the work of an honest writer, the dishonest may borrow from it a *simulacrum* of power which, if his mask were stripped from him, would vanish at once.[7]

Hopkins's objection to the collective anonymity of journalistic rhetoric thus rests not simply on the grounds of its obfuscation of the journalist's 'real' identity, but also on account of the politically charged question of journalistic responsibility. If, on the one hand, the responsible journalist is insufficiently recognized under a system of anonymity, on the other hand, the use of the collective subject confers an unwarranted prestige upon the utterance of the irresponsible. It is this '*simulacrum* of power' which the advocates of the New Journalism characteristically see themselves as unmasking. By endowing the personal interests of the journalist with a false aura of authority, the rhetoric of journalistic impersonality operates as an insidious form of coercion. Seeing itself reflected in this collective subject of discourse, the public is persuaded to accept the newspaper as the authentic voice of public opinion.

It was W.T. Stead, perhaps the foremost advocate of the New Journalism, however, who carried the political implications of this analysis furthest. In his programmatic article 'The Future of Journalism' (1886), Stead makes a direct equation between the 'personal' mode of journalistic address and the ideological function of the newspaper as an instrument of democratic social change. Conversely, the imposing rhetoric of high-Victorian journalism is viewed as an autocratic form of cultural expression, which requires sceptical decoding:

Impersonal journalism is effete. To influence men you must be a man, not a mock-uttering oracle. The democracy is under no awe of the mystic 'We'. Who is 'We'? they ask; and they are right. For all power should be associated with responsibility, and a leader of the people, if a journalist, needs a neck capable of being stretched quite as much as if he is a Prime Minister.[8]

Like Hopkins, then, Stead argues for the necessity of rooting the responsibility of journalistic 'power' in the individual, although, unlike the former, he does not ascribe the success of this illusory aura of impersonality to a gullible public. In this populist account, the journalist appears as an heroic figure: a 'leader of the people', accountable to his followers, but opposed to the constituted authority of the state. Stead's interpretation of the political function of personal journalism, however, must also be set against the conflicting pressures which marked the formation of a mass-circulation press towards the end of the century. While Stead posed as the dynamic, individualistic editor, in fact, as Raymond Williams and more recent historians have shown, the popular press simultaneously became increasingly *impersonal* during the 1880s and 1890s, as a result both of the introduction of new technologies of production and of corporate structures of ownership.[9] Within these new forms of commercial organization, the 'personal' voice of the journalist tended to carry less weight: the political engagement which marked the initial phase of the New Journalism had to be balanced against the private commercial interests upon whose advertising revenue the newspaper press was increasingly dependent.[10]

It was this contradiction between the demands of politically committed investigative journalism, on the one hand, and the increasingly commercialized orientation of the press on the other, which William Dean Howells dramatized (in an American context) in his novel *A Modern Instance* (1882). When the ambitious journalist Bartley J. Hubbard is offered a post on the Boston *Events*, he is warned by Mr Witherby, the owner of the paper, against attacking the private interests which subsidize his own endeavours:

Suppose all the newspapers pitch in – as they sometimes do – and denounce a certain public enterprise: a projected scheme of railroad legislation, or a peculiar system of banking, or a co-operative mining interest, and the counting-room sends up word that the company advertises heavily with us; shall we go and join indiscriminately in that hue and cry, or shall we give our friends the benefit of the doubt?[11]

Witherby's question is a threat to which the weak-minded Bartley is only too willing to submit. Bartley's cynical 'theory of independent journalism', we are told, is to 'hold a course of strict impartiality, and yet come out on the winning side'.[12] Here, the ethos of critical publicity advocated by radical journalists such as Stead is degraded into a spuriously 'de-politicized' journalism, subservient to the corrupt private interests which it is the task of the 'independent' journalist to expose. The investigative impulse, which characterized Stead's campaigning style in the *Pall-Mall Gazette*, was also capable of yielding less subversive objects of 'revelation'.[13] Instead of denouncing the dubious practices of railroad or mining interests, Bartley conducts a series of personal interviews with business tycoons, which, while 'guarded and inoffensive as respects the sanctity of private life', provide a surrogate gratification.[14] In effect, Howells shows how the potentially radical energies of the new, personal journalism were liable to be deflected from their course.

THE REVERBERATOR

If *The Reverberator* seems sketchy in detail beside the meticulous realism of Howells's depiction of the world of commercial journalism, it is no less immersed in the cultural debates which I have been outlining. The relevance of these debates to James's novel may be seen immediately once we recognize that *The Reverberator* takes as its underlying theme a tension between individual and collective forms of identity. There is evidence to suggest, moreover, that this concern was recognized by contemporary readers, familiar with its cultural frame of reference. In his 1889 article on the question of journalistic anonymity, Tighe Hopkins quotes the critic William Archer in support of his own opposition to such impersonal forms of address as 'the *Reverberator* is of such an opinion'.[15] Archer's apparent allusion to the title of James's fictive newspaper suggests that the novel itself was read as a direct contribution to the debate surrounding the appropriate form of journalistic expression: in this instance, the *Reverberator* is invoked as a byword for the overweening rhetoric of 'impersonal' journalism. If this is the case, however, Archer's (and subsequently Hopkins's) reading of *The Reverberator* is also somewhat misleading. Certainly Archer would be correct in supposing that James's text criticizes the rhetorical strategy of concealing the private interests of the journalist through the assumption of an imposing collective voice. By way of authorizing his own discourse, the journalist George Flack constantly invokes the collective subject of the 'American people', which thus functions as a 'democratized' form of Stead's 'mystic "We"'. Archer, however, apparently wishes to enlist *The Reverberator* in support of a cause with which James was equally uneasy. The novel is also, and more obviously, critical of the 'more personal tones' which characterized the New Journalism in both Britain and America: it is Flack's pursuit of scandalous personal 'revelations' which is the main target of its satire.[16]

While *The Reverberator* may be read as a contribution to the journalistic debates of the 1880s, then, it does not offer a programmatic critique along the lines of Stead's polemical opposition between personal and impersonal journalism. Instead, James shows how both these rhetorical strategies are conflated within Flack's journalistic project. This conflation is illustrated early in the novel when Flack outlines his conception of the journalism of the future in the form of a marriage proposal to Francie Dosson. Like the narrator of 'The Aspern Papers', the journalist's personal motives are thinly concealed behind a rhetoric of professional disinterest. The narrator of the novel ironically observes 'the note of the prospectus mingling with the accent of passion'; only at the end of a lengthy statement of his journalistic ambitions does it become apparent that Flack also includes Francie in his future plans (*R* 60). This inability to distinguish between personal and professional goals graphically enacts the 'extinction of all sense between public and private' which James had seen as the underlying tendency of modern journalistic culture in his notebook sketch of the novel. A similar 'extinction' of the difference between private and public interests may be observed in Flack's claim to represent his readership:

> The society news of every quarter of the globe, furnished by the prominent members themselves (oh, *they* can be fixed – you'll see!) from day to day and from hour to hour and served up at every breakfast-table in the United States – that's what the American people want and that's what the American people are going to have . . . I'm going for the secrets, the *chronique intime*, as they say here; what the people want is just what isn't told, and I'm going to tell it. Oh, they're bound to have the plums! That's about

played out, anyway, the idea of sticking up a sign of private and thinking you can keep the place to yourself. (*R* 60–1).

Here, as I have suggested, Flack appropriates the collective identity of the 'American people' as a means of authorizing and, at the same time, obfuscating his individual agency. Hence, he claims to embody a 'public opinion' of which his readers are apparently the subject, but in truth the object, of address. This strategy is one that again recalls the 'estrangement' between artist and audience which Theodor Adorno saw as symptomatic of the emerging conditions of mass culture. For Adorno, the music of Richard Wagner exemplifies this separation by strategically aiming to bridge it: by 'incorporating the public in the work as an element of its "effect"'. While Wagner exhibits a 'democratic considerateness towards the listener', his apparently spontaneous receptivity to the public conceals an orchestration of its 'demands'.[17] If Wagner seems an unlikely figure for George Flack, a similar strategy of incorporation may be witnessed in the journalist's assumption of 'what the American people want'. While Flack insists that he is merely responding to public demand in his pursuit of 'society news', the 'demand' itself is already inscribed within the rhetorical structure of the product which he supplies. Since the consumption of the newspaper is prefigured within its own form, it operates, in Jean Baudrillard's terms, as a 'self-fulfilling prophecy', offering its readers the spectacle of a popular satisfaction which has already been 'foretold'.[18]

The manipulative effect of Flack's journalistic rhetoric is, of course, by no means difficult to detect. As Thomas Strychacz has observed, James's coolly ironic narrative voice functions as a means of contextualizing Flack's statements, even if he is not overtly condemned.[19] More specifically, James's satire works to demystify the power of journalistic rhetoric by prising apart its conflated subjects. In a parenthetic aside, for example, the narrator remarks that 'Mr. Flack was wonderful on all occasions in finding what he wanted (which, as we know, was what he believed the public wanted)', thus demonstrating his ability to distinguish between the individual identity of the journalist and the collective identity which he assumes (*R* 26). If James uses such narrative interjections as a means of indicating a capacity for discrimination superior to that of his characters, and so reinforcing an implicit distinction between 'literature' and 'journalism', as Strychacz contends,[20] it should also be said that this capacity is not dissimilar to the distinction urged by some of the pioneering advocates of the New Journalism. Unexpectedly, perhaps, James's proximity to Stead is, in this respect, quite striking. In 'The Future of Journalism', Stead debunks the pious 'journalistic assumption of uttering the opinion of the public' as 'a hollow fraud'; in reality, he points out, the journalist's knowledge of the public is devised 'in the office, in the club, or in the drawing-room'.[21] To suggest that James attempted to counter the New Journalism by referring back to an earlier and more austere (or 'literary') mode of journalistic discourse would thus be too simple. James would probably have concurred with Stead's critique of the magisterial rhetoric of journalistic impersonality, and this alone suggests the complexity of his critical concerns in the novel.

Superficially, at least, these concerns revolve around a familiar opposition between the cultural assumptions of American democracy and European conservatism. Having refused Flack's offer of marriage, Francie Dosson subsequently becomes engaged to Gaston Probert, a Gallicized American whose aristocratic family despise the vulgarity of newspaper publicity. Then, during a conversation with her rejected suitor, Francie indiscreetly reveals the family secrets of the Proberts, which Flack proceeds to publish. From these elements, James constructs a scenario in which the revelatory discourse of personal journalism is couched in the language of a democratic 'right to know', while the entrenched domesticity of the Proberts is seen as belonging to a corrupt European society, which erects socially exclusive barriers around the private sphere. At the same time, James also shows how this opposition collapses in the absence of a genuinely critical form of publicity. Rather than tearing down the bastions of privilege, as he claims, Flack's model of investigative journalism actively erects a sign of 'privacy' in order to infiltrate it. If the journalistic 'scandal' is to maintain its compulsive interest, the boundary between private and public spheres must be maintained, even as it appears to be threatened. In this sense, Flack's revelatory discourse is fundamentally intransitive: it is aimed not so much at dispelling 'privacy' as reinforcing its presence.

More importantly, though, what James seems to be testing in the novel is the very possibility of an opposition between American and European cultural forms. While *The Reverberator* has usually been read as one of James's more ephemeral 'international' comedies, I would argue that it is very much concerned with questioning the possibilities of cultural difference which this fictional paradigm presupposes. Rather than viewing James's recourse to the 'international theme' as a distraction from his satire of journalistic culture, as Anne Margolis does, I would also suggest that the interaction of these two strands of the novel is entirely congruent with James's critique of the cultural effects of publicity.[22] It is certainly true, as Margolis suggests, that there is a marked shift in emphasis between James's initial notebook sketch and the novel itself. In the passage from the notebook which I quoted earlier, James is primarily interested in questioning the motives of the American woman who betrays the confidence of her European hosts, without scrutinizing the response of the latter. In his preface to the New York edition of *The Reverberator*, James recapitulates this initial assessment of the conflict between American and European cultures. 'The couple of columns in the vulgar newspaper', he insists, 'constituted no document whatever on the manners and morals of the company of persons "betrayed", but on the other hand, in its indirect way, flooded "American society" with light, became on *that* side in the highest degree documentary' (*LC* II 1197). From this standpoint, James adopts a strategy of revelation similar to that of the journalist, but inverts it, so that the 'light of the press' (to use a familiar trope, employed by Flack himself), is directed against the agents of publicity. Far from revealing anything about 'the manners and morals' of its subjects, James argues that publicity illuminates the very culture from which it emanates. The interest of the 'couple of columns in the vulgar newspaper' lies not in what they say about the 'corruption' of Europe, but in what they unwittingly say about America.

Whilst this interpretation of the *donnée* matches James's initial response in the notebook, however, it proves misleading when applied to the novel itself. There, the reader is forced to consider the content of the scandalous revelations as well as their form. Principally, as Margolis observes, the novel shifts our attention towards the problems of cultural difference which attend Francie's impending marriage with Gaston.[23] These problems are not simply incurred by Flack's propagation of a 'scandal', which leads to the rupture between Francie and Gaston's family, and hence to the need for reconciliation if the international marriage is to be happily concluded. More significantly, the response of the Proberts to Francie's part in the scandal raises the question of their own 'manners and morals', which James had earlier refused to countenance. Thus, the central dilemma of the novel is reached by Gaston's recognition that, in order to resolve the conflicting claims of Francie and his family, he must choose between two antagonistic cultures which are equally oppressive and, in some ways, curiously similar.

In James's notebook sketch the problem of resolving the conflicts engendered by publicity is approached in an entirely different manner. Instead of attributing responsibility to the European figures, he proposes a solution which is engineered entirely by the journalist:

> I think the truest and best and most illustrative would be this: that the young interviewer who has *his* virtuous indignation too, learning the scandal he has brought about, the rupture of the marriage, etc., threatens the bloated foreigners with a new horror – that is, to publish the scandal itself, with tremendous headings – the way they have treated the girl, etc. Appalled by this possibility they 'come round' – forgive, conciliate, swallow their grievance, etc., so that the marriage takes place. The newspaper dictates and triumphs – which is a reflection of actual fact. (*NB* 84)

In this projected ending to the story James is able to bring about the marriage between Francie and Gaston with a brilliantly paradoxical sleight of hand. Rather than mute the conflict between American and European manners by accommodating it to the requirements of a reconciliation, he uses the very cause of this conflict as a means of imposing its solution. The interviewer's threat to publish 'the scandal itself' compels the Europeans to 'swallow their grievances' against his naive accomplice, and allows James to achieve a desired narrative closure, while, in the same gesture, reinforcing his satire of publicity. The latter effect is a result of James's recognition that the journalist possesses the power not only to initiate scandal but also to respond to the outrage which it elicits. The journalist is able to incorporate resistance to publicity precisely by representing it. The newspaper 'dictates and triumphs' because it is always capable of having the last word.

James had already noted a similar strategy of publicity in *The Bostonians*, where the reporter Matthias Pardon encourages the conservative Mrs Luna to voice her disapproval, not only of the radical views of her sister Olive, but also of his own journalistic activities. When, in turn, Mrs Luna threatens to protest against the publicizing of her opposition to publicity, Pardon is delighted by the prospect of still further material for publicity. In both novels, then, the journalist thrives upon the hostility which he provokes because opposition to publicity is immediately translated back into the cultural code which it contests. The representation of an exchange between publicity and its material effects is liable to be recirculated indefinitely, even though (or, rather, precisely because) this exchange is entirely asymmetrical. The journalist responds to his own initiatives by promoting the spectacle of publicity itself.

The fact that James did *not* use this proposed ending to *The Reverberator*, however, requires us to consider what is gained by the novel's actual narrative resolution. By allowing Gaston to choose to marry Francie, rather than compelling him by an external threat, James indirectly raises still deeper and more disturbing questions about the cultural effects of publicity. First, Gaston's choice allows him to recognize the deficiencies of his own familial identity, as well as to question the cultural assumptions which lead Francie to accept as natural the intrusive practices of the press. From this recognition, it becomes apparent that the 'privacy' defended by the Proberts is synonymous not with the autonomy of the individual self, as it is elsewhere in James's writings, but, rather, with the closed site of the patriarchal family.[24] The Proberts, we are told, are 'a family in which there was no individual but only a collective property': a family for which Francie, of course, is viewed as a potential acquisition (*R* 39). Thus, Gaston's attempt to break free from this constricting collective identity actually reverses the terms of Flack's rhetorical opposition between American and European cultural forms. Whereas the journalist constructs an opposition between the ethical collective subjectivity of the 'American people' and the corrupt, privatized world of European society, Gaston comes to view American culture as representing an individualistic code of moral responsibility in contrast to the collective structure of the aristocratic French family. In this respect, Gaston's American friend Charles Waterlow is an important, though seemingly minor, figure in the novel's shifting construction of national cultural identities. Waterlow, an impressionist painter, appears to embody an ideal configuration of Gallic (aesthetic) and American (moral) qualities, and significantly urges Gaston to assert his individual will by marrying Francie in spite of the hostility of his family.

This schematic realignment of the polarities of cultural identity would seem to establish a rather more familiar account of the meeting between American individualism and the rigidity of European manners in James's international fiction.[25] In *The Reverberator*, however, this idealized typology of American character can scarcely be sustained. Besides Waterlow, all the other American characters in the novel are marked precisely by their lack of individual identity and independent will. The Dosson family, for example, lead a life of nomadic aimlessness which is aptly signified by their name. If the name 'Probert' offers a sufficient indication of the European(ized) family's oppressive sense of propriety, conversely, the name 'Dosson' marks the affluent vagrancy of the Americans. While Mr Dosson spends his time reading the newspapers, Francie submits to the directions of her sister Delia who, in turn, channels her own desires into Francie's relationship with Gaston. Their conspicuous lack of individual autonomy is suggested by Delia's ambiguous remark that 'My sister *is* myself – I haven't got any other': whether she is referring to a lack of other sisters or, more alarmingly, to the lack of another self which is 'myself' is left unclear (*R* 8).

It could, of course, be argued that Flack himself is an obvious exception to this rule. His purposive pursuit of journalistic material calls to mind the equally energetic figures of Matthias Pardon and Henrietta Stackpole in *The Portrait of a Lady*, and offers a glaring contrast to the lassitude of the Dossons. Yet while Flack clearly embodies a certain kind of manipulative agency, he is equally lacking in the accredited form of individual identity; in his self-proclaimed role as the voice of the people, he is unable, according to the narrator, to possess 'a property of his own' (*R* 13). Flack's lack of the 'property' which defines autonomous identity is a condition curiously similar to Gaston's, except for the fact that it postulates a very different order of commodity relations. The journalist, we are again informed, is not 'a particular person, but a sample or memento – reminding one of certain "goods" for which there is a steady popular demand' (*R* 14). This oddly contradictory conjunction, comparing Flack to a 'sample or memento' (as if the two items did not refer to opposing temporal perspectives), suggests neither a future unfolding of character nor the plenitude of a remembered past, but, instead, a temporal horizon which is bounded by the serialized instance of mass production. Flack's appearance of being simultaneously novel and familiar 'carried with it in general no ability to remember – that is to recall – him: you could not have evoked him in advance, and it was only when you saw him that you knew you *had* seen him' (*R* 14). He exists solely within a present moment which evokes past and future as aspects of its indefinite repetition. It is this repeatable moment of the 'modern', the novel suggests, which constitutes the distinctive temporality of the disposable and anonymous products of mass culture.

It is through these admittedly sketchy delineations of character, then, that James questions the possibility of an 'international theme' which, as in his earlier novels, reveals ironic contrasts between American and European cultural forms. On the one hand, the homogenizing effects of mass culture are shown to have undermined the ideal of individual autonomy which sustains American identity in the face of 'feudal' Europe. On the other hand, James reveals a disturbing similarity between the aristocratic collectivism of the Proberts and the serialized anonymity of Flack and the Dossons. While the novel is ostensibly organized around a conflict between these two polarities of cultural identity, in fact both embody the same absence of individual 'property'.[26] It becomes clear, then, that James's increased interest in the European response to the American 'invasion of privacy' does not diminish his study of the cultural effects of publicity, but deepens it. By shifting his attention in this direction, James is able to show how the ossified manners of the Proberts come to resemble tendencies that are already latently exhibited in American culture. His concern with the erosion of individual autonomy and responsibility under the effects of a burgeoning mass culture is reinforced by the projection of this anxiety on to a self-consciously anachronistic cultural site: the modern, ironically, involves a repetition of the archaic.

That the Proberts should, in this sense, mirror the Dossons is also testimony to James's awareness of the global expansion and dissemination of American culture towards the end of the nineteenth century, and of the ways in which this process tends to subsume cultural difference and the imaginative possibilities which it holds for the writer. James recognized one of the practical problems which ensued from this homogenization of cultural identity at the outset of his conception of *The Reverberator.* In his notebook sketch, he ponders the question of where to situate the outraged victims of the newspaper scandal:

> The application has presented a real difficulty, which, however, I think I have solved: that difficulty was where to find people today in Europe who would really be so shocked as that comes to – shocked enough for my dramatic opposition. I don't in the least see them in England, where publicity is far too much, by this time, in the manners of society for my

representation to have any verisimilitude here. The *World* and *Truth*, etc., stare one in the face – people write to the newspapers about everything – it is in short also a newspaperized world, and allowing for a rather better form, there is about as little delicacy as *là bas* [i.e. in America]. (*NB* 84–5)

James's difficulty in locating 'people today . . . who would really be so shocked' by the intrusiveness of the newspaper anticipates the wider questions of cultural identity pursued in the novel itself. His solution to this problem lies in the exaggerated reactionary hauteur of the Gallicized American: a figure who seems more 'European' than any actually existing European people. This figure is required in order to construct a 'dramatic opposition' between America and Europe which can no longer be sustained with any 'verisimilitude'. Ironically, then, James is forced to turn to an American simulation of 'European' cultural values in order to evoke the archaic otherness of 'Europe'. For as he is aware, the 'newspaperized world' of American culture has already penetrated this other space, rendering it largely immune to shock. His recourse to the figure of the Gallicized American thus implies a process of desensitization which renders resistance to publicity increasingly difficult to envisage.

Historically, this process may be seen as an effect derived, in part, from the formation of extensive networks of transatlantic communication during the nineteenth century. Over the course of the century, the utilization of these new technologies of communication radically altered both the discursive form and the cultural function of the press. James, of course, alludes to these communicative practices in the title of his novel. According to the OED, the word 'reverberation' signifies the repeated iteration and circulation of a story or rumour: although it may be applied to the senses of heat or light, it is primarily used to denote the transmission of sound through multiple refractions, as in an echo chamber.[27] Indeed, the word itself, with its long sequence of even, repetitive syllables and indistinct, slurred phonemes, evokes this passage of sound onomatopoeically. James evidently saw this word as peculiarly expressive of the way in which information is disseminated through modern media of communication. In the preface to the *The Reverberator*, for instance, he alludes to the mimetic function of the novel's title by way of recalling its original *donnée*. Whereas in his notebook sketch James had been alarmed by a betrayal of confidence which appeared to be symptomatic of the modern 'mania for publicity', in the preface he recalls having been most struck by the shocked response of the persons betrayed:

> Strange, it struck me, to tell the truth, the fact itself of 'anybody's knowing', and still more of anybody's caring – the fact itself, that is, of such prompt repercussion and recognition: one would so little, in advance, have supposed the reverberation of the bomb, its heeded reverberation, conceivable. No such consequence, clearly, had been allowed for by its innocent maker, for whose imagination, one felt sure, the explosion had not been designed to be world-shaking. The recording, slobbering sheet, as an object thinkable or visible in a medium so non-conducting, made of actual recognition, made even of the barest allusion, the falsest of false notes. (*LC* II 1196)

Here, in fact, James makes the opposite assumption from his earlier recognition of the difficulty of locating people who would be 'shocked enough' by publicity. Yet while he expresses surprise that in 'a medium so non-conducting' as Venice the 'revelations' of an American newspaper should meet with 'such prompt repercussion and recognition', this is precisely because the expected absence of response would, in this instance, constitute a still more authentic sign of cultural difference. The fact that the Venetians *are* shocked by the behaviour of their American guest only reinforces James's awareness of the pervasive scope of modern communications. What May McClellan, the 'innocent maker' of the 'bomb', fails to take into account is the 'reverberation' of publicity: its capacity to return upon its original source. Scandal is no longer spread simply by word of mouth, but by a print media which is circulated rapidly in time and indefinitely through space; hence, its effects are not easily localized according to the intentions of its initiator. In this sense, the shock of the Venetians signals their incorporation into the network of modern communications, rather than offering an authentic gesture of resistance to it. In expressing outrage at the manners of American culture, they bear witness to the difficulty of remaining outside the communicative circuits through which these manners are disseminated.

The incorporation of seemingly 'non-conductive' regions of geographical and cultural space may, indeed, be seen as one of the primary cultural effects of the utilization of new communications technology within nineteenth-century journalism. Probably the most important of these technological innovations was telegraphy. By the 1860s the laying of transatlantic telegraph cables had enabled the almost instantaneous transmission of information between Europe and North America. Initially, these cables were few in number and expensive to use, but American newspapers, in particular, were prepared to spend an increasing proportion of their resources on ensuring that they were quickly informed of world 'events'.[28] In the following decade, according to Frank Luther Mott, the larger American newspapers also began to adopt the telephone as a means of communicating with their reporters in the field.[29] The establishment of these global news networks, however, was not simply an unmediated effect of technological innovation. The advent of telecommunications enabled the formation of new organizational structures for the transmission of information, which, in turn, shaped the ways in which technology was utilized. The creation of news agencies in the 1860s, for example, centralized the process by which journalistic information was collated and circulated in both the United States and Great Britain. These organizations provided standardized reports for the various newspapers which they represented, and thus lessened the cost of the new communications technology while widening access to it. As a result of this process of centralization, it might be argued, the newspaper press was homogenized at the very moment that it became viable to expand the range of different titles. As private companies, the news agencies enjoyed a virtual monopoly on the news, and fears were expressed in both countries about their power to control access to information.[30]

The cultural effects of the new communications technology cannot, therefore, be derived automatically from what might be deemed to be its inherent function. It is important to recognize that the use of telegraphy as a means of opening up space and time was dialectically related to the formation of bureaucratically controlled networks of communication. Or, to put it another way, the decentring of space and time was harnessed to a centralized administration of information, at least in terms of the newspaper press. The unfolding of this dialectic of communicative expansion and closure is responsible, one might argue, for some of the characteristic tensions and ambiguities in James's handling of the 'international theme'. As both a metaphor of cultural exchange and the material basis of its new possibilities, telegraphy is clearly an important figurative and structural element in James's international fiction. One obvious example of this enabling function of telegraphy is the opening scene of *The Portrait of a Lady*, in which Mrs Touchett's telegram serves not only to announce Isabel Archer, but also seemingly to transmit her immediate physical presence. Here, the telegram is used both as a means of signifying Isabel's geographical and cultural remoteness from Europe and as a way of collapsing distance. It heralds the almost instantaneous arrival of the character whom it introduces into the novel, even if, for that reason, James exploits the rapidity of telegraphy in order to note the still greater rapidity and energy of Isabel herself.[31] Through the medium of the telegram, absence is rendered magically present, thus enabling a constant exchange between different cultural milieus.

James recognized this positive effect of modern communications technology, more explicitly, in an 1898 review of Henry Harland's *Comedies and Errors.* Situating Harland's 'cosmopolitan' fiction within the new era of global communication, he hailed the fact that the modern writer was no longer bound 'to draw his sap from the soil of his origin'. Whereas earlier novelists such as Scott, Dickens, Hawthorne and Balzac had all been famed for their representation of 'local' manners, it was now possible, James observed, to be 'an author without a country' (*LC* I 282). 'The forces that are changing all this', he specifies, 'need scarce be mentioned at a moment when each day's breakfast-table – if the morning paper be part of its furniture – fairly bristles with revelations of them. The globe is fast shrinking, for the imagination, to the size of an orange that can be played with' (*LC* I 283). The resonance of these remarks is, of course, not confined to Harland's fiction. It was the imaginative shrinking of the 'globe', exemplified by the regular appearance of the 'morning paper', which also provided the necessary conditions for James's success as 'an author without a country'. This choice of example, however, is profoundly ambivalent. The capacity of the newspaper to gather information from around the world and assemble it within the confines of the reader's home echoes George Flack's aim of providing 'The society news of every quarter of the globe . . . from day to day and from hour to hour and served up at every breakfast-table in the United States' (*R* 60–1). If James would have acknowledged the liberating possibilities of this technological reconfiguration of space and time, he also perceived a negative side to the same process.

The most likely source of James's understanding of how the newspaper adversely alters the temporal and spatial boundaries of experience is his reading of Emerson. In 'Works and Days' (1870),

Emerson had commented upon the nineteenth century's fascination with the technological mastery of nature, and, by way of example, upon 'the newspaper, which does its best to make every square acre of land and sea give an account of itself at your breakfast-table'.[32] Like James, then, Emerson was struck by the newspaper's capacity to compress disparate regions of geographical space into the intimate sphere of the reader. The image of the 'breakfast-table', which both Emerson and James use to evoke this sphere of private consumption, does not, however, simply denote a cultural *space*. What is equally remarkable is the newspaper's power to compel global space into a simultaneous reading experience. Space comes to be perceived as a virtual effect of time, forced to 'give an account of itself' to the consumer in daily instalments. This reconfiguration of space and time positions the consumer in the same way that it represents the geographical space of the news. On the one hand, the reader of the newspaper is located in the privacy of the home; on the other hand, each reader shares the 'breakfast-table' with a simultaneous community of others. Just as the global space of the news is both fragmented and homogenized, so the image of the breakfast-table figures both the atomization and the massification of the consumer. Daniel Boorstin offers an apt description (if not an adequate analysis) of this phenomenon with his use of the term 'consumption community'. Referring to the emergence of consumer culture in late-nineteenth-century America, Boorstin defines a 'consumption community' as a group of privatized individuals whose collective identity is forged through their consumption of the same brand of commodity.[33] As I have already suggested, a similar strategy of assembling a collective body of consumers informs Flack's rhetoric in *The Reverberator*. The journalist's invocation of the 'American people' as the authorizing subject of his discourse is designed to forge a sense of communal identity, even though this community can only inhabit the time of its consumption, and not (as the rhetoric suggests) a space of unmediated presence.

Of more importance to the novel, however, is the clear suggestion that Flack's manipulative rhetoric marks an asymmetry within modern practices of communication in general. If *The Reverberator* (both in James's various commentaries on the text and in its 'completed' form) traces an expansion in the technology of communication, it also suggests that the proliferation of communicative media gives rise to a corresponding impoverishment of social interaction. This asymmetry is spelled out by the relationship between the Dossons, who are seen as naively receptive to the influence of the newspaper, and Flack. While the latter is figured as a master of modern communications, the former are chronically incapable of making connections. The Dossons' passage through Europe is marked by a series of comically inept attempts to meet their fellow American tourists:

> They were continually looking out for meetings and combinations that never came off, hearing that people had been in Paris only after they had gone away, or feeling convinced that they were there but not to be found through their not having registered, or wondering whether they should overtake them if they should go to Dresden, and then making up their minds to start for Dresden, only to learn, at the eleventh hour, through some accident, that the elusive party had gone to Biarritz. (*R* 26)

The inability of the Dossons to link up with the circuit of European travel is part of a general communicative incompetence which is implicitly ascribed to their inculcation of the habits of American mass culture. Even their temporary residence at the 'Hôtel de L'Univers et de Cheltenham' appears to signify this disabling effect of modern communicative practice: the globalization of space promised by the name of the hotel is ironically coupled with a provincial location, suggesting perhaps the discrepancy between the aspirations and the reality of the Dossons' 'international' situation (*R* 25). The Dossons' communicative incompetence, moreover, forces them into a relationship of dependence with Flack whose mastery of communications, modern or otherwise, assumes a magical quality. For the Dossons the journalist possesses an uncanny ability to decipher the 'mystic clue' of visiting cards, telegrams and hotel registers: unlike themselves, he 'generally knew where they were, the people who were "somewhere in Europe"' (*R* 27). Significantly, however, Flack's 'knowledge' is itself incommunicable, since it comes to him 'by a kind of intuition, by the voices of the air, by indefinable and unteachable processes' (*R* 27). His ability to tap into the informational resources of modern technology is preserved as an esoteric skill, unavailable to less favoured individuals.

The journalist's privileged access to the media of modern communications thus allows him to stand at the centre of a communicative network which James characteristically examines in terms of its distribution of power. Similarly, in *The Bostonians*, the ineffectual publicist Selah Tarrant views the offices of newspapers as 'national nerve-centres', controlling (in Jennifer Wicke's phrase) the circulation of 'knowledge and visibility' (*B* 123).[34] Likened to the nervous system of the body, the network of modern communications is organized around central nodal points, to which Selah is irresistibly drawn, but from which he remains pathetically excluded. For Selah, however, the allure of the newspaper office lies precisely in its impenetrability: in his recognition that such cultural spaces contain a knowledge which is not universally accessible. If the newspaper office is a site from which publicity issues, it does not apply the principle of publicity to itself. Indeed, ironically, the fascinating '*penetralia* of the daily press' offer one of the very few instances of authentic private space within the entire novel (*B* 123).

The terms of James's critique of this asymmetrical distribution of knowledge and power, however, may be elicited further by considering the alternative model of communication which is inscribed within *The Reverberator*. Although I have argued that James ironically collapses his 'dramatic opposition' between the Dossons and the Proberts, there remains at least one sense in which this opposition holds true. In spite of their aversion to the 'vulgar' noise of the newspaper, the Proberts, unlike the Dossons, are not incapable of communication. Indeed, as Gaston suggests, the members of his family are 'all social animals':

> That was doubtless part of the reason why the family had acclimatised itself in France. They had affinities with a society of conversation; they liked general talk and old high *salons* . . . where there was a circle round the fire and winged words flew about and there was always some clever person before the chimney-piece, holding or challenging the rest. (*R* 98–9)

In contrast to the communicative practice of the newspaper, then, the Proberts' 'society of conversation' centres around a reciprocal exchange of opinions. According to this view, the aristocratic salon offers the possibility of social relations which are at once intimate and 'challenging'. Both these aspects of the salon are important for the distinction which James wishes to make. Unlike the intimacy of Flack's journalistic discourse, the intimacy of the salon is not fundamentally intransitive in form: it apparently facilitates argument and disagreement, rather than cementing a false accord which refuses to recognize the boundaries between self and other. Gaston, for example, recalls that his father 'liked to take possession of the hearthrug' and hold forth his views, but he also notes that 'he never triumphed in argument': 'His word on most subjects was not felt to be the last (it was usually not more conclusive than a shrugging, inarticulate resignation, an "Ah, you know, what will you have?")' (*R* 99). Thus, while M. Probert is fond of delivering his opinions, he does not use his position as speaker to impose them on others. His speech is not designed to preclude further discussion; unlike the newspaper (in James's view), he does not always have the last word.

James's model of an alternative discursive community, centred around the 'old high *salons*' of aristocratic French society, is similar in many ways to those offered by more recent critics of the mass media. Both Jürgen Habermas and Richard Sennett have, in their different ways, offered versions of a narrative in which the French salons and English coffee-houses of the eighteenth and early nineteenth centuries function as a paradigmatic communicative space, from which it becomes possible to measure the subsequent 'distortions' of the mass media.[35] Like these contemporary critical narratives, moreover, James's evocation of the Proberts' 'society of conversation' is predicated upon an undoubtedly idealized vision of a space of pure communicative transparency. Not only is it obviously possible to point to the social exclusivity of the aristocratic salon, and hence to level the familiar charge of cultural elitism at James, but it is also clear that such historical narratives tend invariably, though by no means simply, to privilege the (supposed) immediacy of oral communication over the irretrievably mediated condition of mass culture.[36] Yet having said that, it would be a mistake to assume that James's 'dramatic opposition' is conceived simply out of nostalgia. Certainly, Gaston is not unmindful of the limitations of the salons frequented by his father. If the intimacy of the salon is its virtue, it is also indicative of the narrow interests which it represents. Although these sites may not have been 'too small' for meaningful communication, neither were they 'too large, though some of them supposed themselves to be very great institutions' (*R* 99). This ironic note in Gaston's judgement of the provincialism of salon society counters his otherwise idyllic recollections. What is concealed by M. Probert's seemingly 'transparent' public speech is the closed structure of the patriarchal family over which he presides. But if the salon cannot be conceived as an entirely neutral communicative space, free from all relationships of power and interest, its characteristic distortions are, at any rate, different from those of the mass media. While the mass media expands the field of communicative possibilities at the cost of interaction, salon society is interactive within narrower confines. By situating Gaston's recollections of his father on the periphery of the text, James invokes the salon, not as a means of proposing a positive alternative to the 'newspaperized world' of the present, but as a way of signalling (and memorializing) the vestigial status of the past.

'THE PAPERS'

In his preface to *The Reverberator*, James retrospectively recast the novel's *donnée* as a fable of the changing geopolitical relationship between Europe and America. Like many nineteenth-century observers (writing primarily, of course, from a European perspective), James saw the United States as the birthplace of mass culture. Advocates of the New Journalism in Britain, for example, were often accused of assisting an insidious process of 'Americanization' by importing such innovative practices as the interview and the 'scarehead' (headline).[37] Appropriately, then, the *donnée* is used to exemplify this wider process of American cultural expansion, and, in particular, the American 'colonization' of Europe. To employ a metaphor of colonization in this comparatively weak sense might seem disingenuous, were it not for the fact that James himself authorizes such a reading in the preface. Displacing a conventional view of British imperialism, he conceives of the American attitude towards Europe as both innocent and predatory in nature. Figured as 'remote adventurous islanders', it is the Americans who, by virtue of their geographical isolation, lack any sense of 'give-and-take between their bustling archipelago and the far, the massed continent' (*LC* II 1200). Here, James translates the asymmetrical structure of the mass media into the language of an encounter between colonizer and colonized. As the colonizing power, America appropriates the cultural material of Europe without conceding a reciprocal effect to its representational practices. It assumes that these representations can remain sealed from their object, even though the globalizing technologies upon which American cultural expansion rests dictate otherwise.

James's use of the metaphor of colonization thus helps to explain his understanding of the way in which publicity incorporates forms of cultural difference by subjecting them to representation. If we compare *The Reverberator* with some of James's later fiction, we can see this process of cultural colonization unfolding along a wider historical trajectory. In the tale 'Flickerbridge' (1902), for example, James presents a conflict of cultural values similar to that of the earlier novel, but situates it within an even more phantasmic light. The tale concerns an American magazine writer named Addie, who discovers that she has a distant cousin (Miss Wenham) living in the remote English village of Flickerbridge. Addie's fiancé, Frank Granger, pays a preliminary visit to Miss Wenham so as to report back his impressions to her. Observing the unspoiled, cloistered world of Flickerbridge, however, Granger has second thoughts about exposing it to Addie's keen journalistic eye. Flickerbridge is 'untouched, untouchable, indescribable': a virgin territory which has thus far escaped the destructive gaze of modernity (*CT* XI 336). Once again, James inverts the topography of European colonial expansion. Granger informs Miss Wenham that she is like 'Niagara before the first white traveller – and you know, or rather you can't know, what Niagara became *after* that gentleman' (*CT* XI 344). Once it has been witnessed by Addie, Flickerbridge will be invaded by hordes of American journalists and tourists in search of an experience of cultural 'authenticity' that will, of course, be negated in the very process: 'You'll be too exactly the real thing and to be left too utterly just as you are, and all Addie's friends and all Addie's editors and contributors and readers will cross the Atlantic and flock to Flickerbridge, so, unanimously, universally, vociferously, to leave you' (*CT* XI 344). The otherness of Flickerbridge, Granger perceives, will not survive its representation as 'other' in the media of publicity.

In this tale, then, James pursues his earlier insight into the increasing difficulty of envisaging a site of resistance to the pervasive practices of the mass media. The receding horizon of cultural difference is pushed still further back into the microcosmic world of Flickerbridge. Towards the end of the tale, Granger offers an apocalyptic vision of the cultural forces which are ranged against Miss Wenham's unspoiled and uncharted existence:

> We live in an age of prodigious machinery, all organised to a single end. That end is publicity – a publicity as ferocious as the appetite of a cannibal. The thing therefore is not to have any illusions – fondly to flatter yourself, in a muddled moment, that the cannibal will spare you. He spares nobody. He spares nothing. (*CT* XI 348)

In this final twist of the colonial metaphor, it is publicity itself which stands revealed as the threatening 'other': as the 'cannibal' which devours its human subjects. Granger's outburst, moreover, points towards the totalization of publicity as a cultural experience which nobody and nothing can escape. Rather than serving simply as a means of realizing the commercial interests of the press, publicity is envisaged as the 'single end' of modern culture. With this suggestion, James comes close to anticipating the nightmare scenario of Adorno and Horkheimer's vision of a fully-fledged 'culture industry'. Writing in the 1940s, Adorno and Horkheimer discerned a similar shift from means to ends in the function of 'culture as publicity'. Advertising, they contend, can no longer be understood solely as a means of selling commodities: more insidiously, it has become a form of '*l'art pour l'art*, advertising for its own sake, a pure representation of social power'.[38] Capable of being detached from its external referents – the commodities which it claims to represent – advertising constitutes an increasingly self-referential system of cultural codes. Accordingly, it is no longer only the objects of publicity which are consumed, but also publicity itself: the language and signs of advertising which are reproduced in the habitual manners of the consumer.

In his later fiction, James, too, suggests that the manner of publicity has become ingrained within everyday cultural consciousness. It is perhaps for this reason that in 'The Papers', the long short story which James published alongside 'Flickerbridge' in his 1903 collection, *The Better Sort*,[39] he entirely forgoes the attempt to construct a conflict between the modernizing forces of publicity, on the one hand, and a residual site of cultural difference, on the other. In this text, there is no longer any historical trace of an organized community of speech, such as Gaston Probert's recollections of salon society, operating outside the boundaries of modern communications. Instead, James presents an apocalyptic, if grotesquely comic, vision of publicity as a well-nigh universal ontological condition, in which, as David Howard has observed, 'To live is to be published, to have come out, to have appeared.'[40] Far from facing the resistance or 'shock' which attended Flack's pursuit of scandalous revelations, the journalists in 'The Papers' discover that their subjects are willing victims. While James constructs an initial opposition between the successful publicist Howard Bight and the unsuccessful Maud Blandy, it is Howard's experience of the universal hunger for publicity which proves to be the more accurate: 'Specimens indeed of human greed – *the* greed, the great one, the eagerness to figure, the snap at the bait of publicity, he had collected in such store as to stock, as to launch, a museum' (*CT* XII 17). Within this phantasmagorical world, publicity is conceived to be the sole source of desire and meaning. To 'figure', or be figured, in the medium of the Papers is a cultural imperative which, through offering visibility to the subject, also offers existence itself; conversely, to be excluded from this source of value is to experience a form of cultural invisibility equivalent to death.

Playing upon this equivalence between publicity and ontology, James constructs an elaborate conceit around the metaphysics of absence and presence, which also forms the ironic structural principle behind the events of the narrative. At the centre of this conceit is the fact that the figure who dominates the visual and auditory horizon of 'The Papers' is not 'present' at all, in the sense usually belonging to fictional characters. The celebrity, Sir A.B.C. Beadel-Muffet, is literally a pure fabrication of publicity, made present only through the two journalists' reading of the Papers and the choric cries of the newsboys who recurrently announce the events of his 'Mysterious Disappearance', death, and resurrection. Beadel-Muffet's absence as a character, however, allows him to enjoy a form of presence which is greater than any conferred by mere 'fictional' representation. As the narrator remarks after his apparent death, 'He had been, poor Beadel, public and prominent, but he had never affected Maud Blandy at least as so marked with this character as while thus loudly committed to extinction' (*CT* XII 66). The point of this elliptical joke, of course, is to suggest that the representational practices of the Papers are more powerful than those of James's fictional tale (which, naturally enough, recuperates its powers precisely by representing its own comparative insufficiency when set against the medium of the press). The mystery of Beadel-Muffet's disappearance and death only nourishes his status as a celebrity and enhances his presence within the text.

What is so remarkable about James's visionary narrative of a world entirely determined by the 'greed' for publicity, however, is the way in which it draws, quite precisely, upon traditional conceptions of the desire for literary fame. As Leo Braudy reminds us, the word 'fame' comes from the Latin *fama* (or *Fama* in its personified form), which is etymologically derived from *fames*, meaning hunger or, in a cognate sense, famine. Thus, the very notion of fame appears to inscribe both a desire for plenitude and an apprehension of lack;

throughout the history of its representation, as Braudy has shown, writers have lamented the insufficiency which attends its attainment.[41] Whether consciously or not, James recalls a similar dialectic of desire and fear in his apprehension of the cultural imperatives of modern publicity. If, in his notebook sketch for *The Reverberator*, James had protested against 'the devouring *publicity* of life', in 'The Papers' he acknowledges that publicity is both devouring and devoured. Publicity is no longer conceived simply as an external force, imposed upon its victim from the outside, but is instead a medium so powerful that it is capable of engineering the 'inner' consent of its subjects.

Ironically, though, as David Howard notes, this shift actually leads to a more sympathetic treatment of the journalist.[42] As the shock of journalistic sensation becomes routine, so James's interest in the figure of the journalist evolves from the relatively crude satire of *The Reverberator*. Here, I would disagree with Peter Conn's reading of 'The Papers' as a wholly negative, and ultimately reactionary, response to the burgeoning world of mass culture, and to journalism in particular.[43] In fact, the thinly-veiled contempt in which the narrator of the earlier novel holds the figure of George Flack is conspicuously absent from the later tale. In *The Reverberator*, the journalist appears as a demagogic embodiment of the forces of publicity, even though James also questions the authenticity of Flack's individual identity. By contrast, in 'The Papers', publicity assumes the character of an autotelic force, functioning beyond the control of its individual agents. The journalists are subjected to the impersonal machinery of the Papers as much as (if not more than) the celebrities whom they interview. Despite the initial confidence of his claim to have mastered the 'strange logic' of the 'great forces of publicity', Howard, in particular, is forced to concede that he too has been 'sold' by the case of Beadel-Muffet (*CT* XII 86, 121). His individual impotence is comically suggested when the celebrity (apparently) expresses a wish to retire from public life. Howard is engaged to secure the removal of Beadel-Muffet's presence from the Papers, only to find that by carrying out his desire not to be publicized, he unwittingly creates the ground for further publicity: 'He *can't* disappear; he hasn't weight enough to sink; the splash the diver makes, you know, tells where he is' (*CT* XII 58). This bemused apprehension of the self-generating mechanisms of mass media publicity alludes to, but significantly rewrites, Alexander Pope's satire of literary fame in *The Dunciad* (1728).[44] Whereas Pope had subjected his dunces to a parodic spectacle in which their mediocrity is tested and exposed through the gravitational pull of literary obscurity, Howard discovers that the modern celebrity is positively unable to sink into the mire of anonymity. Thus, James ironically disjoins the traditional assumption that fame could be demonstrably linked to merit. As his name suggests, Sir A.B.C. Beadel-Muffet KCB, MP is literally an anonymous, serialized figure whose degree of 'presence' bears no conceivable relationship to any intrinsic identity.[45] Modern publicity, in other words, is perceived as a grotesquely irrational condition: as a fate which cannot be divorced from its chosen subject, either by force of will or critical judgement.

It is for this reason that the question of individual journalistic responsibility, which surfaced in the New Journalism debates of the 1880s and in James's novel of that period, is markedly absent from 'The Papers'. By the turn of the century, it would seem, the axis of publicity had shifted from the journalist to the celebrity, or from the site of production to that of consumption. This is not to suggest that James was no longer concerned with the agency of journalistic publicity; rather, it is to observe that this agency is itself figured as an anonymous, collective organization, symbolized by its generic nomenclature, the Papers. Indeed, in a sense, it is in this story that James's critique of the mystifying strategies of what Stead termed 'impersonal journalism' is taken to its extreme. Rather than pointing simply to a rhetorical form of address, as in *The Reverberator*, James represents the entirety of the press as a single, monolithic, collective subject. The individual agents of the Papers are subsumed within this collective entity, which is capitalized throughout the text. Thus, when Maud and Howard see an approaching newsboy, for example, they recognize only that 'The Papers had come into sight in the form of a small boy bawling the "Winner" of something' (*CT* XII 78). The identity of the boy is expressed solely by his function as a bearer of the Papers: as a single molecule within a complex organism. Likewise, in an almost physical sense, the two journalists inhabit, and are inhabited by, the Papers, which represent 'all the furniture of their consciousness' (*CT* XII 14). As in *The Reverberator*, the journalists' position within the organization of the Papers allows them to gain a privileged knowledge of its workings. In this instance, however, their reluctance to divulge the 'inside story' in their possession is not so much an act as an effect of coercion:

> It was known certainly to all who had to do with the Papers, a brotherhood, a sisterhood of course interested – for what was it, in the last resort, but the interest of their bread and butter? – in shrouding the approaches to the oracle, in not telling tales out of school . . . The Papers, taken together the glory of the age, were, though superficially multifold, fundamentally one, so that any revelation of their being procured or procurable to float an object not intrinsically buoyant would very logically convey discredit from the circumference – where the revelation would be likely to be made – to the centre. (*CT* XII 18–19)

Although Maud and Howard are well aware that the celebrity of Beadel-Muffet is a manufactured product of the Papers, rather than 'intrinsically buoyant', they are nevertheless compelled to represent the collective interests of this shadowy organization. Viewed from the margins of its 'circumference', moreover, the central intelligence of the Papers remains opaque, even for the journalist.

At this point, it is worth noting that James's representation of the Papers as a monstrous organic totality registers in phantasmagorical form the real process of incorporation which began to transform the newspaper industry in the 1890s. The structure of the corporate organization forges a single, indivisible legal identity out of diverse constituent elements which are related to each other through a central administrative body. In this way, the identity of the corporation is diffused throughout its mass, while it retains a compact chain of command. James's recognition that the Papers are 'though superficially multifold, fundamentally one' takes on further resonance when we consider that commercial syndication led to a dramatic concentration of newspaper ownership around the turn of the century. Press barons such as Harmsworth and Pearson (in Britain) and Pulitzer and Hearst (in the United States) took control of large sectors of the market by amassing chains of newspapers. Thus, in spite of the proliferation of new publications which took place towards the end of the nineteenth century, the economic and ideological interests of the press became increasingly homogenous.[46] As I suggested earlier, this organizational transformation of the press led to a form of 'impersonality' which far exceeded the journalistic anonymity derided by advocates of the New Journalism. If, during the mid nineteenth century, the newspaper had maintained a code of collective identity that was expressed rhetorically by its use of the plural 'We', it was, generally speaking, produced by small numbers of journalists and subject to individual editorial influence or control.

In a sense, the newspaper which emerged towards the end of the century reversed this model: while the language of journalism became personalized, its mode of production involved an increasingly complex division of labour. As responsibility for the final product became less easy to locate, so, ironically, the 'more personal tones' of journalistic discourse diverted attention away from the very forms of power and interest which they had been designed to expose.

It is this immanent contradiction between the form (impersonal) and the content (personal) of the New Journalism which James demonstrates, most graphically, in 'The Papers'. If the tale evokes a world that is entirely governed by sinister, collective agencies, it also shows how the same world is suffused by images of 'personality' which conceal the truth of its anonymity. By the same token, if visibility is conceived as the ultimate source of value in the tale, this value is signally absent from the forces which produce it. As a result, the image of the celebrity attracts the attention of 'the public' in a way that is quite literally figured as a distraction from the collective experience of modern life. The dramatist Mortimer Marshal, for instance, has an intense desire to 'feel the great murmur surrounding one's name . . . the great city, the great empire, the world itself for the moment, hanging literally on one's personality and giving a start, in its suspense, whenever one is mentioned' (*CT* XII 82). Marshal aspires to attain Beadel-Muffet's capacity to fixate the amorphous crowds which congregate in the urban space of London. In this respect, James appears to substantiate Richard Sennett's belief that the late-nineteenth-century fascination with 'personalities' expressed the need to preserve a domain of intimacy against the conditions of inarticulacy and impersonality which were felt to be characteristic of modern urban experience.[47] As Sennett suggests, however, the value placed on 'personality' was itself a symptom of these conditions, rather than offering an escape from them, as was widely supposed. Interestingly, in his preface to *The Reverberator*, James offers a similar insight. Expressing his opposition to the dominant valuation of visibility, James proposes the positive utility of anonymity as a possible refuge from the impositions of the newspaper. This possibility, he suggests, may arise from the very saturation of publicity: 'for supreme, more and more, is the blest truth – sole safety, as it mostly seems, of our distracting age – that a given thing has but to be newspaperised *enough* (which it may, at our present rate of perfection, in a few hours) to return, as a quick consequence, to the common, the abysmal air and become without form and void' (*LC* II 1201). Here, it is precisely on account of its increasing familiarity, James perceives, that publicity loses its distinctness as a mode of cultural visibility, and so leaves its subject less exposed. The 'sole safety' of this 'distracting age' lies in the rapidity of its production cycles, which lead to a virtual implosion of visibility and the return of the publicized matter back into a formless 'void'.

The possibility of escaping publicity by vanishing into 'the common, the abysmal air' is one that is also explored in 'The Papers'. Much of the interest of the tale lies in James's evident fascination with contemporary motifs of obscurity: with the indeterminate figure of the crowd and the fictive theme of detection. In particular, this fantasy of anonymity is evoked towards the end of the tale when Maud imagines Howard as a fugitive from the very glare of publicity which he has been guilty of serving. Having apparently provoked Beadel-Muffet's sensational disappearance and death, the journalist is implicated in a crime which must, in turn, be exposed:

> He showed to her, at these strange moments, as blood-stained and literally hunted; the yell of the hawkers, repeated and echoing round them, was like a cry for his life, and there was in particular a minute during which, gazing down into the roused Strand, all equipped both with mob and with constables, she asked herself whether she had best get off with him through the crowd, where they would be least noticed, or get him away through quiet Covent Garden, empty at that hour, but with policemen to watch a furtive couple, and with the news, more bawled at their heels in the stillness, acquiring the sound of the very voice of justice. (*CT* XII 92–3)

At this moment in the text, Howard is transformed from hunter to hunted: from the agent of publicity to its object. The crime for which he is to be punished, though, is both twofold and contradictory. If Howard is ostensibly pursued for his suspected part in the mysterious case of Beadel-Muffet – a pursuit which invokes publicity as a suitably ironic punishment *for* publicity – what is also being punished here is the very thought of escaping into the refuge of anonymity. It is Maud's suggestion of spiriting Howard away from the attentions of both policemen and mob which, in fact, simultaneously invokes the means of his detection. What also occurs at this moment, then, is nothing less than a transfiguration of the meaning of publicity itself. The apparatus of the mass media, signified by the 'yell of the hawkers', seems to merge into an apparatus of surveillance, incorporating the police, the mob, the 'very voice of justice'. As Susan Sontag has observed, these agencies might well be taken to represent the twin axes of modern social visibility, both equally 'essential to the workings of an advanced industrial society: as a spectacle (for masses) and as an object of surveillance (for rulers)'.[48] In this instance, however, any difference between the two agencies is lost: the sinister organization of the Papers assumes the same function as the equally anonymous body of 'The Authorities', as it is figured in Maud's imagination (*CT* XII 105). The mass media, in short, becomes an instrument of authority itself.[49]

The scene which I have just described is also, therefore, a particularly ambivalent moment in the story. On the one hand, it may be read as a moment of resistance within the text, since it is here that James questions the desire for publicity by transforming it into a nightmare of exposure, and where, conversely, he elevates the anguish of anonymity into a place of refuge. On the other hand, the subversive potential of this strategy is compromised by its epistemological incitement of the countervailing practice of detection. If, as Walter Benjamin argued, 'The original social content of the detective story was the obliteration of the individual's traces in the big-city crowd', then the fantasy of social control inscribed within detective fiction may be seen as a direct response to the threatening opacity of urban experience.[50] Likewise, Maud's recourse to the motifs of detective fiction, in projecting Howard's 'hunted' flight from publicity, binds the allure of escaping the visible traces of personal identity to the techniques which were designed to circumvent it. More insidiously, though, the desire to escape into the anonymity of the crowd may also be seen to mark a reinscription of publicity beyond the limits of visual representation. This is true of both 'The Papers' and the preface to *The Reverberator*, where James takes consolation in the prospect that publicity may reach a kind of vanishing point in the very moment of its saturation. There, James's anticipation of disappearing into 'the common, the abysmal air', of becoming 'without form and void', inadvertently echoes his earlier evocation of one of the most significant forms of modern publicity: namely, the disembodied acoustics of telecommunications technology. In 'The Papers', this invisible network of communication seems, oppressively, to saturate the very atmosphere of the city: the recurrent metaphor of 'the voices of the air', which James had already used to indicate the source of Flack's seemingly intuitive knowledge, connotes the unseen, but ever-present, technological resources at the disposal of the Papers.

Ultimately, it is this invisible network of communication, rather than the production of visibility itself, which constitutes the tale's most disturbing manifestation of the power of publicity. In an interesting discussion of the development of telecommunications in the late nineteenth century, Asa Briggs has shown how these technologies were understood to have rendered the intangible matter of the 'ether' susceptible to human manipulation. The air itself, in other words, was seen as capable of functioning as a medium of communication and, potentially, of surveillance.[51] In 'The Papers', James evokes a similarly heavy and opaque ethereality, weighed down by the codes which it transmits. The action of the narrative revolves around the presence of the Papers within the communicative interstices of the city: on street corners, in railway news-stands, in Fleet Street and the Strand. Maud and Howard are constantly drawn to these spaces, as if by some centripetal impulse. The 'voices of the air', the 'howl of the Strand', the 'roar' of the Papers emerge periodically from the silent, empty crowds through which the two journalists pass (*CT* XII 15, 65, 77–8, 90, 103, 118, 120–1). Thus, the saturation of publicity in the tale extends far beyond the realm of visibility which the discourse of journalism appears to privilege. If James saw this moment of saturation as an opportunity for escaping the coercive strategies of journalistic 'revelation', equally it may only serve to reinstate publicity in a different guise.

In 'The Papers', then, James consummates his vision of publicity as the 'single end' of modern culture. The darkness of his satire in this tale represents a grotesque apotheosis of the historical narrative which I have traced in this chapter. Following the trajectory outlined in his earlier fiction, James envisages a world in which the presence of publicity is so pervasive that it cannot even be located within the referential space of fictional realism. Whereas, in *The Reverberator*, it was still possible to demarcate and delimit the agency of publicity from the forces which claimed, at least, to oppose it, in 'The Papers' the amorphous and phantasmic agencies which take the place of fictional characters signify the fluidity and anonymity of an increasingly corporatized mass media. If this reading of the story is correct, however, one must also ask how James is able to locate his own critical stance within the text. By positioning the two journalists as if they inhabited the very body of the Papers, James seems to concede that it is no longer possible to constitute an external space of opposition to publicity. Yet the very fact that Maud and Howard remain capable, in some measure, of articulating resistance to the Papers also implies the formulation of an authorial stance which recognizes its own immanence in the object of its critique. It is this recognition which marks the difference between the Olympian narrative of *The Reverberator* and the (paradoxically) more sympathetic tone of 'The Papers'. In the later fiction, it might be argued, James finally identified himself with the figure of the journalist. Indeed, in his transfigured situation as both agent and object of publicity, Howard Bight may be said to embody the ambivalent status of the Jamesian text.

CHAPTER FIVE

The secret of the spectacle: advertising 'The Ambassadors'

By his own account, *The Ambassadors* (1903) was the novel which gave James the least trouble to write. In his preface to the New York edition, James was effusive in recollecting the triumphant facility of its composition, claiming that he could 'recall . . . no moment of subjective intermittence, never one of those alarms as for a suspected hollow beneath one's feet, a felt ingratitude in the scheme adopted, under which confidence fails and opportunity seems but to mock' (*LC* II 1306). As he proceeds to unfold the history of the novel's conception, however, it becomes clear that such statements of unbounded 'confidence' are not entirely accurate. Later in the preface James confesses that there did come a time when a 'shade for a moment fell across the scene' (*LC* II 1312). Recognizing that the interest of Lambert Strether's Parisian adventure lies primarily in the fate of 'a moral scheme of the most approved pattern which was yet framed to break down on any approach to vivid facts', James appears suddenly to experience a revelation of the obvious, which forces him to question the singularity of his own narrative (*LC* II 1311):

> There was the dreadful little old tradition, one of the platitudes of the human comedy, that people's moral scheme *does* break down in Paris; that nothing is more frequently observed; that hundreds of thousands of more or less hypocritical or more or less cynical persons annually visit the place for the sake of the probable catastrophe, and that I came late in the day to work myself up about it. There was in fine the *trivial* association, one of the vulgarest in the world; but which gave me pause no longer, I think, simply because its vulgarity is so advertised. (*LC* II 1312)

James is clearly, if momentarily, disturbed by the affinities between his own project for *The Ambassadors* and the vulgar 'tradition' of popular mythology. That he is engaged in writing the story of an American whose inflexible 'moral scheme' inevitably collapses in the dissolute ambience of Paris risks being not only a belated exercise (as 'belated' as Strether's own appearance on the Parisian scene), but one, moreover, which can scarcely maintain the aura of heightened aesthetic experience and fine moral discrimination with which it is to be charged.

Indeed, in their most rudimentary form, all the elements of this story were already in common usage. As Jean Méral has shown, *The Ambassadors* was written at a time of increased American interest in the exotic bohemian life of Paris: a world which was explored in the travel writings and tourist guides of Frank Berkeley Smith, Richard Harding Davis and Theodore Childs.[1] More significantly, perhaps, the myth of the 'American in Paris' had been repeatedly promoted by the arch-publicist, Oscar Wilde, over the course of the preceding decade. Wilde was fond of quoting Thomas Appleton's epigrammatic remark that 'All good Americans, when they die, go to Paris', and incorporated it into both *The Picture of Dorian Gray* (1891) and *A Woman of No Importance* (1894).[2] By the time that James came to write his initial notebook sketch of *The Ambassadors* in October 1895, he had already sensed 'the *banal* side of the revelation of Paris': 'it's so obvious', he conceded, 'so usual to make Paris the vision that opens his eyes, makes him feel his mistake' (*NB* 226). From the beginning of his conception of the novel, then, James seems to have been anxious about the banality of the cultural resonances upon which he was proposing to draw. Later, in the preface, he attempted to distinguish between Strether's 'drama of discrimination', in which Paris serves only as the catalyst to a 'lifelong trick of intense reflexion', and the '*bêtise* of the imputably "tempted" state', which might conventionally be expected of his situation (*LC* II 1311–12). Strether, he insists, is not to be seduced by the sensuous allure of Paris, at least not in any immediate fashion; and in this claim James has been followed by many readers of the novel. F.O. Matthiessen, for instance, repeated almost word for word the terms of James's preface, affirming that *The Ambassadors* had succeeded in 'avoiding the banal by not making Paris the usual scene of seduction but instead the center of an ethical drama'.[3] Likewise, Albert E. Stone praised the novel for avoiding the expected 'Parisian passions', and thus steering well clear of the degraded archetypes of popular romance.[4]

Such strenuous denials of James's recourse to the myth of the 'American in Paris', however, tend merely to confirm the suspicion that they wish to allay. It is noticeable that James's summary dismissal of this suspicion in the preface is less a resolution of his concern than a definitive restatement of the problem. The '*trivial* association' may be forgotten, James elliptically asserts, because 'its vulgarity is so advertised'. The use of the word 'advertised' at this juncture is not without significance, since it may be said to crystallize the anxiety that has momentarily been revealed. James is evidently concerned by the embarrassing resemblance between his own fiction and a myth that, in its casual notoriety and popular dissemination, bears all the hallmarks of an advertisement. It is this concealed proximity between the apparently antithetical projects of high culture and mass culture, I shall argue, which allows us to glimpse the one 'suspected hollow' beneath James's authorial 'feet'. *The Ambassadors* is a novel which, from the very moment of its inception, is forced to incorporate a realm of value, and a set of mounting cultural pressures, which it takes to be its opposite. James's efforts to distance himself from the domain of advertising, however, do not merely result in an unwitting complicity. Advertising is not only a theme which is broached (and thus distanced) within the referential confines of the novel, as Jennifer Wicke has ably shown; it can also be taken to represent the most visible manifestation of a prolonged and reflexive examination of the material conditions of James's own literary production.[5] What is finally at issue in this enquiry is James's recognition of the extent to which the literary text may itself be seen to function as an object of publicity.

'THE ART OF ADVERTISEMENT'

One of the most remarkable and puzzling scenes in *The Ambassadors* occurs towards the end of the novel, when Chad Newsome abruptly informs Strether that he has recently 'been getting some news of the art of advertisement'. What is striking about Chad's 'announcement' is the seemingly arbitrary, unmotivated manner in which the question of advertising is introduced into the text (*A* 341). The reader is, of course, already aware of Mrs Newsome's desire to persuade Chad to return to Woollett so that he may 'boss the advertising department' of the family business, as Jim Pocock puts it (*A* 216). Yet it is only with Chad's later declaration that the nature of his prospective career is treated (comically enough) as a serious object of concern:

He appeared at all events to have been looking into the question and had encountered a revelation. Advertising scientifically worked presented itself thus as the great new force. 'It really does the thing, you know.' (*A* 341)

Chad's 'revelation' concerning the power of advertising as a modern cultural 'force' visibly shocks Strether, even though the latter has himself acted as an emissary on behalf of the interests of the Woollett business. With its strangely bathetic appeal, the scene violates the subdued, dignified tone which the narrative consciousness, filtered primarily through Strether, has sought to maintain. On the spot, Strether's idealized vision of Chad as a model of refined Parisian culture is shattered, 'quite as if, there on the pavement, without a pretext, he had begun to dance a fancy step', an 'irrelevant hornpipe or jig' (*A* 341–2). Transformed already by Madame de Vionnet, Chad now undergoes a second transformation, this time into the guise of the showman, the manifest face of the future advertising man.

Yet the real force of this scene may be gathered from the way in which, as Wicke has observed, it 'reshapes the contours of the novel', allowing us to reinstate advertising into the text as an 'erased or suppressed term'.[6] Chad's experience of 'revelation' is precisely the effect which the scene in which it is recounted bears upon the novel as a whole. The significance of the theme of advertising is disclosed in an act of naming which then permits the retroactive inscription of this content into earlier textual lacunae, from which, we begin to realize, it has been carefully evacuated. For instance, it is made clear only at this point in the novel that it was Strether himself who ironically implanted the seeds of Chad's enthusiasm for advertising during their first meeting in Paris. By referring back to their 'original discussion', which James refrains from representing directly, Chad lifts the silence which has surrounded Strether's projection of this scene, and thus ensures that the 'content' of the narrative, if not its mode of representation, travels full circle (*A* 342). As Chad reminds Strether, his experience in London 'doesn't amount to much more than what you originally, so awfully vividly – and all, very nearly, that first night – put before me'; in broaching the matter again, he wishes only to 'wind up where we began' (*A* 341–2). In other words, Chad's 'revelation' is not quite the arbitrary interruption of the narrative which it is made to appear; rather, it is the mirror-image, or delayed reciprocal exchange, of a speech first uttered by Strether. Chad's new-found fascination with 'the art of advertisement' simply renders visible the liminal presence of what Strether has written out of the narrative consciousness.

The question of naming is, of course, one which explicitly marks Strether's flight from the commercial concerns of Woollett. As several critics have recently argued, Strether's imaginative project in Paris may be understood as an attempt to escape the rigid principle of identity which is represented paradigmatically by the form of the standardized commodity produced at the Woollett manufactory.[7] Thus, he pointedly refuses to name the 'small, trivial, rather ridiculous object of the commonest domestic use' which is the source of the Newsomes' wealth (*A* 48). Maria Gostrey evidently recognizes the significance of Strether's refusal when she finally agrees not to question him further on the matter: 'In ignorance she could humour her fancy, and that proved a useful freedom. She could treat the little nameless object as indeed unnameable – she could make their abstention enormously definite' (*A* 48).

By complying with Strether's 'abstention', Maria paradoxically secures a 'useful freedom' for speculation about the precise nature of the object, while ensuring that their mutual silence is 'enormously definite'. The demarcation of this textual lacuna is such that the finality of revelation is suspended, without being erased. If the later exchange between Chad and Strether on the subject of advertising may thus be read as a veritable return of the repressed, it is also clear that such 'repression' is never unknowingly accomplished in the text. The audible silence which surrounds the source of the Newsomes' wealth is, indeed, symptomatic of the way in which the novel as a whole works in tracing the suppressed connections between the worlds of culture and commerce. Concealed to the last, the 'unnameable' identity of the Woollett commodity maintains a constant subtextual joke about the determining presence of 'business' concerns. The world of commerce figuratively underlies the domain of culture, and it is the knowledge of this shameful dependence which, to varying degrees, both Strether and Mrs Newsome attempt to elude.

In the preliminary 'Project' for *The Ambassadors*, which James sent to his publishers in 1900, the shame which is attached to the source of the Newsomes' wealth is dwelt upon extensively and explicitly. It is Mrs Newsome's 'fine expiatory or compensatory nature', conditioned by her husband's exploitative business practices, that leads her to subsidize 'an expensive Review, devoted to serious questions and inquiries, economic, social, sanitary, humanitary'.[8] Likewise, in the novel itself, Strether recognizes the Review as Mrs Newsome's 'tribute to the ideal' (*A* 51). Assiduously courting unpopularity, the Review provides Mrs Newsome with a channel into which her dubiously acquired capital can be diverted, but not permitted to reproduce itself in the form of profit. Here, James images the relationship between cultural and economic production in its most damning form: culture is a product which gains its autonomy only by denying itself the very principle of utility upon which it is secretly dependent. In the process, money – the abstract equivalent form of commodities – is hypostatized as a pure social resource. For Maria Gostrey, Mrs Newsome's wealth is momentarily transfigured into 'a vision of gold', a vision of the 'bright dollars shovelled in[to]' the Review, thus illustrating the ease with which money, as Marx observed, constantly erases its origins (*A* 51).[9]

Strether, of course, is only too aware of what lies behind Mrs Newsome's desire to separate 'culture' from the process of economic exchange. He is himself the visible sign of this attempted autonomization of culture, employed by Mrs Newsome as editor of the Review, and serving as its suitably unworldly front. It is Strether's name which is inscribed upon the green cover of the Review, while Mrs Newsome preserves her anonymity. Yet as he acknowledges to Maria, it is Mrs Newsome who 'peeps out': 'She's behind the whole thing; but she's of a delicacy and a discretion – !' (*A* 50). Rather than confirming an existing authorial presence, then, Strether experiences the sign of his name on the cover of the Review as an attenuation of identity. For, in this respect, to be named is to be reminded precisely of his lack of substance; the name being both literally and figuratively a 'cover' for the essential but 'unnameable' depths beneath it.

What is less recognizable for Strether, however, is the extent to which this same structural and epistemological relationship between commerce and culture obtains in the relationship between Woollett and Paris. If the Woollett Review is simply too meagre a product to sustain the ideological weight of investing it with a credible cultural autonomy, this is evidently not the case with the products of European culture. For Strether, Paris holds out the promise of an authentic aesthetic experience, cut free from all moorings within the domain of economic rationality. Here, surely, is a site of pure culture, or, as Maud Ellmann has argued, a realm of sensuous difference, released from the constricting self-identity of American society.[10]

Ellmann's overly rhapsodic account of Strether's European experience, however, ignores both the way in which Paris is constructed as a site of new forms of economic value (as I suggest later), and the way in which its apparent cultural autonomy can only function in relation to a banished other. In this latter sense, Paris stands in the same relationship to Woollett as the Woollett Review does to the business which finances it. James constantly reminds us of the fact that Strether's experience of European culture is itself an object of purchase, contingent upon the financial backing of American capitalism.

This contingency is suggested, not long after his arrival in Paris, when Strether begins to experience a strange sublimation of the sordid reality of economic accumulation. Once again, money is aesthetized into a static hoard from which he prepares to draw: 'Strether hadn't had for years so rich a consciousness of time – a bag of gold into which he constantly dipped for a handful. It was present to him that when the little business with Mr Bilham should be over he would still have shining hours to use absolutely as he liked' (*A* 76). Strether's surrender to the ostentatious expenditure of time involves a dramatic shift from the temporal economy of Woollett. Here, Benjamin Franklin's famous dictum, '*time* is money', which Max Weber found so emblematic of the protestant ethic of modern capitalism, is explicitly reversed.[11] But while Strether begins to savour time as a resource to be spent, rather than to be saved, or otherwise subjected to rational calculation, this does not mean that time is liberated from economic value *per se*. Writing of America's burgeoning 'leisure class' in 1899, Thorstein Veblen observed that the 'non-productive consumption of time' did not signify mere 'indolence or quiescence', but, rather, functioned as a means of exhibiting 'the pecuniary ability to afford a life of idleness'.[12] While Strether can scarcely be described as a member of Veblen's complacent cultural elite, his new-found leisure is, nevertheless, not so much a pure expenditure (or wastage) of time, as Ellmann suggests, as the realization of a surplus value – a figurative and literal 'bag of gold' – which constitutes his *allowance* of time. Quite literally, it is money which buys time, as James, so often vilified as an uncritical historian of the leisure class, was well aware.

In this regard, Terry Eagleton's remarks on the 'historical secret' determining the characteristic form of Jamesian consciousness are suggestive, if somewhat misleading. Eagleton is surely right to observe that, in much of James's fiction, 'negativity is the abyss which opens up between consciousness itself and the suppressed, supportive economic base of which it is finely oblivious – an abyss inscribed within consciousness itself as a blank freedom from financial constraint';[13] but he fails to see that this 'oblivious' consciousness is precisely what James's own more knowing authorial stance ironically scrutinizes. Certainly, in *The Ambassadors*, James situates the domain of consciousness in what we might call a 'superstructural' relationship to the economic base. Indeed, it is this binary structure, articulated variously in terms of the oppositions between Paris and Woollett, culture and commerce, surface and depth, which permeates the entire novel. The realm of culture, even in the guise of Paris, is never fully able to escape the gravitational pull of the material basis of its production, as Mrs Newsome's persistent telegraphic correspondence with Strether conspicuously demonstrates.

At the same time, James's strategy of representing the 'abyss' between base and superstructure both mimetically re-enacts the illusion of their separation, and problematizes the assumption of a singular mode of determination between the two. It is in these respects that James bears witness, most closely, to the historical moment in which his later fiction must be placed, and in which the centrality of advertising as a cultural phenomenon most clearly emerges. For if James consciously refuses to banish the liminal presence of Woollett's 'unnameable' commodity, *The Ambassadors* also traces the emergence of new economic and cultural practices, in which the old lines separating base and superstructure begin to dissolve. Advertising, as Wicke has observed, plays a crucial intermediary role within the historical narrative adumbrated by James: in order to distinguish its anonymous commodity from other products of the same kind, and thus to attain a monopoly status, the Woollett manufactory 'stands in need of the auratization . . . that only advertisement will be able to provide'. As the organized practice of representing the world of commodities, advertising is both a purely instrumental economic strategy and a 'new aesthetic system'.[14] Within the novel, then, advertising is the term which simultaneously bridges and reinforces the separation between the opposed worlds of culture and commerce. Not only does its belated naming allow us to glimpse the connections between Strether's seemingly divergent experiences of Woollett and Paris, it also illuminates the very process by which Woollett's 'vulgar' business concerns are buried beneath a surface of sensuous, aesthetic impressions. The cultural 'surface' of advertising (and its related practices of commodity representation) may now be seen to operate at the 'deepest' levels of economic determination.

Thus, one of the cultural effects of advertising which James's novel clearly registers is an uncertainty as to the site of precisely that 'historical secret' which Eagleton so confidently locates. Marx himself likened the sphere of circulation to a surface upon which the exchange of commodities takes place in open view, while beneath it lies 'the hidden abode of production', the site which must be penetrated if the 'secret of profit-making' is to be 'laid bare'.[15] Yet while James, as I have suggested, maintains Marx's scrutiny of the 'depths' of production, he also reveals the complexity of this hermeneutic procedure within the culture of modern consumer capitalism. In response to Chad's 'revelation' towards the end of the novel, for example, Strether concedes that 'Advertising is clearly at this time of day the secret of trade' (*A* 341), thus echoing (but also reversing) his earlier remark to Maria Gostrey, that in disclosing the financial basis of Mrs Newsome's Woollett Review, he has revealed 'the very secret of the prison-house' (*A* 51). Strether's later remark suggests not that commercial activity is the generative source behind cultural phenomena, but, conversely, that the cultural form of advertising is itself the 'secret' behind modern commercial practices. Chad's understanding of this 'secret' promises to give him access to a set of practices which control the production of a highly articulated world of visual appearances and representations, symbolized by Paris, seemingly from below its surface. Yet a further irony prevents us from simply installing advertising within the text as the concealed, manipulative practice which it is often thought to be. For both Chad's and Strether's claims on behalf of the efficacy of advertising may themselves prove to be nothing more than a further rhetorical flourish, symptoms of a characteristically double illusion by which the truth of the hidden power of advertising is unveiled through the very language of advertising, and thus called into question.[16]

Here, there are notable similarities between the language of James's text and the rhetorical mode of contemporary advertising discourse. The advertising agent Thomas Smith, for instance, titled his periodical trade manual *Successful Advertising: Its Secrets Explained*. Published throughout the 1880s and 1890s, each issue contained numerous testimonials to the efficacy of the manual, many of them heralding Smith's accomplishment in finally revealing the 'secrets' of advertising.[17] Likewise, in a manual entitled *The Art of Advertising* (1899), William Stead, Jr proclaimed his intention of unveiling the 'great secrets of the Art of Advertising'.[18] In texts of this kind, such language functions as a sign of access to a corpus of ostensibly privileged knowledge: the readers of these manuals – the potential clients of the advertising agent – will, it is promised, discover the arcane strategies that make advertising work. Yet, plainly, this invocation of the 'secret of advertising' is itself part of the rhetoric of marketing, designed to sell the literature of selling. The assertion that advertising has its hidden 'depths' – that the technology of advertising exists below the surface of the spectacle which it produces – is in itself epideictic: it partakes of the very strategies which it claims to unveil.

By echoing a turn of phrase which was, by the turn of the century, common currency, Strether's enigmatic utterance thus furthers, rather than resolves, the epistemological problems which he has encountered in the course of the novel. In doing so, however, it does at least identify the terms in which this problem can be articulated. By the end of the novel, Chad's choice of future profession reflects not simply upon the changing economic and cultural practices of the American society to which he will return, but also, and more insidiously, upon the European culture which he will leave. In *The Art of Advertising*, William Stead wrote that 'The day is fast approaching when the best literary and artistic ability will be called in to aid the advertiser in his appeal to the public.'[19] While hardly living up to this exalted billing, the significance of Chad's decision to return to America may also, as Wicke has observed, be seen to lie in a particular historical conjunction of economic and aesthetic interests. For James, however, this conjunction does not simply entail a renewed contrast between an increasingly commodified American culture and an authentic European culture. The resonance of the cultural forms to which advertising finally gives a name cannot be confined to the business world of Woollett, as Wicke tends to suggest.[20]

Indeed, as William Greenslade has shown in an important article on *The Ambassadors*, it is European culture which imbues Chad with the aesthetic sensibility which fits him for his new role within American society.[21] Chad's refashioning at the hands of Madame de

Vionnet offers an uncanny prefiguration of the entire lexicon of cosmetic 'improvement' and personal 'transformation' which encodes the malleability of the self within modern advertising discourse. 'Do I strike you as improved?', Chad asks Strether at their first meeting (*A* 95), to which Strether can only respond in wonderment:

> The effect of it was general – it had retouched his features, drawn them with a cleaner line. It had cleared his eyes and settled his colour and polished his fine square teeth – the main ornament of his face; and at the same time that it had given him a form and a surface, almost a design, it had toned his voice, established his accent, encouraged his smile to more play and his other motions to less . . . It was as if in short he had really, copious perhaps but shapeless, been put into a firm mould and turned successfully out (*A* 97).

The new 'improved' Chad whom Strether encounters in Paris is himself the product of an aesthetic redesigning, which reproduces the effects of advertising practice, though not at the level of referential narrative commentary. Strether's initial astonishment at the sight of Chad's transformation, moreover, encapsulates his perpetually bewildered response to the spectacle of Paris itself. At the end of the novel, Strether finally realizes that his own conception of Chad has been an illusion: 'Of course I moved among miracles. It was all phantasmagoric', he tells Maria (*A* 333). It is precisely this disorientation of visual perception, an effect of the 'phantasmagoric' play of 'form' and 'surface', which best describes the phenomenal experience of Paris.

THE 'SHOW-WINDOW EFFECT'

By choosing to retain Paris as the primary site of Strether's experience of European culture, James was, of course, drawing upon a host of contradictory cultural resonances. If Paris is seen as capable of offering Strether a plausible alternative to the impoverished culture of Woollett, James was well aware that 'Paris' might also be read as a site of material luxury which, far from abolishing the presence of the commodity form, represented its apotheosis. This is the Paris of the *Expositions Universelles*, the series of international trade fairs held at regular intervals in the city since 1855 and culminating, most spectacularly, in 1900. In a letter to Edward

Warren, dated 25 February 1898, James explicitly alludes to this 'extraordinary' visual aspect of Paris:

> with its new – I mean more and more multiplied – manifestations of luxurious and extravagant extension, grandeur and general chronic *expositionism* . . . it strikes me as a monstrous massive flower of national decadance [sic], the biggest temple ever built to material joys and the lust of the eyes, and drawing to it thereby all the forces of the nation as to a substitute for others – I mean other than Parisian – achievement. It is a strange great phenomenon – with a deal of beauty still in its great expansive symmetries and perspectives – and *such* a beauty of light.[22]

What is curious about this statement is the way in which James seems to be rehearsing (or miming) the very language of moral disapproval which he clearly satirizes in *The Ambassadors.* James's response to the 'chronic *expositionism*' of Paris directly anticipates Strether's uneasy recognition of the emblematic status of Maria Gostrey's richly appointed apartment, wherein 'the lust of the eyes and the pride of life had indeed thus their temple' (*A* 80). In both instances, however, what is coded as a 'puritanical' shock at the sin of visual pleasure is immediately followed (and, in Strether's case, also preceded) by a perverse counter-reaction. In spite of its 'decadent' and 'materialistic' character, James is struck with the luminous beauty of the Parisian spectacle.

James's specific emphasis upon the sensory quality of light radiated by the spectacle of Paris also anticipates subsequent responses to the Paris *Exposition* of 1900, which might even be thought to include his own novel. According to Paul Greenhalgh, the *Exposition* of 1900 'was the first in Europe to extensively use electric lighting to evoke a fairy-tale environment, invariably in conjunction with water cascades, glass and mirrors'.[23] Indeed, the *Exposition* was specifically promoted as a spectacle of light: amongst the buildings specially constructed for the occasion were Le Palais Lumineux, Le Palais des Illusions, and Le Palais de L'Electricité. These attractions were designed to offer the visitor a dazzling, and even disorientating, experience of visual pleasure. Commenting upon the glass edifice of Le Palais Lumineux, for example, one contemporary observer likened the Protean quality of its material to the hallucinatory effects of an opium-induced dream. Just as in James's letter to Warren, where the luminous beauty of Paris is disentangled from its grossly 'material joys', so, here too, the dream-like immateriality (*immatérialité du rêve*) of the Palais Lumineux is seen not as the product of a specifically modern cultural condition ('*la matérialité brutale*), but as its direct opposite.[24] The spectacular form of the *Exposition* is used as a means of occluding its status as a site and bearer of the material value of commodities. As Susan Buck-Morss has suggested, the significance of the *Expositions* did not simply, or even primarily, lie in their facilitation of direct forms of commercial exchange. Their real function was, rather, to offer a means, as another observer of the *Exposition* of 1900 put it, of 'combining business with pleasure'.[25] By constructing a phantasmagoric world in which economic rationality became inseparable from new forms of aesthetic experience, the *Expositions* (alongside their British and American counterparts) contributed to the refashioning of visual perception itself.[26] In these sites of commodity display, the pleasure of seeing was not simply conjoined with the act of consumption, but was itself the very object consumed.

If James does not refer directly to the *Exposition* which was actually taking place as he began work on *The Ambassadors* in 1900, the novel is nevertheless 'chronically' saturated with images and figures of the luminosity of Paris. During the scene in Gloriani's garden, for instance, the habituated Parisian Miss Barrace says of her circle that 'We're all looking at each other – and in the light of Paris one sees what things resemble. That's what the light of Paris seems always to show. It's the fault of the light of Paris – dear old light!' (*A* 126). Precisely what the light of Paris does show, however, is left uncertain by these elliptical remarks. For Miss Barrace, as for Strether, the act of 'looking' implies an effort to decode the visual signs which constitute the surface of Parisian manners, and, in this particular case, to discover the true character of Chad's relationship to Madame de Vionnet and her daughter, Jeanne. Yet rather than revealing the truth of objects in themselves – rather than showing Madame de Vionnet 'for what she is', as Strether wishes – the light of Paris reveals only the metaphorical resemblances between objects (*A* 127). Under these conditions, visual perception is strangely specular and reflexive, and its object constantly deferred.

The epistemological uncertainty which ensues from this phantasmagoric play of luminous effects is perhaps best illustrated, however, in the novel's most celebrated image of Paris itself:

> It hung before him this morning, the vast bright Babylon, like some huge iridescent object, a jewel brilliant and hard, in which parts were not to be discriminated nor differences comfortably marked. It twinkled and

trembled and melted together, and what seemed all surface one moment seemed all depth the next. (*A* 64).

This image has been characterized as belonging to a number of different 'ways of seeing': impressionistic, aestheticist and symbolist, to name only the most salient.[27] What has been less remarked upon, however, is the extent to which Strether's apprehension of Paris registers the same disorientation of vision which contemporary observers of the Paris *Exposition* noted in referring to its 'hallucinatory enterprise' and 'fantastic apparition'.[28] Strether's inability to distinguish sufficiently between surface and depth reminds us not only of the way in which such supposedly objective properties are conditioned by a subjective process of seeing, but also reveals how, in turn, the subject's manner of seeing may itself be (albeit in a somewhat different sense) objectively determined. The very same play of effects was rhapsodically ascribed to the *Palais Lumineux*: a construction which was designed to combine opacity and transparency in appearance, and durability and fluidity in its use of materials.[29] It is possible, therefore, to view James's concern with registering both the process of Strether's vision and, through this process, the particular visual field which it takes as its object as a response to the emergence of new and problematic forms of visual experience around the turn of the century. The difficulties which Strether experiences in attempting to make sense of the relationship between visual signs and their apparently concealed meanings may be less a commentary on his own interpretive naivety, and more a reflection of the form of the spectacle itself.

James's understanding of this relationship between visual experience and commodity spectacle is confirmed by a wealth of apparently inconsequential textual detail, which often goes unnoticed in readings of the novel. From its very beginning, Strether's encounter with European culture is mediated by his vision of objects on display; Europe is primarily construed as an 'empire of "things"' (*A* 80). Indeed, perhaps more than any other Jamesian character, Strether is directly figured in the role of consumer, absorbed by the 'arts' of representation and display, which might otherwise go by the name of advertising. During his brief stay in Chester, for example, Strether is immediately drawn to the window displays of 'frivolous' items of fashion. While his American 'comrade' Waymarsh 'most sensibly yielded to the appeal of the merely useful trades . . . Strether flaunted an affinity with the dealers in stamped letter-paper and in smart neckties' (*A* 38). The appeal of such commodities lies, of course, in their apparent freedom from the principle of utility in which both Strether and Waymarsh have been educated. At this point in the novel, though, Strether's liberating desire is not exempt from the judgement of his own 'previous virtue':

> Do what he might, in any case, his previous virtue was still there, and it seemed fairly to stare at him out of the windows of shops that were not as the shops of Woollett, fairly to make him want things that he shouldn't know what to do with. It was by the oddest, the least admissible of laws demoralising him now; and the way it boldly took was to make him want more wants. (*A* 37).

Indeed, it might be thought that the inhibiting effect of Strether's New England conscience, apparently so much in evidence here, offers a sufficient explanation for his continuing hesitation, and even ultimate failure, as a consumer. Yet as this passage reveals, Strether's inculcated 'virtue' cannot strictly be opposed to his illicit desire. Rather, it is precisely the admonitory image of his 'previous virtue', reflected in the mirror of the shop window, which appears to act as a stimulus to its own transgression, leading to a proliferation rather than an abnegation of 'wants'. By forbidding desire, Strether's conscience initiates a process of deferred gratification which only serves to intensify the energies of his visual consumption. The circuit of compulsion by which Strether is left only to 'want more wants' may be read as an exemplary representation of the infinitely receding horizon of 'satisfaction' which is functional to the workings of modern consumer culture.[30]

Both the pleasurable and the functional elements of Strether's characteristic vacillation between wanting and deferring are made explicit in the case of a different object of desire: that of the numerous 'lemon-coloured volumes' displayed in the shop windows of Paris. Not long after his arrival in the city, Strether finds that '[H]is conscience had been amusing itself for the forty-eight hours by forbidding him the purchase of a book' (*A* 63). By the time of his first visit to Madame de Vionnet's apartment in book sixth, however, we discover that Strether has 'for a fortnight now altogether succumbed' to 'the opportunity of a further acquaintance' with the 'lemon-coloured covers with which his eye had begun to dally from the hour of his arrival' (*A* 147). Far from acting as a limit to desire, Strether's initial deferral – 'he held off from that, held off from everything' – allows him to gauge the extent of what he lacks (*A* 63). The present occasion calls to mind a previous visit to Paris in the 1860s, when his purchase of a dozen 'lemon-coloured volumes' of French fiction had seemed to represent the promise of a 'finer taste': a promise which, in the intervening years, has remained unfulfilled (*A* 63). Hence, as Jonathan Freedman has observed, Strether's positive moments of desire appear inseparable from the negative instances of his loss.[31] It is this peculiarly twofold movement – both self-negating and self-affirming – which causes him to 'hover and wonder and laugh and sigh, [makes] him advance and retreat, feeling half ashamed of his impulse to plunge and more than half afraid of his impulse to wait' (*A* 63).

The fact that Strether is often seen in the act of refraining from consumption should not by itself, then, be interpreted as a gesture of resistance to the spectacle of the commodity. It was through the act of looking, rather than through an immediate appropriation of the object, that organized spectacles such as the *Expositions* and arcades of the late nineteenth century succeeded in inculcating the cultural codes of mass consumption.[32] Moreover, as Rachel Bowlby has suggested, it is precisely this moment of apparent distance from the object of display – a moment in which the consumer is 'just looking' – that marks the extent of the subject's absorption in the spectacle. The reflective medium of the shop window allows the consumer to project an ideal imago on to the objects contained behind the glass, while investing these objects with autonomous properties.[33] In a similar fashion, the allure of French fiction is mediated by Strether's 'hungry gazes through clear plates behind which lemon-coloured volumes were as fresh as fruit on the tree' (*A* 63). The erotic and organic metaphors in which this scene of Edenic temptation is couched recall precisely the language of Marx's definition of 'commodity fetishism', in which the material substance of the products of human labour appears to assume independent life in the eyes of its producers.[34] Rather than discerning the artifice of their display, Strether naturalizes the objects of his desire, viewing them as organic produce rather than manufactured commodities. As a consequence, the medium of the shop window is assumed to be genuinely transparent.

James himself, however, was always extraordinarily alert and responsive to the epiphenomena of mass culture. While *The Ambassadors* does not follow the example of Theodore Dreiser's contemporaneous novel *Sister Carrie* (1900), in which the narrator self-consciously digresses upon the 'nature' of the department store and the use of plate glass in the windows of Chicago offices and shops, the two texts may, nevertheless, be seen as exploring the same cultural experience.[35] If Dreiser draws attention to the material processes which shape the commodification of desire in late-nineteenth-century urban space, James offers a less conspicuous, but no less perceptive, representation of the cultural frameworks of contemporary visual experience. One such framing device was facilitated by technological developments in the 1880s and 1890s, which led to the production of much larger expanses of glass, and hence to its systematic use as a medium of display.[36] It is not coincidental, then, that the metaphor of the 'frame', which most critics locate only within the Lambinet landscape scene, is such an important one in *The Ambassadors.* Nor is it coincidental that James elsewhere delineated an explicit connection between pictorial frames and the framing of commodity consumption.

In 'The Beldonald Holbein', published in the same year as *The Ambassadors* (1903), the narrator of the story is invited to paint the portrait of Lady Beldonald, but on first seeing his prospective subject he realizes that 'her life had its centre in her own idea of her appearance' (*CT* XI 285). Since Lady Beldonald is already the product of her own narcissistic self-fashioning, any attempt to represent her in painting must take account of this prior mediation. The effect of this mediation, however, is to conceal its artifice; Lady Beldonald 'looks *naturally* new', as if her youthful beauty had been 'preserved' in a 'plate-glass case' (*CT* XI 285; italics in the original). Thus, the narrator's project in painting Lady Beldonald is not to render his subject as though she were, in truth, spontaneously accessible to the observer, but, rather, to convey the very fabrication of transparency: 'The thing was to paint her, I perceived, *in* the glass case – a most tempting, attaching feat; render to the full the shining, interposing plate and the general show-window effect' (*CT* XI 285). This 'most tempting, attaching feat' might also serve as an appropriate metaphor for James's mimetic strategy and achievement in *The Ambassadors.* By faithfully recording 'the rare condition of . . . [the] surface', the artist demystifies the illusion of transparency which naturalizes the construction of the commodity spectacle (*CT* XI 285). Yet whereas the narrator of 'The Beldonald Holbein' consciously expounds the artifice of his painting, which in turn reflects the artifice of his subject, in *The Ambassadors* James refrains from such direct narratorial intervention. What is reproduced in the novel is the 'show-window effect'; an effect which works to efface its 'interposing' presence.

THE SPECTACLE OF THE BOOK

If James was very much aware of the cultural conditions which frame Strether's visual consumption of objects, as a tale such as 'The Beldonald Holbein' indicates, then I would also argue that the nature of the objects themselves bears similar scrutiny. It is surely worth asking why it is that, of all the different objects of display encountered in the novel, James should pay most attention to Strether's impressions of books. The text of *The Ambassadors* is, in fact, littered with references to books of different forms and appearances: not only to the standard 'lemon-coloured' paper bindings of French fiction and the green cover of the Woollett Review, but also to Strether's purchase of the works of Victor Hugo in seventy volumes of 'red-and-gold' (*A* 175), and to the 'pinkish and greenish' volumes which he discovers in Madame de Vionnet's apartment (*A* 145). Even the characters of the novel are to be understood through an act of 'reading' which is centred upon this site of graphic inscriptions: the transformed Chad, for example, is compared to 'the new edition of an old book that one has been fond of' (*A* 111), while Mrs Newsome's rigid thought figures as a book that has 'no margin, as it were, for any alteration' (*A* 300). What is common to all of these instances is James's evocation of the material character of the book, or, more precisely, of the phenomenal apprehension of its materiality. The appearance of the book may thus be referred to the practices of advertising and display which the novel itself reflexively – that is to say, as a book – dramatizes.

That books are themselves cultural commodities, and hence subject to the proliferation of publicity that enveloped other literary 'products' in the commercial economy of the late nineteenth century, should come as no surprise. While the literary text is not reducible to its status as a commodity, neither was James under any illusions about its capacity simply to transcend this status, as we have seen in previous chapters. What needs to be considered further, however, is the extent to which James explored the relationship between the commercial practice of publicity and the form of his own fiction, thus blurring the boundaries of what is properly conceived as intrinsic and extrinsic to the work of art, and displacing relationships of causality and anteriority between the literary text and its contexts.

During the latter half of the nineteenth century, the material form and visual display of books was increasingly recognized as one of the most important marketing techniques available to publishers and booksellers. In his trade manual *The Profession of Bookselling* (1893), Adolf Growoll, for example, advised American booksellers on the best means of constructing interior and window displays. Growoll's meticulous demonstration of the ways in which extrinsic colour and lighting could be used to enhance the allure of books for prospective consumers reveals the degree of calculation with which the aesthetic form of the book was capable of being construed as 'Window Dressing' (to quote the title of one of Growoll's chapters). Fixed at a precise distance behind the window, Growoll informed his readers, the 'play of light and shade is much more varied and pleasing, the light being softened and diffused'.[37] A similar abstraction of the sensory properties of colour and light appears to inform Strether's impressions of the 'lemon-coloured volumes' set behind the 'clear plates' of Parisian shop windows. As Wicke has noted, we are not informed of the titles or authors of these books:[38] their covers construct the appearance of a pure surface, detached from any interior content. By contrast, the equivalent green cover of the Woollett Review is exposed by Strether as a 'specious shell', containing a 'mere rich kernel of economics, politics, ethics' (*A* 63). Whereas, in the case of the Review, surface is clearly separated from depth, appearance from essence, in the case of the lemon-coloured volumes the surface of the object saturates the horizon of visual signification. This is a phenomenon which, according to Wolfgang Haug, marks the emergence of commodity aesthetics: what is initially conceived as the sensuous form of the commodity is abstracted from its body to the point at which it loses its character as mere 'surface'.[39]

Strether's attempt to rebuild a 'temple of taste' on the basis of the lemon-coloured volumes can thus be seen as flawed from the start (*A* 63). For while he sees these books as offering the possibility of an authentic cultural experience, in contrast to the fatally compromised Review, the former are no more autonomous in their aesthetic value than the latter. Indeed, it is the Review which, by virtue of the shameful knowledge which it contains, is forced to disavow its status as an object of consumption, whereas the lemon-coloured volumes of French fiction openly flaunt it. The literary text thus takes its place within the general spectacle of Paris. It is perhaps for this reason that, of all the different books encountered within the novel, Strether attaches most value to those which he glimpses amongst the objects of Madame de Vionnet's apartment. It is only here that Strether discovers a different mode of possession: one in which the collector has not relied 'on any contemporary method of acquisition', as in the case of both Maria and Chad, but where 'the mistress of the scene before him, beautifully passive under the spell of transmission – transmission from her father's line, he quite made up his mind – had only received, accepted and been quiet' (*A* 146). Madame de Vionnet's passive accumulation seems designed to preclude any vulgarly active form of consumption, and so, through time, the objects of her collection are divested of their commodity character. The same aura extends to her possession of 'copies of works presented, with inscriptions, by authors now classic' (*A* 146); here, the book appears purely as a gift, inscribed with the signature of its author and removed from the anonymous sphere of exchange. It is only the emerging visibility of Madame de Vionnet's own status as an object of patriarchal exchange which hints at the forms of power which underlie this 'spell of transmission'.

This fleeting idyllic vision constitutes the ideal form of the book as it is manifested in the novel. Elsewhere, however, a recognition of the hidden flaw within Strether's imaginative construction of an autonomous high culture appears to pervade its symbolic usage. As an object of hermeneutic desire, the book corresponds precisely to the trajectory of Strether's adventure, promising a moment of consummate understanding only to culminate (however provisionally) in frustration. Outside their visual frame of display, books unfold their inner 'depth' only to reveal a constitutive lack at their core. This recurrent eventuality of Strether's experience of Parisian culture is encapsulated early on in the novel when, strolling past the bookstalls of the Latin Quarter, he endeavours to 'reconstruct' Chad's bohemian lifestyle, as well as his own youth, by observing the browsers. Momentarily, the 'stray spirit of youth' revives 'in the turned page of shock-headed slouch-hatted loiterers whose young intensity of type, in the direction of pale acuteness, deepened his vision, and even his appreciation, of racial differences, and whose manipulation of the uncut volume was too often, however, but a listening at closed doors' (*A* 67–8). Here, Strether's vision of books is itself enclosed within a scene of 'bohemian life' taken from a prior act of reading (the reference being to Murger's *Scènes de la vie de bohème*). The empirical and the metaphorical figure of the book appear to merge. Yet while Strether's imaginative effort of reconstruction is initially assisted by the 'turned page' of the readers, the scene ends with the ominous closure of the 'uncut volume', signalling his inability to fully inhabit or understand the desired text.

In this instance, Strether's response to the 'charming open-air array of literature classic and casual' is again one of self-restraint:

> He found the effect of tone and tint, in the long charged tables and shelves, delicate and appetizing; the impression – substituting one kind of low-priced *consommation* for another – might have been that of one of the pleasant cafés that overlapped, under an awning, to the pavement; but he edged along, grazing the tables, with his hands firmly behind him. He wasn't there to dip, to consume – he was there to reconstruct. He wasn't there for his own profit – not, that is, the direct. (*A* 67).

Yet, here, a more complex motive also informs Strether's refusal to consume. Appetitive consumption is conceived as a form of self-interest which, as in the tradition of Kantian aesthetics, threatens both to abolish the autonomy of the object and to enslave the desire of the subject. In this definition, consumption is incompatible with aesthetic experience since what is particular to the substance of the aesthetic object is thereby obliterated.[40] Strether's concern that he should accrue no 'profit' from his experience (which is later described as his fear of 'acting in an interested way') is thus neither simply a denial of pleasure nor simply a functional instance of its deferral, but rather a means of preserving the pleasure of aesthetic experience which consumption itself prematurely forecloses (*A* 203). To gain 'profit' would be to achieve the form of positive value most appropriate to the utilitarian economy which Strether wishes to evade. In his recent discussion of *The Ambassadors*, Ross Posnock has also argued that for Strether (and, by implication, for James) desire cannot be understood as a teleological pursuit of plenitude. If desire founders (and is founded) upon the necessity of lack, as Baudrillard has insisted, the consumerist ideology of satisfaction in desire is itself radically untenable. Strether's inability to achieve the object of his desire – or even to know what he desires, as he confesses to Maria towards the end of the novel – may thus be seen to expose an irreducible flaw at the heart of modern systems of exchange: namely, the belief that desire can be fulfilled through a complete identity between the subject and object of consumption. Posnock's reading of the novel, then, allows us to account for Strether's resistant and, in a certain sense, dysfunctional negotiations of consumer culture, although I would also argue that this reading tends to over-accentuate the subversive import of Strether's '"counter-economy" of lack and difference'.[41]

This sense of lack may also be witnessed in Strether's final encounter with the lemon-coloured volumes. Returning to Chad's apartment after his break with Sarah Pocock, Strether enjoys one last vision of 'the novel half uncut, the novel lemon-coloured and tender, with the ivory knife athwart it like the dagger in a *contadina's* hair' (*A* 283). By this time, of course, Strether is already aware that his European adventure 'probably *was* all at an end' (*A* 282). The condition of the book, however, with its pages only 'half uncut', and the paper-knife suspended across it, offers a telling image of the prematurely arrested state of Strether's erotic and hermeneutic awakening. This is not so much a scene of 'seduction', as Wicke has described it, but more one of castration.[42] Or, rather, these two possibilities are perpetually suspended on the brink of consummation as the phallic act of cognitive 'penetration' is enfolded in the feminized contours of the book. Likened to 'the dagger in a *contadina's* hair', the knife which threatens the book with violation is itself threatened with emasculation.

In its ultimate 'undecidability' this image of the 'half-uncut' book recalls Mallarmé's use of similar tropes in *Quant au livre* (1895). In 'Le Livre, instrument spirituel' Mallarmé likewise conceived of the book in feminized terms, while explicitly rejecting the masculine model of cognitive possession, symbolized by the violent penetration of the paper-knife. Yet it is precisely the feminine form of the book which, in Mallarmé's account, both produces and confounds the claim to interpretive mastery. As the cutting of the folds leaves 'a mark which remains intact', the book can be seen as both inviolable and always already violated.[43] Thus, commenting on Mallarmé's text, Jacques Derrida has argued that the fold or 'hymen' of the book cannot be used as a metaphor for the definitive rupture of hermeneutic understanding since it is already self-divided: the space of the 'hymen' does not conceal meaning as a 'secret', but irretrievably disperses it.[44] In this respect, the most important similarity between Mallarmé and James lies in their distrust of the positivistic claims which accompany the representation of the book as a metaphor for knowledge or experience. James's figure of the book, as much as Mallarmé's, forestalls the possibility of a satisfying cognitive plenitude and even the realization of a constitutive lack, at least as Strether finally sees it. Where James instructively differs from Mallarmé, however, is in his reading of the cultural status of the book. Mallarmé's call for a revolution in the practice of typographical spacing is an explicit response to the standardized products of modern mass culture. The ideal form of the book is opposed to the formlessness of the newspaper, whose flat surface and linear type gives it the 'vulgar advantage' of being suited to the techniques of 'mass production and circulation'. Hence, for Mallarmé, the ideal book, which would differ from the derivative products of commercial publication, must assume the capacity to elude its value as commodity.[45] By implication, literature must be distinguished from mere journalism.

For James, on the other hand, this differential evaluation and separation of textual forms is an ambition which his own text conspicuously confuses. It is certainly true that the newspaper comes to be seen as the paradigmatic cultural form of Woollett, just as the material object of the book comes to represent the 'higher culture' of Europe. On more than one occasion, Strether himself feels that his letters to Mrs Newsome are either written or read in the spirit of 'some showy journalist, some master of the great new science of beating the sense out of words' (*A* 196). The constant transatlantic traffic in telegraphy between Woollett and Paris is, to a still greater extent, a reminder of the alternative technologies of writing with which the book is forced to compete. Significantly, however, the use of these technologies is not confined to America. Towards the end of the novel, Strether encounters a different aspect of Parisian life when he enters the office of the Postes et Télégraphes. In composing his response to Madame de Vionnet's *petit bleu*, Strether is compelled to use 'the dreadful needle-pointed public pen at the dreadful sand-strewn public table: implements that symbolized for Strether's too interpretative innocence something more acute in manners, more sinister in morals, more fierce in the national life' (*A* 317). It is the publicity which attends this act of 'private' communication which, by way of contrast, reveals the aura of intimacy which is expected of the book. Yet what Strether's fascination with this public scene of writing forgets is that the intimacy of the book is itself construed through the medium of display. Unlike Mallarmé, then, James does not allow the artefactual allure of the book to exempt it from complicity with the conditions of mass culture.

It is James's recognition of this complicity, I wish to argue, which helps to explain the innumerable references to books which fill the pages of *The Ambassadors*. For rather than elaborating an ideal totality of The Book, as in Mallarmé's *Quant au livre*, these references reflexively inscribe the material existence of James's novel itself.[46] As I suggest in chapter 3, James was intensely concerned with the processes by which texts pass from the private sphere of production to the increasingly public sphere of consumption; often to the extent that, as in 'The Death of the Lion', the knowledge of the text's dissemination inhabits the prior moment of its inscription.

A similar knowledge may be located at different stages of James's writing of *The Ambassadors*. It is worth noting, for example, that in his preface to the novel James returns to the metaphors of framing and display which play such a large part in the novel itself. There, James explained his reasons for not employing a 'first person' narrative form in *The Ambassadors* in the following manner:

> The 'first person' then, so employed, is addressed by the author directly to ourselves, his possible readers, whom he has to reckon with, at the best, by our English tradition, so loosely and vaguely after all, so little respectfully, on so scant a presumption of exposure to criticism. Strether, on the other hand, encaged and provided for as *The Ambassadors* encages and provides, has to keep in view proprieties much stiffer and more salutary than any our straight and credulous gape are likely to bring home to him, has exhibitional conditions to meet, in a word, that forbid the terrible *fluidity* of self-revelation. (*LC* II 1316).

In this context, James's resistance to the self-revelatory form of 'autobiography' is interesting because of the way in which it seems to register certain anxieties which materialize thematically in the novel itself. He is concerned to avoid a first-person narrative since it would appear to construct the kind of relationship between author and public which gives the latter an unmediated access to the private subjectivity of the former. This seemingly transparent, confessional mode of communication is particularly problematic given James's views on the credulous nature of his potential readership. James's proposed solution to this dilemma is to impose more stringent 'exhibitional conditions' upon his protagonist: to 'encage' Strether within an impersonal narrative form. But what is significant about this proposal is its duplication of the very framing of visual perception which Strether himself encounters in the Parisian world of display. If James's statement on autobiography may be read autobiographically, as William Goetz has suggested, then a number of analogies between the authorial and narrative positions of James and Strether begin to emerge.[47] On the one hand, James's anxiety about the 'terrible *fluidity*' of autobiographical 'self-revelation' echoes Strether's uneasy fascination with the forms of commodity display which characterize the visual experience of Paris. On the other hand, James's desire to protect Strether from the conditions of unmediated publicity ironically reproduces the very strategies of representation which channel Strether's vision as a consumer. As it appears in the preface, the central architectonic principle of the novel's form seems to mirror the process by which Strether's perception is literally framed within the novel. In other words, James's authorial framing encloses, and is enclosed within, the 'exhibitional conditions' which it is designed to avoid.

In the novel itself, of course, this metaphor of framing is most vividly realized in Strether's excursion to the French countryside in book eleventh. On this occasion, the object disclosed within the frame is not a book but a painting. Strether's vision of the rural scene is modelled upon a landscape by Emile Lambinet which he has seen years before in a Boston auction room; hence the perceptual metaphor of 'picture' and 'frame' is superimposed on to the 'real' landscape. Yet while Strether wishes to see the Lambinet painting 'resolved back into . . . [the] elements' from which it was drawn, the temporal and epistemological thrust of this scene lies clearly in a different direction (*A* 303). Far from reinstating a romanticized genesis of experience in which the material of art is recovered in its original state of nature, Strether's impression tends to show the reverse. This is not simply to note, as critics have often done, the primacy of representation over 'the real' (or 'art' over 'life') in James's aesthetic thought. Rather, it is to suggest that what is striking about this episode is the way in which Strether keeps returning to the scene of his original vision of the painting:

It had been offered, he remembered, at a price he had been instructed to believe the lowest ever named for a Lambinet, a price he had never felt so poor as on having to recognize, all the same, as beyond a dream of possibility. He had dreamed – had turned and twisted possibilities for an hour: it had been the only adventure of his life in connexion with the purchase of a work of art. The adventure, it will be perceived, was modest;

but the memory, beyond all reason and by some accident of association, was sweet. The little Lambinet abode with him as the picture he *would* have bought – the particular production that had made him for the moment overstep the modesty of nature. (*A* 303)

It is specifically the auction room in Tremont Street which provides the cultural framework of Strether's memory of the Lambinet, and although this 'background' cannot wholly determine the proliferation of spatial and temporal perspectives in which the painting can be located, it exercises an ineliminably material presence. The painting remains with Strether precisely because it is 'the picture he *would* have bought': the fact of his not having bought it again forestalling the closure of consumption, and allowing desire to circulate in the inverted form of regret. But even in this negative instance, the painting itself cannot be entirely separated from the context of its exhibition. Strether's recollection of this scene indiscriminately merges the 'picture' and its 'frame', fusing together 'the dusty day in Boston, the background of the Fitchburg Depot . . . the maroon-coloured sanctum, the special-green vision, the ridiculous price, the poplars, the willows, the rushes, the river, the sunny silvery sky, the shady woody horizon' (*A* 303). Rather than construing the Lambinet as an autonomous work of art (or for that matter as merely a 'copy' of nature), Strether inextricably dissolves the boundary between what is inside and what is outside the frame.[48] As much a part of the painting itself are the 'exhibitional conditions' in which it is situated. Moreover, James goes further by suggesting that at the very heart of Strether's impression of the French countryside is its most external 'frame'. Strether, we are told, is in danger of 'boring so deep into his impression and his idleness that he might fairly have got through them again and reached the maroon-coloured wall [of the auction room]' (*A* 304). Here, the passage from an exterior 'frame' of aesthetic apprehension to an interior 'picture' of the real landscape is dialectically negated by the re-emergence of the surface under its own depth.

By locating the apparently peripheral and trivial 'maroon-coloured wall' at the very centre of Strether's heightened aesthetic experience, James ironically deflates the hermeneutic model which, to use Tzvetan Todorov's terms, proceeds from the 'unessential' to the 'essential'.[49] The real irony of this inversion, though, lies in the fact that Strether's most resonant image of European high culture is seen to offer the greatest testimony to the power of American finance. The value of the Lambinet (both economic and cultural) derives more from its exhibition in a Boston auction house than it does from the painting's immanent signification of French culture, and indeed it is only within the medium of the former that Strether is able to apprehend the prestige of the latter. James presumably locates Strether's experience of the Boston exhibition at around the same time that he himself was a direct witness to the first major American acquisitions of European art, and in his reviews of the 1870s the accompanying shift in the balance of cultural capital was duly noted. Commenting upon the private purchase of Meissonier's *Friedland* in 1876, for example, James confessed to taking 'an acute satisfaction in seeing America stretch out her long arm and rake in, across the green cloth of the wide Atlantic, the highest prizes of the game of civilization'.[50] By the turn of the century, of course, James's national perspective had itself shifted, as his decidedly uneasy portrayal of the American art collector, Adam Verver, in *The Golden Bowl* (1904) suggests. The very fact that Strether's recollection of the exhibition is at the same time a recollection of his inability to purchase gives a sufficient indication of his ambivalent relationship to America; while his consumption of European culture remains dependent upon the resources of American capitalism, he is simultaneously alienated from these resources, capable only of engaging in their aesthetic sublimation.

More importantly, though, the conspicuous virtuosity of the Lambinet scene adds further weight to the view that *The Ambassadors* is a novel concerned with the status of the aesthetic object in a modern economy of commodity display. For James, the object itself cannot be detached from the cultural context which constructs its appeal to the viewer, and this applies both to pictorial art and, more insidiously, to the literary artefact. Thus, through its oblique handling of the theme of 'advertising', it is possible to reconstruct the deeply self-referential concerns of the novel. *The Ambassadors* is a book that represents books as material objects of display; at the same time, these books themselves reflect, as in the shop window, the book in which they are displayed. Similarly, James is a writer who claims to have fashioned the character of Strether in order to control the conditions of his exhibition while figuring him in the novel as a consumer of this spectacle. Strether's consciousness is not simply a mirror which reflects the world of display within the text, but is also, in an important sense, the very object of textual display. It is this dual function of consciousness which James also ascribed to Prince Amerigo in the preface to *The Golden Bowl*:

> Having a consciousness highly susceptible of registration, he thus makes us see the things that may most interest us reflected in it as in the clean glass held up to so many of the 'short stories' of our long list; and yet after all never a whit to the prejudice of his being just as consistently a foredoomed, entangled, embarrassed agent in the general imbroglio, actor in the offered play. (*LC* II 1323)

According to this formulation, the Prince is both a medium by which the reader sees what *he* sees and yet, by virtue of his role as 'agent' within the 'play', he is also precisely what the reader sees in the act of seeing. Moreover, as Jean-Christophe Agnew has suggested, what *The Golden Bowl* itself registers is a 'deeply internalized commodity world' comparable in its scope to that of *The Ambassadors*.[51] James's ambiguous metaphor of the 'clean glass' of consciousness is modelled upon the literal medium of the shop window through which the Prince gazes in the opening chapter of the novel: a medium which both allows the gaze of the consumer to pass through it (transparently) and reflects it back (like a mirror).[52]

Like Prince Amerigo, then, Strether is both consumer and object of consumption. While he is used to displace the exposed position of his creator, subject to the threat of autobiographical 'self-revelation', he also assumes an antithetical position as the spectator of books. Hence, we are entitled to ask the question: what are these anonymous books that Strether sees behind the glass of the shop window? Is Strether perhaps the fascinated spectator of his own display, gazing at the very scene that awaits him? This would be to suggest that Strether's vision of the lemon-coloured volumes draws attention to the materiality of his own fictive status. As a character in a book that already encodes the conditions of its commodification, Strether is simultaneously and self-consciously inside and outside the frame of his own representation. 'We know you as the hero of the drama, and we're gathered to see what you'll do', Miss Barrace informs him on one occasion (*A* 267). Even such an habitual observer as Strether cannot remain entirely outside the boundaries of his projected world, evading the luminosity of the spectacle. For in his capacity as the 'hero of the drama', Strether bears witness to the 'exhibitional conditions' faced by *The Ambassadors* itself.

Strether's dual status within the text is also symptomatic of the position which *The Ambassadors* occupies in relation to the apparently irreconcileable cultural milieus, which it takes as its central theme. To the extent that Chad's decision to return to America at the end of the novel can be seen to represent the triumph of an increasingly powerful and alluring mass culture over the visibly attenuated promise of Madame de Vionnet's 'higher culture', James dramatizes the growing apprehension of cultural rift which was to pervade much early twentieth-century critical thought. Yet while there is undoubtedly a sense in which James mourns the passing of Strether's ideal of cultural authenticity, he is also covertly engaged in uncovering the collusions and repressions which underpin this ideal. The series of oppositions around which the novel is structured may appear to endorse a secure polarization of cultural values, but they cannot remain unscathed by this ironic enquiry. As both cultural and economic practice, advertising is the term which mediates between the opposing sites of Woollett and Paris, dissolving, even while appearing to congeal, the bifurcation of 'high' and 'low' art. It is this reconciliation of a divided social totality which, for Theodor Adorno, marks the distinctive achievement of the modern 'culture industry': an achievement which is to be regretted since, by proclaiming its own universality, it occludes the negative truth of cultural division.[53] In James's later fiction, it is already possible to witness the process by which the world of advertising is offered to consciousness as the horizon of a new social totality. The form of the commodity spectacle is inscribed both within the projected world of James's fiction and in the projection itself, saturating even the spaces from which it is signally excluded. It was the very extent of James's saturation in this spectacle, however, which allowed him to confront the difficult truths which faced him as a writer. The literary text could no longer simply be used as a medium 'in' which advertising was held up as an object of critique: it had also to recognize itself in the image of its other.

POSTSCRIPT

'The pinnacle of publicity'

Over the course of this study, I have attempted to chart James's complex and ongoing negotiation of the distinctive cultural terrain of the modern public sphere. While I have situated his writings within a series of interrelated (and largely synchronic) cultural contexts, rather than pursuing a single developmental line of enquiry, a certain historical trajectory has, nevertheless, emerged. If, during the 1880s and 1890s, James undertook to offer an explicit, 'full-frontal' analysis of the symptomatic modern phenomenon of publicity in such texts as *The Bostonians*, *The Reverberator* and his many tales of the literary life, his later novels appear to retreat from this confrontation only to reinscribe it in more oblique and insidious ways. Thus, in a more or less direct relation to the historical expansion and saturation of the mass media, James devised strategies of representation which registered the necessity of an increasingly immanent critical stance. While this shift in critical strategy marks an important juncture in his engagement with the formation of mass culture, however, it should not necessarily be seen as a definitive or culminating moment. Throughout the remainder of his career, James continued to articulate many of the same critical concerns, and at no time more so than during and immediately after his return to the United States in 1904. In *The American Scene* (1907), the most immediate product of his visit, James offered both a virtual résumé of these existing concerns and a significantly different analysis of the first and most developed 'mass society'.

In the American scene of 1904, James was confronted with a social spectacle 'so completely outward' that its cultural significance was literally insusceptible to concealment (*AS* 8). Where American society differs from the Parisian scene of 1900 is not, as I have shown, in the mere fact of its spectacular commodification, but, rather, in its apparent capacity to dispense with the mystification of its own lack of hermeneutic 'depth'. Whereas Paris employs the 'art(s) of advertisement' in order to appear 'all surface one moment . . . all depth the next', the American spectacle, James suggests, is simply all surface (*A* 341, 64). This is one of the reasons why James's response to the exhibition of American society is at once more direct and more disturbed than his ironic representation of Strether's impressions of Paris. In stark contrast to the alluring appeal of the Parisian shop window, for example, is James's vision of the 'American shop' and its 'tendency to swarm, to bristle, to vociferate' (*AS* 168). It is in the 'lurid light' of American consumption, indeed, that a comparison with the seductive ambience of the earlier novel is almost explicitly drawn: 'So it was, therefore, that while the imagination and the memory strayed – strayed away to other fiscal climates, where the fruits of consumption so engagingly ripen and flush – the streets affected one at moments as a prolonged show-case for every arrayed vessel of humiliation.' The American shop, with its 'combination' of inflated prices and impersonal exchange, appears to represent an entirely different economic order: an order of ' "protected" production' which registers the contemporary historical shift from liberal to monopoly capitalism (*AS* 168–9).

If interpretive bewilderment is the effect of the phantasmagorical spectacle of Paris, however, the very transparency of the American scene seems only to exacerbate the same problem. Indeed, it is precisely because the American scene lacks 'depth' that it appears to offer such a challenge to James's interpretive resources. While his stance as the 'restless analyst' compels him to 'keep on asking, from the force of acquired habit, what may be behind, what beneath, what within' this spectacle, such conventional interpretive procedures are frustrated by the sheer exteriority of their objects (*AS* 32). Thus, ironically, James is forced to assume the significance of this very absence of signification in a manner which recalls the manipulative practice of the narrator of 'The Aspern Papers'. 'The illustration might be, enormously, of something deficient' or 'absent', he concedes, but, none the less, '[a]s an explication or an implication the democratic intensity could always figure', if only as an 'aching void' (*AS* 40). For the same reason, the American spectacle is also figured as a medium of pure publicity: as a surface which cannot even be deemed superficial since there nothing 'behind' or 'beneath' it. Almost from the very moment of his disembarkation in New Jersey, James – like Matthew Arnold some twenty years earlier – was struck by the 'blaring publicity' of American life.[1] One of his first significant impressions of New York, for example, occurs during a drive along the Jersey shoreline in which he surveys the surrounding *villeggiatura*. While these suburban villas testify vociferously to the expense of their construction, they reveal nothing, according to James, of the 'manners' of their occupants:

> the most as yet accomplished at such a cost was the air of unmitigated publicity, publicity as a condition, as a doom, from which there could be no appeal; just as in all the topsy-turvy order . . . there was no achieved protection, no constituted mystery of retreat, no saving complexity, not so much as might be represented by a foot of garden wall or a preliminary sketch of interposing shade. (*AS* 7)

Whereas James's 'acquired habit' of interpretation assumes that the social display of wealth functions as a means both of representing and of concealing a particular mode of domestic manners, the extrusion of the American spectacle precludes all possibility of 'inward' projection. Without the 'basis of privacy', he insists, the imputation of 'manners' is inconceivable (*AS* 7).

Thus, everywhere, in the material environment of America, James finds evidence of the process which he had long since identified as one of the most symptomatic phenomena of modern culture: the 'extinction of all sense between public and private' (*NB* 82). In its 'fresh, frolicsome' architecture, he discovers a 'diffused vagueness of separation between apartments, between hall and room, between one room and another, between the one you are in and the one you are not in' which 'the public institution shares impartially with the luxurious "home"' (*AS* 119). Yet whereas, in *The Bostonians*, James had largely attributed this reconfiguration of the boundaries of social space to an insidious 'invasion of privacy', here he is no longer capable of differentiating between 'private' and 'public' space. The 'extinction' of these boundaries is encoded within the fabric of American society as 'the very law of the structural fact':

> Thus we have the law fulfilled that every part of every house shall be, as nearly as may be, visible, visitable, penetrable, not only from every other part, but from as many parts of as many other houses as possible, if they only be near enough. Thus we see systematized the indefinite extension of all spaces and the definite merging of all functions; the enlargement of every opening, the exaggeration of every passage, the substitution of gaping arches and far perspectives and resounding voids for enclosing walls, for practicable doors, for controllable windows, for all the rest of the essence of

> the room-character, that room-suggestion which is so indispensable not only to occupation and concentration, but to conversation itself, to the play of the social relation at any other pitch than the pitch of a shriek or a shout. (*AS* 119–20)

James's horror at the absence of interiority within American architecture need not be dismissed as a merely conservative complaint about the erosion of genteel privacy. For, in fact, what is at issue here is not the extinction of privacy *per se*, but rather an extinction of the possibility of difference between private and public spheres. It was precisely this possibility, moreover, which nineteenth-century practitioners of publicity so assiduously exploited. The barrier of the door facilitates revelation as much as it does concealment, and, as the frustration of his 'acquired habit' of interpretation ought to remind us, James is himself in search of 'revelations' in *The American Scene*. By contrast, the 'law' of American architecture represents a condition of publicity so general and pervasive that it might almost be said to mark the end of publicity as it had been conceived in James's earlier writings. With the 'indefinite extension of all spaces and the definite merging of all functions', there is no longer anything to reveal. Above all, perhaps, it is the possibility of conflict between the pursuit of publicity and the defence of privacy which the American scene seems to erode.

James's acknowledged liking for the 'enclosures' and '*penetralia*' which he finds missing in both 'private' and 'public' buildings in America is, without question, charged with political implications. One of the conclusions at which he arrives during his visit to the Boston Public Library is that 'social democracies are unfriendly to the preservation of *penetralia*' because they appear to function as symbolic guardians of institutional prestige (*AS* 179). The existence of *penetralia* forms a barrier between the authority of the public institution and the public itself, and thus reinforces 'the distinction between a benefit given and a benefit taken' (*AS* 179). By contrast, in the public institutions of America, James acknowledges his inability to rise 'to the height of the native argument, the brave sense that the public, the civic building is his very own'; he is reluctant to adopt an unmediated identity between the private citizen and the representative institution (*AS* 70). On his own testimony, then, James's antipathy towards the 'publicity' of American society would also appear to make him ill-suited to the conditions of a modern democratic public sphere. Yet while there is no doubt some truth to this common criticism of *The American Scene*, the accusation of haughty conservatism again proves misplaced.[2] If it is possible to construe James's defence of the value of 'enclosure' as a plea for the maintenance of spatial boundaries which are designed, in effect, to prevent public access, it should also be observed that such boundaries function primarily as a means of demarcating *public* – and not private – space. Indeed, one of the paradoxes of *The American Scene* is that while James is concerned ostensibly with charting the erosion of privacy in American society, most of his examples refer specifically to the status of public buildings and monuments.

As I have argued throughout this study, James's understanding of the value of privacy is itself far from straightforward. On occasions, throughout *The American Scene*, he contemplates the possibility of evading the 'general glare' of the spectacle by retreating into a space of absolute seclusion (*AS* 210); Harvard, for instance, seems briefly to offer the refuge of the 'cloister', 'the place inaccessible . . . to the shout of the newspaper, the place to perambulate, the place to think, apart from the crowd' (*AS* 41). By this account, James's response to the 'American gregarious ideal' would take the familiar form of a desire to demarcate the boundaries of the individual pysche against the external socializing agencies of 'mass' society (*AS* 66). Spatial interiority, as James implies in his comments upon the 'law' of American architecture, both facilitates and corresponds to the 'concentration' of the autonomous bourgeois ego, whereas in 'mass' society it was precisely the inability 'to build and protect a personal, private realm' which, according to Herbert Marcuse, threatened the individual's critical 'power of negation'.[3] Yet to assume that James's critique of the massification of American culture arises purely from the anachronistic imperatives of bourgeois individualism would be a mistake. While there are clearly a number of similarities between James's analysis of mass culture and that of a later twentieth-century sociology, James himself cannot be accommodated within the typological schema which David Riesman, for example, used to describe a similar shift in the form of 'American character'. Whereas, in Riesman's model, the 'gregarious ideal' of mass society generates an 'other-directed' character which triumphs over the 'inner-directed' type of an earlier American individualism, James's ideal of privacy is both solitary and social.[4] Indeed, as Ross Posnock has extensively argued, James is himself committed to a form of 'other-direction'; one which is implicitly set against the homogenizing forces of mass culture.[5] From this perspective, his pursuit of privacy may be viewed not as a desire for pure solipsistic interiority, but as a means of tracing marks of individual and cultural difference.

Another way of putting this would be to say that, for James, the value of privacy is not in itself private. If, on occasions, privacy is envisaged as a state of solitary refuge in *The American Scene*, it can also facilitate 'the play of the social relation' in a way which distinguishes between different sites of social intercourse. In this sense, James's ideal of privacy is not external to the realm of 'society' since it is, in itself, an ideal of sociability. Conversely, American public culture is deficient, for James, not simply because it privileges social aggregation over the individual, but also because it is *insufficiently* social. This is one of the reasons for his 'scandalized' response to the groups of youths who treat the public space of the Pullman car 'as familiar, domestic, intimate ground, set apart, it might be, for the discussion and regulation of their little interests and affairs, and for that so oddly, so innocently immodest ventilation of their puerile privacies at which the moralizing visitor so frequently gasps' (*AS* 309). While it could certainly be argued that such a reaction reveals the patrician bias of James's ethos of sociability, the fact that he considers such conduct unsociable, rather than merely gregarious, is, nevertheless, interesting to note. In other words, James is concerned not so much with the erosion of privacy which the incident might be taken to represent, as with an erosion of the normative function of public space. By treating the Pullman car as 'intimate ground' for the 'ventilation' of their own private interests, the youths refuse to recognize the boundaries not only between private and public domains but also, and by the same token, between the self and others. While such conduct scales 'the pinnacle of publicity', as James remarks of a similar incident, earlier in the text, it remains self-absorbed, oblivious of the existence of any 'concurrent presence', any 'human or social function' (*AS* 24).

It is for this reason that *The American Scene* deserves to be read not as a nostalgic lament for the disappearance of 'privacy' within the environment of urban modernity, but as a sustained and serious engagement with the characteristic conditions of democratic public life. This engagement is certainly not unique in James's canon since it refers us back, in many ways, to *The Bostonians*. As in the earlier novel, for instance, James is concerned with a deformation of American civil society which he links to a perceived polarization between the masculine sphere of 'business' and the feminine sphere of 'culture'. That James should envisage 'society' as an empty field – as a 'boundless, gaping void' – metaphorically awaiting the impregnation of the male presence, is again, no doubt, indicative of the anxious correlation between 'feminization' and mass culture which I examined in earlier chapters (*AS* 247). Yet, as Posnock has argued, James also suggests that the apparent autonomy of female society conceals its dependence upon the interests of commodity production. Civil society is thus reduced to the task of adorning – without disturbing – the rapacity of the market.[6] By contrast, James himself devotes much of *The American Scene* to a critical scrutiny of the unbridled operation of private capitalism, and, in his observations on New York, writes of the need for a new 'civic conscience' (*AS* 102). It is characteristic of the complexity of James's critique that, even when he is concerned primarily with the massification of American culture and its concomitant erosion of individual difference, this does not entail a wholesale rejection of the possibility of collective endeavour. Surveying the New York skyline, for instance, offers 'the vividest of lectures on the subject of individualism, and on the strange truth, no doubt, that this principle may in the field of art – at least if the art be architecture – often conjure away just that mystery of distinction which it sometimes so markedly promotes in the field of life' (*AS* 101). Even 'under the icy breath of Trusts and the weight of the new remorseless monopolies' which begin to mark the corporatization of American capital, capitalist economic development remains a form of rampant individualism, and it is this principle, James suggests, rather than an apparently countervailing collectivism, which hinders the exercise of civic responsibility (*AS* 98). Indeed, if 'conformity and subordination' are authoritarian tendencies 'in the name of which our age has seen such dreary things done', an 'assent to collectivism', he acknowledges, '[may] 'become on a given occasion the one *not* vulgar way of meeting a problem' (*AS* 101). Collectivism, in the planning of urban development, would at least counter the ubiquitous privatization of public space to which the landscape of New York so stridently testifies.

Thus, while recent critics have rightly emphasized James's prescient remarks on the 'American genius for organization', encountered in the administered culture of the hotel, equal weight should be given to his sense of the disorganization of American public life (*AS* 75).[7] James identifies the contradictory logic inherent within the trajectory of capitalist modernization, and the object of his critique is, accordingly, twofold. In his analysis of the 'amazing hotel-world', for instance, James recognizes 'a conception of publicity *as* the vital medium' of social exchange (*AS* 73, 75). The inhabitants of the hotel enter a public stage, but one that has already been prepared for them; 'they were as perfectly in their element', he notes, 'as goldfish in a crystal jar: a form of exhibition suggesting but one question or mystery. Was it they who had invented it, or had it inscrutably invented *them*?' (*AS* 328). Although James does not deny the possibility of reciprocity between the bureaucratic administration of the hotel and the 'ingenuous joy' of its inhabitants, the hotel-world is, nevertheless, a graphic figure for the 'representative' form of publicity, directed solely to the display of its own institutional prestige, which, for Habermas, marks the 'refeudalization' of the modern public sphere (*AS* 76).[8] Of central importance to James's understanding of this modern form of publicity, however, is its contradiction of the positive principle of publicity inscribed within his own ethos of civic responsibility. As Mark Seltzer suggests, the visibility of the hotel also represents a form of surveillance, since the exhibition of its public is orchestrated by an 'absolute presiding power' which itself remains invisible (*AS* 76).[9] In this sense, modern 'publicity' is a decidedly private affair. The 'supremely gregarious state' of its public is not an unconditioned effect of urban 'mass' society, but a phenomenon which is mediated by the play of private – and literally unseen – interests (*AS* 75). It is for this reason that I would disagree with Posnock's 'insistence on the primacy of interest' as the basis of James's cultural criticism in *The American Scene.*[10] Certainly, James acknowledges the interested nature of his own critical stance, and thus avoids the Arnoldian assumption of disinterest which he satirized in many of his fictional narrators. In itself, however, the unfettered play of private interests, which Posnock equates with James's political pluralism, is incompatible with his simultaneous cultivation of a 'civic conscience'. By definition, the very fact that James is capable of recognizing that he *has* a private interest implies the possibility of transcending (without necessarily erasing) these limits, and it is this possibility which his reading of the public monuments and institutions of America constantly endeavours to elicit.

In this respect, one of the most interesting moments in *The American Scene* occurs during James's record of his visit to New York's

City Hall. There, as I have mentioned, James notes the difference between European and American conceptions of the appropriate relationship between the private citizen and the public institution, and suggests that the absence of *penetralia* in the case of the latter erodes the distinctive character of public space. Ironically, as we have also seen, James's argument in favour of preserving the constitutive difference of the public institution looks like an argument for preserving its privacy. What makes the public institution seem public is the existence of those boundaries which can also function as a means of guarding the prestige of a privileged social elite. A further irony, however, is that as James proceeds to explore City Hall, he also begins to exercise – and to enjoy – the rights of the democratic citizen who feels that 'the public, the civic building is his very own'. Unlike in Europe, he is able to enter 'unchallenged' the 'old official, the old so thick-peopled local, municipal world', and penetrate the very heart of administrative power (*AS* 70). Yet instead of leading to a comfortable accommodation with the representatives of public office, with the 'portraits of past worthies, past celebrities and city fathers, Mayors, Bosses, Presidents, Governors, Statesmen at large', James uses this opportunity as an occasion for exposing their 'frankest responsibility' for the rapacious exploitation of the city (*AS* 70, 71). Contrary to our initial expectations, perhaps, the 'florid ghosts' of City Hall do not embody an earlier ideal of civic society, in opposition to the urban development of modern New York, but are themselves directly implicated in 'those monsters of the mere market' (*AS* 71, 57). The 'collective presence' of the portraits 'becomes a kind of copious tell-tale document signed with a hundred names', and the place where this evidence may be read is not in the impressive architectural achievement of City Hall, but 'all the way from river to river and from the Battery to Harlem, the place in which there is most of the terrible town' (*AS* 71). City Hall itself is thus no longer the aesthetic oasis which it initially appeared to be, but a space that is directly 'continuous', as Seltzer observes elsewhere, with the more extrusive manifestations of economic and social power.[11]

What is most significant about James's recognition of the complicity between civic authority and private commercial interests, however, is his exemplary practice of a certain kind of critical publicity. By exposing the concealed corruption of the public officials within his own published text, James enters City Hall, one might argue, in the true spirit of the 'muckraking' journalist. But in order to do so, he must adopt a stance of critical scrutiny which neither congeals nor entirely collapses the difference between private and public space. If James takes advantage of the democratic accessibility of City Hall in a way that the prestige of European institutions would have precluded, his investigative posture is, nevertheless, distinctly different from the assurance of intimacy which derives from the American theory of a complete identity between private citizen and public authority. It is this sense of 'safe sociability, as all equally initiated and interested – not as in a temple or a citadel, but by the warm domestic hearth of Columbia herself' that James was to recognize in the national civic centre of Washington (*AS* 259). The 'national relation' to the Capitol also appears to relinquish the majesty of public authority with the effect 'of a certain large, final benignity' (*AS* 259). But the cost of such familiarity, as James also sufficiently indicates, is a calculated 'social indifference' towards the exercise of political and administrative power on the part of the 'City of Conversation' (*AS* 245). The extinction of all difference between private and public interests leads to a complacent assumption of commonality, which limits the space for critical scrutiny. By contrast, James's unexpected access to City Hall produces an experience of estrangement from (rather than one of intimacy with) the 'personal look' of authority, which allows him both to preserve the particularity of the public interest and to recognize its absence in the corridors of power (*AS* 71). Whereas intimacy would perpetuate the occlusion which persists at the centre of City Hall's apparent public accessibility, estrangement, conversely, is the means by which James counters the conditions of American culture with his own practice of publicity.

THE BIRTH OF A LION

If James's return to the United States was an opportunity for the novelist to record his impressions of the publicity of American culture, however, it was also an occasion on which the practitioners of publicity recorded their impressions of James. Besides generating an enthusiastic response to his series of public lectures, James's visit also attracted considerable attention in the American press. Ironically, much of this attention was manifested in a form which James himself had previously satirized in such tales as 'The Death of the

Lion' and 'John Delavoy'. During the visit, at least two interviews with James were published, as well as a number of illustrated articles on his home at Rye.[12] By way of concluding this study, then, it is worth recalling the fact that James was by no means detached from the forms of publicity which his own fiction and criticism so persistently challenged. In assessing the significance of James's critique of mass culture, it is also worth remembering that this perspective can always be reversed.

What is most striking about the American press coverage of James's visit is its open acknowledgement of his resistance to the cultural practices embodied by the journalists themselves. In an interview published in the *New York Herald* on 2 October 1904, Florence Brooks, for example, declared that 'Henry James has never been "interviewed". It is one of his cherished habits to keep out of the sort of gaze that follows the limelight.'[13] Interestingly, exactly the same claim was made in another journalistic 'exclusive' eleven years later. In 1915 the *New York Times* published an interview with James under the headline: 'Henry James's First Interview / Noted Critic and Novelist Breaks his Rule of Years to Tell of the Good Work of the American Ambulance Corps'.[14] James's 'rule' of refusing interviews was thus more flexible, it would seem, than was claimed by those who endeavoured to break it. Indeed, it is tempting to suggest that James's desire to avoid 'the sort of gaze that follows the limelight' was magnified by the very journalists whose interests might appear to have been threatened by it. Like some grim parody of 'John Delavoy', the idea of James's aversion to publicity was actively fostered within the media of publicity: the scarcity of his interviews became the measure of their commercial value.

A different response to the discrepancy between such journalistic claims and the media in which they were articulated, however, would be to observe that James himself was more willing to comply with the demands of personal publicity than his fictional stories of beleaguered artists would lead us to believe. Such publicity was an increasingly important commodity for authors wishing to enhance the visibility of their work, and although James privately complained about the journalistic attention which surrounded his return to America, he clearly consented to much of it.[15] Evidence of this consent is provided in an article entitled 'Mr. Henry James at Home', written by Sidney Brooks and published in *Harper's Weekly* on 8 October 1904. This article consisted of a brief written text and a series of illustrative photographs displaying various interior and exterior views of Lamb House. The photographs were clearly commissioned with this particular purpose in mind, since in one of them James is shown posing frontally in the garden, and in another he can be seen, from a distance, seated outside the house.[16] Such images were a familiar component of contemporary literary interviews: authors were often represented in a proud, proprietorial relationship to their homes, inviting, rather than resisting, the gaze of the camera.[17] Indeed, while Brooks's article is not strictly an interview, it offers a straightforward example of the 'author at home' genre which James had parodied in 'The Death of the Lion'. In this instance, however, it is James himself who plays host to what he had termed 'the art of finding people at home' (*CT* IX 78).

What is also interesting about this article, though, is the way in which Brooks sets out to represent James (in writing) as a solitary, reclusive figure, whose domestic environment tangibly inscribes his distance from the self-promotional world of publicity. As a representative of this world, Brooks appears to lack any sense of irony in declaring that James 'has made his home, far enough away from the distractions and multitudinous inroads of London life', and that '[h]ere he can work and live in peace and possess himself'.[18] The fact that James's private idyll is not 'far enough away' from Brooks himself sufficiently reveals the oxymoronic strategy by which the journalist evokes a world that is other than the world of publicity and yet only realized through the mediation of publicity. This is essentially the same strategy which James himself was to detect during a visit to the 'home' of Washington Irving, which he records in *The American Scene*. Sunnyside, James observed, 'is inevitably, today, but a qualified Sleepy Hollow . . . for "modernity", with its terrible power of working its will, of abounding in its sense, of gilding its toy – modernity, with its pockets full of money and its conscience full of virtue, its heart really full of tenderness, has seated itself there under pretext of guarding the shrine' (*AS* 110–11). The fate of such 'shy retreats of anchorites' is not simply that they are 'doomed to celebrity', but that celebrity itself is 'dedicated to the history of the hermit' (*AS* 111). The tourist industry which surrounds Irving's home – like the journalist who records James's idyll – simultaneously dispels and exploits the possibility of a refuge from publicity, and thus, in effect, the possibility of its own negation.

Florence Brooks offers an even more striking example of this rhetorical strategy than her namesake Sidney. In the *New York Herald* interview, the mediating presence of the journalist is similarly effaced by her representation of a world which appears distant from, or even hostile to, the world of publicity. Thus, she observes that James's 'life of seclusion for twenty years in England and on the Continent has kept him personally out of the public eye, which he very much prefers to the amiable habit we have of advertising celebrity'. Indeed, it is precisely James's refusal to court publicity, according to Brooks, which has created such a great public interest in him. In a passage which bears a strong resemblance to Sidney Brooks's representation of James's home at Rye, she encodes this principle within the very landscape in which James (allegedly) moves. Upon his arrival in America, she insists, the novelist 'retired at once into the background', where 'Crowds either curious or critical have not yet seen him, hidden as he is in the gentle hills, inaccessible, removed from railway, from all publicity in the heart of New England, miles north of Boston.' Here, Brooks emphasizes the gesture of concealment in order to reinforce the revelatory strategy of her text: hidden within the folds of the landscape, James seems to disappear from common view, only to re-emerge before the privileged gaze of the interviewer. Similarly, recalling the moment of her meeting with James, Brooks claims that 'after a kindly if bewildered welcome from this man who is called intensely shy, he was found to relinquish himself with delightful confidence to that profane rite, an interview'.[19] While Brooks is keen to stress James's eventual compliance with the 'profane rite' of the interview, and so to secure its claim to the authentic 'intimacy' of confession, she also attempts to preserve the aura which separates the celebrity from the 'ordinary' reader. Something inscrutable in James's 'shyness' prevents him from becoming a merely transparent presence within the text.

According to Leo Braudy, this enigmatic quality is entirely characteristic of modern representations of literary (and other forms of) fame. It is precisely that which seems to be concealed beneath the surface of the public persona, Braudy suggests, which signifies the 'authenticity' of the celebrity.[20] Thus, what seems to elude the cultural visibility of fame is, in fact, what defines it. In a story by Max Beerbohm, set in the 1890s but not published until 1927, Braudy finds a telling illustration of this point. 'Felix Argallo and Walter Ledgett' shows how the nephew of a famous author astutely manages his uncle's reputation by seeming to neglect it: 'It was he that sent interviewers and photographers empty away. "Privacy is the biggest Ad", he once said to me, with a wink.'[21] By refusing publicity on behalf of Argallo, the nephew, George Batford, realizes that the scarcity of the commodity will cause its value to rise. The cultivation of 'private' experience, so often conventionally opposed to the 'artifice' of publicity, is itself, Beerbohm suggests, another form of artifice. If it seems unlikely that James was as cunning an exploiter of his 'privacy' as Beerbohm's character, the same principle of publicity may, nevertheless, be applied. It was James's (apparent) reluctance to be interviewed that proved to be his most valuable asset as a subject for interviewers, just as his own resistance to publicity was incorporated into the medium of publicity, not covertly, but through its open acknowledgement.

Indeed, one gathers from reading Florence Brooks's interview with James that the subject of publicity was raised in the course of their meeting. In defence of his aversion to celebrity, James is quoted as remarking that 'One's craft, one's art, is his expression . . . not one's person, as that of a great actress or singer is hers' [sic]. Moreover, Brooks concedes that James's reticence does not arise from his inability to 'understand the journalistic life', since 'he has done it wonderfully in a bit of fiction called "The Papers"'. Her acknowledgement of James's opposition to publicity, however, does not disturb the self-assurance of the text. James's characteristic objection to the excessive interest in literary 'personalities' is accommodated within a discursive practice which exemplifies that very interest; likewise, Brooks seems unconcerned that James's 'bit of fiction' satirizes the very activity – the interviewer's pursuit of 'Personal Peeps' into the lives of celebrities – in which she is engaged (*CT* XII 52). Without effacing the resistance of its subject, then, the medium of the interview appears capable of absorbing or dispelling it. This dual strategy has the effect of creating radically discontinuous propositions within the text. At one point, for instance, Brooks demands why 'the public' should expect James 'to splash himself, reveal his person on paper?', to which she replies that 'The kindly manner of the author . . . refutes his demand to be let alone.'[22] If the reply seems scarcely adequate to the question, its very incoherence remains functional, dramatizing as it does the dialectic of concealment and revelation which allows James's 'private' self to be more teasingly unveiled.

The tendency of interviewers to thematize the reticence or

resistance of their subjects is also exemplified in a second interview with James, published during his American visit. Witter Bynner's article 'A Word or Two with Henry James' was published in the literary journal *The Critic* in February 1905, and, in terms of its style and medium, is certainly very different to Florence Brooks's text. Yet despite its more august setting, and the fact that Bynner was himself a poet and critic rather than a 'journalist', the article adopts strategies that are not dissimilar to those of the popular celebrity interview. Most notably, Bynner again acknowledges (or produces) his subject's antipathy to being interviewed during a dramatized encounter, at the end of which he quotes James's valedictory words:

> May I add, since you spoke of having been asked to write something about me, that I have a constituted and systematic indisposition to having anything to do myself personally with anything in the nature of an interview, report, reverberation, that is, to adopting, endorsing, or in any other wise taking to myself anything that anyone may have presumed to contrive to gouge, as it were, out of me? It has, for me, nothing to do with *me* – *my* me, at all; but only with the other person's equivalent for that mystery, whatever it may be. Thereby if you find anything to say about our apparently blameless time together, – it is your little affair exclusively.[23]

As in Florence Brooks's interview, one can only speculate as to the authenticity of the speech which is here attributed to James. In later years, Bynner himself revealed that this so-called 'interview', which had appeared to represent the transcript of a particular occasion, was, in fact, compiled from notes which he had previously taken of James's conversation. The scripted nature of the 'interview' was such that, when James gave Bynner permission to publish his notes in the form of a dialogue, he initially suggested that the proofs be sent to him for correction.[24] If one accepts that Bynner's quotation is, to some degree, accurate, however, it also offers an interesting (and ironically appropriate) statement of James's awareness of the distinction between what he terms '*my* me' and the representation of this 'me' within the medium of the interview. By refusing to endorse the figure which the interviewer will have 'contrive[d] to gouge . . . out' of him, James, in effect, withdraws his sanction from Bynner's interview at the end of the interview itself. Similarly, in a letter which Bynner quotes in his later recollection of the circumstances surrounding the 'interview', James finally urged Bynner not to submit the proofs of the article to him on the grounds that 'I shouldn't know how to participate little *enough*, and I had much rather participate, frankly and freely, in you as yourself than in you – as not yourself!'[25] By deciding not to correct the proofs of the 'interview', and thus not to collaborate in what is 'nothing to do with *me*', James deliberately refrains from authorizing a representation of himself which is, more accurately, Bynner's self-representation. The interview's figuration of him, he suggests, belongs properly to Bynner's 'you', rather than to his own 'me'.

By denying that Bynner's interview has anything to do with himself, James is also refuting the primary function of the interview, as it was commonly conceived at the time. As a particular form of 'investigative' journalism, the interview, as I suggested earlier, claimed implicitly to reveal an inner truth about its subject. It was the 'private' experience of the celebrity which was valued as a sign of authenticity. Through the tortuous language of his correspondence with Bynner, however, James suggests that the medium of the interview re-presents the interiority of the private self in a manner which only reveals its oxymoronic project. Committed, rhetorically, to the preservation of an inner self, the interview is simultaneously the agent of its dispersal or 'reverberation'. Yet the very fact that it is possible to elicit this reading of Bynner's interview is also symptomatic of the same process. The fact that James's refusal to sanction Bynner's text is staged within the text itself allows both for this possibility of reading the interview 'against the grain' and of further reinforcing its own signifying strategies. Significantly, in the concluding line of the quotation, James hands over all responsibility for the interview by conceding that 'it is your little affair exclusively'. With this pun on the journalistic 'exclusive', the note of renunciation, upon which the article itself ends, simultaneously appears to license Bynner's text by giving it a free interpretive rein. James's rejection of the interview is finally made to look like its endorsement.

In many respects, then, these journalistic texts reveal the rather ironic fate of James's own literary celebrity. The publicity surrounding James's return to America in 1904 took as one of its principal themes his life-long resistance to publicity. The cultural critique which he had elaborated over the course of the preceding thirty years came to be incorporated into the very cultural practices against which it was directed. Yet perhaps the deeper irony of this fate is that James himself had so often anticipated its occurrence within his own fiction and criticism. If an interview with James might seem to be the last place in which to find an approving reference to 'The Papers', this story had itself acknowledged the impossibility of evading the cultural forms which it satirized. Having vainly attempted to master the 'strange logic' of the 'great forces of publicity', the journalist Howard Bight is finally forced to confront the fact that the Papers are capable of appropriating all forms of resistance to themselves, including such gestures of negation as silence or anonymity (*CT* XII 86). To this extent, the incorporation of 'The Papers' into the context of the *New York Herald* verifies James's prior apprehension of the accumulative energies of the mass media. If James had consistently recognized the extent to which modern publicity functions as a metalanguage, capable of translating other voices into its own frame of reference, then Florence Brooks literally enacts this insight by extending the chain of self-referential texts. The interview, in short, confirms what James had already suspected.

Notes

INTRODUCTION

1 For an interesting discussion of this rhetorical function of 'public' discourse, see Michael Warner, 'The Mass Public and the Mass Subject' in *The Phantom Public Sphere*, ed. Bruce Robbins (Minneapolis and London: University of Minnesota Press, 1993), pp. 234–6.

2 Thus, during the eighteenth century, according to Habermas, the formation of the literary public sphere was paradoxically accompanied by a proliferation of publications which purported to express the realm of 'private' subjectivity. See Jürgen Habermas, *The Structural Transformation of the Public Sphere: An Inquiry into a Category of Bourgeois Society*, tr. Thomas Burger with the assistance of Frederick Lawrence (Cambridge: Polity Press, 1992), pp. 32–51.

3 For an interesting, and by no means unsophisticated, exposition of this claim, see Richard Sennett, *The Fall of Public Man* (London and Boston: Faber and Faber, 1993), pp. 259–68.

4 This is an argument which Leon Edel's influential interpretation of the pivotal significance of James's reaction to his traumatic experience of the theatre did much to consolidate. See, for example, Leon Edel, *Henry James: A Life* (London: Collins, 1987), pp. 481–2.

5 For somewhat different versions of this argument against James's withdrawal into a purely private realm of aesthetic value, see Jean-Christophe Agnew, 'The Consuming Vision of Henry James' in *The Culture of Consumption: Critical Essays in American History, 1880–1980*, ed. Richard Wightman Fox and T.J. Jackson Lears (New York: Pantheon, 1983), pp. 87–91; Marcia Jacobson, *Henry James and the Mass Market* (Alabama: University of Alabama Press, 1983), pp. 18–19, 92–9, 142–4; and Michael Anesko, *'Friction with the Market': Henry James and the Profession of Authorship* (New York and Oxford: Oxford University Press, 1986), p. 25.

6 See Jacobson, *Henry James and the Mass Market*; Anesko, *'Friction with the Market'*; and Anne T. Margolis, *Henry James and the Problem of Audience: An International Act* (Ann Arbor: UMI Research Press, 1985).

7 See Fredric Jameson, 'Reification and Utopia in Mass Culture', *Social Text: Theory, Culture, Ideology*, 1, 1979, pp. 133–4; and also, by the same

author, *The Political Unconscious: Narrative as a Socially Symbolic Act* (London and New York: Routledge, 1989), pp. 206–8.

8 On this point, see Theodor Adorno and Max Horkheimer, *Dialectic of Enlightenment*, tr. John Cumming, 2nd edn (London and New York: Verso, 1986), p. 135; and Adorno's letter to Walter Benjamin, dated 18 March 1936, in Ernst Bloch *et al.*, *Aesthetics and Politics*, tr. and ed. Rodney Taylor (London: NLB, 1977), p. 123.

9 See Agnew, 'The Consuming Vision', pp. 79, 83, 76.

10 See Guy Debord, *Society of the Spectacle* (Detroit: Black and Red, 1983).

11 For contributions to this debate, see Craig Calhoun, ed., *Habermas and the Public Sphere* (Cambridge, Mass. and London: The MIT Press, 1992); and Bruce Robbins, ed., *The Phantom Public Sphere* (Minneapolis and London: University of Minnesota Press, 1993).

12 See Habermas, *Structural Transformation*, pp. 14–36, 51–6, 79–117.

13 Ibid., pp. 141–201.

14 See Alexis de Tocqueville, *Democracy in America*, 2 vols., tr. Henry Reeve (New York: Alfred A. Knopf, 1945), vol. II, p. 10.

15 Matthew Arnold, *Letters of Matthew Arnold 1848–1888*, 2 vols., collected and arranged by George W.E. Russell (London and New York: Macmillan, 1895), vol. II, p. 221.

16 See Matthew Arnold, *The Complete Prose Works of Matthew Arnold*, 11 vols., ed. R.H. Super (Ann Arbor: University of Michigan Press, 1960–77), vol. X, p. 7; and James, *LC* I, pp. 719–31. For details of the extensive private exchanges between Arnold and James during this period, see the editorial notes to 'A Word about America' in Arnold, ibid., vol. X, pp. 449–50.

17 See Alfred Habegger, *Gender, Fantasy, and Realism in American Literature* (New York: Columbia University Press, 1982), p. 301, and *Henry James and the 'Woman Business'* (Cambridge: Cambridge University Press, 1989), pp. 58–61, 225–8.

18 See Andreas Huyssen, *After the Great Divide: Modernism, Mass Culture, Postmodernism* (Houndmills: Macmillan, 1988), pp. 44–62.

19 On James's attitude towards the perceived predominance of women writers within the literary market, see Habegger, *Henry James and the 'Woman Business'*, pp. 15–26, 63–125; and Margolis, *Henry James and the Problem of Audience*, pp. 6–10, 152–3.

20 Although Habermas is aware of the fact that women were excluded (both in principle and often in fact) from the institutions of the bourgeois public sphere, he neglects the ramifications of this insight. For a discussion of this failure, see Nancy Fraser, 'Rethinking the Public Sphere: A Contribution to the Critique of Actually Existing Democracy' in *The Phantom Public Sphere*, ed. Bruce Robbins (Minneapolis and London: University of Minnesota Press, 1993), pp. 5–23.

21 For Kant's conception of the *sensus communis* (or '*public* sense') necessarily involved in judgements of taste, see Immanuel Kant, *The Critique of*

Judgement, tr. James Meredith Creed (Oxford: Clarendon Press, repr. 1992), pp. 42–50, 84–5, 150–4. For Arnold's emphasis on critical 'disinterest', see 'The Function of Criticism at the Present Time' (1865) in *Complete Prose*, vol. III, pp. 268–83.

22 See Pierre Bourdieu, *Distinction: A Social Critique of the Judgement of Taste*, tr. Richard Nice (London: Routledge, 1989), pp. 485–500.

23 See Ian F.A. Bell, *Henry James and the Past: Readings into Time* (Houndmills: Macmillan, 1991), pp. 1–11; and for a similar emphasis on James's dissolution of boundaries, see Ross Posnock, *The Trial of Curiosity: Henry James, William James, and the Challenge of Modernity* (New York and Oxford: Oxford University Press, 1991), pp. 6–24.

24 See Bell, *Henry James and the Past*, p. 11.

25 For an interesting reading of the figure of the 'newspaperman' in *The Sacred Fount*, see Thomas Strychacz, *Modernism, Mass Culture, and Professionalism* (Cambridge: Cambridge University Press, 1993), pp. 73–4.

1 TRANSFORMATIONS OF THE PUBLIC SPHERE IN *THE BOSTONIANS*

1 Rita Felski uses the term 'counter-public sphere' to refer to the oppositional status of feminist discourse. See Felski, *Beyond Feminist Aesthetics: Feminist Literature and Social Change* (London: Hutchinson Radius, 1989), pp. 9–12.

2 See Habegger, *Henry James and the 'Woman Business'*, pp. 189–90, 225–6.

3 Ibid., pp. 182–9.

4 See Bell, *Henry James and the Past*, p. 65.

5 See Jennifer Wicke, *Advertising Fictions: Literature, Advertisement, and Social Reading* (New York: Columbia University Press, 1988), pp. 90–6.

6 For a discussion of this form of advertising, see Wicke, *Advertising Fictions*, pp. 92–3.

7 See Bell, *Henry James and the Past*, pp. 84–5; for Marx's discussion of 'commodity fetishism', see Karl Marx, *Capital: A Critique of Political Economy*, vol. I, tr. Ben Fowkes (Harmondsworth: Penguin, 1990), pp. 163–77.

8 The naturalistic elements of *The Bostonians* may well have been derived from James's reading of Zola's novel, *Nana*, which he reviewed in 1880, the year of its publication. Like James's novel, *Nana* may be read as a study of the histrionic 'character' (in this case, that of an actress) and the surrounding influence of her theatrical milieu. See Emile Zola, *Nana*, tr. George Holden (Harmondsworth: Penguin, 1987); for James's review, see *LC* II, pp. 864–70.

9 Marx, *Capital*, p. 165.

10 Roland Barthes, *Mythologies*, tr. Annette Lavers (London: Vintage, 1993), p. 90.

11 As examples, see Agnew, 'The Consuming Vision', pp. 81–97; Wicke,

Advertising Fictions, pp. 90–102; and Bell, *Henry James and the Past*, pp. 173–205.

12 Agnew, 'The Consuming Vision', p. 70.

13 For Baudrillard's definition of 'sign-value', see *Le Système des objets* (Paris: Gallimard, 1968), pp. 276–7. Wicke points out that, prior to the use of brand names in advertising, commodities were commonly represented by generic symbols, which denoted a particular class of otherwise undifferentiated goods. See *Advertising Fictions*, pp. 29–30, 59–60.

14 For a similar argument with regard to the complicity of Basil's oppositional stance, see Bell, *Henry James and the Past*, p. 81.

15 See Sennett, *The Fall of Public Man*, pp. 211–13. For a discussion of feminist responses to Sennett's book, see Laura Marcus, *Auto/biographical Discourses: Theory, Criticism, Practice* (Manchester and New York: Manchester University Press, 1994), pp. 174–5.

16 See Max Weber, *On Charisma and Institutional Building: Selected Papers*, ed. S.N. Eisenstadt (Chicago and London: University of Chicago Press, 1968), pp. 48–54.

17 See Brook Thomas, 'The Construction of Privacy In and Around *The Bostonians*', *American Literature*, 64 (4), December 1992, pp. 740–1.

18 See 'The Speech of American Women' in Henry James, *French Writers and American Women*, ed. Peter Buitenhuis (Branford, Conn.: Compass, 1960), pp. 32–53; and *The Question of Our Speech, The Lesson of Balzac: Two Lectures* (Boston and New York: Houghton, Mifflin, 1905), pp. 3–51. For Habegger's comments on 'The Speech of American Women', see *Henry James and the 'Woman Business'*, p. 235.

19 James, *The Question of Our Speech*, pp. 11–12, 29–30, 14.

20 Ibid., pp. 33, 34, 51–2.

21 In *The American Scene*, James argued that the American businessman had 'abdicated' his cultural responsibilities, leaving the field of 'society' to be occupied by women (*AS* 247–8). Yet James's position in relation to the gendered spheres of business and culture was ambiguous, not least in terms of his own masculinity. On this point, see Habegger, *Gender, Fantasy and Realism*, pp. 263–5. For James's references to contemporary changes in the status of women in his essays on Sand and Serao, see *LC* II, pp. 774–5, 780–2, 956–7; and for his involvement in *Votes for Women*, see Elizabeth Robins, *Theatre and Friendship* (London and Toronto: Jonathan Cape, 1934), pp. 263–9.

22 See Marx, *Capital*, pp. 187, 198.

23 See Richard Godden, 'Some Slight Shifts in the Manner of the Novel of Manners' in *Henry James: Fiction as History*, ed. Ian F.A. Bell (London: Vision, 1984) p. 175.

24 See Thorstein Veblen, *The Theory of the Leisure Class: An Economic Study of Institutions* (New York: Random House, 1934), pp. 22–4.

25 A similar reconfiguration of interior and exterior space is suggested by Walter Benjamin's description of the nineteenth-century arcade as 'a

cross between a street and an *intérieur*'. See *Charles Baudelaire: A Lyric Poet in the Era of High Capitalism*, tr. Harry Zohn (London and New York: Verso, 1989), pp. 36–7. For a more recent discussion of the shop window and its mediation of subjectivity and desire, see Rachel Bowlby, *Just Looking: Consumer Culture in Dreiser, Gissing and Zola* (New York and London: Methuen, 1985), pp. 32–4.

26 See Veblen, *Theory of the Leisure Class*, pp. 81–5.

27 For a discussion of this ideological separation, see Carole Pateman, 'Feminist Critiques of the Public/Private Dichotomy' in *Public and Private in Social Life*, ed. S.I. Benn and G.F. Gaus (London and Canberra: Croom Helm, 1983), pp. 281–303.

28 See Habermas, *Structural Transformation*, pp. 27–31, 45.

29 As Michael Warner has suggested, the American tradition of civic republicanism may be seen as a specific variant of the bourgeois public sphere, as defined in general terms by Habermas. See Warner, *The Letters of the Republic: Publication and the Public Sphere in Eighteenth-Century America* (Cambridge, Mass. and London: Harvard University Press, 1990), pp. x–xiii.

30 See Habermas, *Structural Transformation*, pp. 28–30, 46–7, 55–6, 74–5, 87–8, 109–11. On the inadequacy of Habermas's attention to gender as a determining category of the bourgeois public sphere, see Introduction, n. 20.

31 See Habermas, *Structural Transformation*, pp. 36–43, 52–5, 84–8. Ian Bell finds a similar insistence upon maintaining the 'necessary otherness' of the public domain in James's reading of Emerson and Sainte-Beuve. See *Henry James and the Past*, p. 131.

32 For an account of these journalistic and biographical representations of authorship, see Daniel H. Borus, *Writing Realism: Howells, James, and Norris in the Mass Market* (Chapel Hill, NC and London: University of North Carolina Press, 1989), pp. 127–8; and also Richard D. Altick, *Lives and Letters: A History of Literary Biography in England and America* (New York: Alfred A. Knopf, 1966), pp. 117–18, 259–60.

33 For a discussion of this common accusation, see Hazel Dicken-Garcia, *Journalistic Standards in Nineteenth-Century America* (Madison, Wis.: University of Wisconsin Press, 1989), pp. 190–6.

34 De Tocqueville, *Democracy in America*, vol. 1, p. 318.

35 See Habermas, *Structural Transformation*, pp. 129–40.

36 Unlike Basil, de Tocqueville was a broadly sympathetic observer of American democracy, as he states in his preface to the second volume of *Democracy in America*.

37 See Fraser, 'Rethinking the Public Sphere', pp. 21–3.

38 Habegger makes a similar point about the apparent conflation of journalism and the women's movement in the novel, but assumes that this strategy is entirely authorized by James. See *Henry James and the 'Woman Business'*, p. 226.

39 Ann Douglas, *The Feminization of American Culture* (New York: Alfred A. Knopf, 1979), p. 254.

40 Ibid., pp. 6–13.

41 For a reading of *The Bostonians* which emphasizes the importance of Verena's performative self in a different context, see Philip Fisher, 'Appearing and Disappearing in Public: Social Space in Late-Nineteenth-Century Literature and Culture' in *Reconstructing American Literary History*, ed. Sacvan Bercovitch (Cambridge, Mass. and London: Harvard University Press, 1986), pp. 155–88.

42 See Mary Jean Corbett, *Representing Femininity: Middle-Class Subjectivity in Victorian and Edwardian Women's Autobiographies* (New York and Oxford: Oxford University Press, 1992), pp. 129, 141.

43 See Henry James to Mrs. Humphrey Ward, 9 December 1884 in *L* III, pp. 58–60; for Edel's interpretation of this letter, see *Henry James: A Life*, p. 294. Bell also notes the 'distance' between James's comments on *Miss Bretherton* and his concerns in *The Bostonians*, although without reading the former as a challenge to the latter. See *Henry James and the Past*, pp. 141–2.

44 Bell, *Henry James and The Past*, p. 11.

45 Charles Knowles Bolton, *The Reign of the Poster: Being Comments and Criticism* (Boston: Winthrop B. Jones, 1895), [p. 1] (no pagination).

46 For the most celebrated definition of the *flâneur*, see Benjamin, *Charles Baudelaire*, pp. 53–6.

47 Agnew offers a similar description of the twentieth-century urban environment. See 'The Consuming Vision', p. 67.

48 Richardson Evans, *The Age of Disfigurement* (London and Sydney: Remington & Co., 1893), pp. 6, 72–3.

2 WHAT THE PUBLIC WANTS: CRITICISM, THEATRE AND THE 'MASSES'

1 F. Marion Crawford, *The Novel: What it Is* (London and New York: Macmillan, 1893), pp. 20, 13.

2 See Leon Edel, *Henry James: The Treacherous Years 1895–1901* (London: Rupert Hart-Davis, 1969), pp. 15–88; and 'Henry James: The Dramatic Years' and 'Editor's Foreword' to *Guy Domville* in *The Complete Plays of Henry James*, ed. Leon Edel (London: Rupert Hart-Davis, 1949), pp. 19–69, 465–83. While otherwise attempting to de-mythologize James's dramatic career, Michael Anesko also remains close to Edel's pyschological mode of interpretation. See *'Friction with the Market'*, pp. 11–24.

3 Anesko is primarily concerned with the changing relationships between authors and publishers; Margolis with those between authors and readers.

4 Henry James, *The Princess Casamassima*, ed. Derek Brewer (Harmondsworth: Penguin, 1986), p. 478.

5 See Nigel Cross, *The Common Writer: Life in Nineteenth-Century Grub Street* (Cambridge: Cambridge University Press, 1985), pp. 213–16.
6 Robert Buchanan, *A Look Round Literature* (London: Ward and Downey, 1887), p. 359.
7 See Henry James, 'The Science of Criticism', *The New Review*, 4 (24), 1891, pp. 398–402. Page numbers cited in the text refer to *LC* 1.
8 See Francis Whiting Halsey, *Our Literary Deluge and Some of its Deeper Waters* (London: Grant Richards, 1902), p. 107.
9 Anesko, *'Friction with the Market'*, p. 34.
10 Buchanan, *A Look Round Literature*, p. 360.
11 See Peter Keating, *The Haunted Study: A Social History of the English Novel 1875–1914* (London: Fontana, 1991), pp. 71–2.
12 See Halsey, *Our Literary Deluge*, pp. 3–8.
13 Frederic Harrison, *The Choice of Books and Other Literary Pieces* (London: Macmillan, 1886), pp. 11, 15, 16.
14 Henry James, *Notes of a Son and Brother* (London: Macmillan, 1914), p. 19.
15 Walter Benjamin, 'The Work of Art in the Age of Mechanical Reproduction' in *Illuminations*, tr. Harry Zohn (Bungay: Fontana, 1982), p. 224.
16 James, *Notes of a Son and Brother*, p. 22; emphasis in the original.
17 Bourdieu, *Distinction*, p. 488.
18 Walter Besant, *Autobiography of Sir Walter Besant* (London: Hutchinson, 1902), p. 237.
19 See Walter Besant, 'How Can a Love and Appreciation of Art be Best Developed among the Masses of the People?' in Rev. W. Tuckwell, Charles Godfrey Leland and Walter Besant, *Art and Hand Work for the People: Being Three Papers Read Before the Social Science Congress, September 1884* (Manchester: J.E. Cornish, 1885), pp. 19–32.
20 Buchanan, *A Look Round Literature*, p. 360. For a useful overview of the educational reforms of the 1870s and their perceived role in the formation of a mass reading public, see Keating, *The Haunted Study*, pp. 140–3; and also Raymond Williams, *The Long Revolution* (London: The Hogarth Press, 1992), pp. 137–44, 173–8.
21 For a critique of this separation of production and consumption in early twentieth-century theories of the mass media, see Paolo Carpignano, Robin Andersen, Stanley Aronowitz and William Difazio, 'Chatter in the Age of Electronic Reproduction: Talk Television and the "Public Mind"' in *The Phantom Public Sphere*, ed. Bruce Robbins (Minneapolis and London: University of Minnesota Press, 1993), pp. 93–120.
22 James's adoption of a posture of passive martyrdom is, of course, entirely consonant with the kind of imaginary modernist identification, which, as Huyssen observes, leaves the stigmatization of mass culture as feminine intact. In my view, however, such identifications allow for a less univocal discourse on mass culture than Huyssen suggests. See Huyssen, *After the Great Divide*, pp. 44–55.
23 Ibid., p. 52.

24 Harrison, *The Choice of Books*, p. 66. For an explicit example of this endemic association between the phenomenon of the literary deluge and the quantity of women writers, see 'Advertisement as a Gentle Art', *The National Review*, 26 (155), 1896, p. 655. There is, no doubt, a certain continuity between these late-nineteenth-century assumptions and the similar anxieties which had accompanied the growth of the circulating libraries in the late eighteenth century. On this latter point, see Richard D. Altick, *The English Common Reader: A Social History of the Mass Reading Public 1800–1900* (Chicago: University of Chicago Press, 1957), pp. 63–6.

25 For an early example of James's ascription of the 'fatal gift of fluency' to female writers, see his 1864 review of Harriet Prescott's *Azarian* (*LC* I 610). While such comments might seem to suggest that James advocated an aesthetic economy of rigorous formal control, in line with the stable boundaries of the bourgeois male ego, recent critics have pointed to the existence of contrary impulses in his own fiction and criticism. See, for example, Ross Posnock, *The Trial of Curiosity*, pp. 18–24.

26 This is not to say that James was hostile to Sand's 'fluidity': on the contrary, he was evidently fascinated by it. For further references, see *LC* II, pp. 739, 748, 749–51, 754–5, 758–60, 768, 773, 777, 797.

27 See Habegger, *Henry James and the 'Woman Business'*, pp. 12–26; and Margolis, *Henry James and the Problem of Audience*, pp. 6–10.

28 On the identification of women writers with 'mass audiences' during the late Victorian period, see also Gaye Tuchman with Nina E. Fortin, *Edging Women Out: Victorian Novelists, Publishers, and Social Change* (London: Routledge, 1989), p. 78.

29 This phrase is taken from an essay in which Adorno compares the theatre of Richard Wagner to the rhetorical strategies of mass culture. See *In Search of Wagner*, tr. Rodney Livingstone (London: NLB, 1981), pp. 30–1.

30 Matthew Arnold, 'Numbers: or the Majority and the Remnant' in *Complete Prose*, vol. x, pp. 162, 163.

31 See Keating, *The Haunted Study*, pp. 340–4.

32 See Margolis, *Henry James and the Problem of Audience*, pp. 81–5.

33 Q.D. Leavis, *Fiction and the Reading Public* (London: Chatto and Windus, 1978), p. 163. In a similar vein, see F.R. Leavis, 'Mass Civilization and Minority Culture' (1930), published as an appendix to *Education and the University: A Sketch for an 'English School'* (Cambridge: Cambridge University Press, 1979), pp. 143–71.

34 Arnold, *Complete Prose*, vol. x, p. 164. On the project of establishing an Anglo-American 'Race Union', see Keating, *The Haunted Study*, p. 438.

35 See Posnock, *The Trial of Curiosity*, pp. 276–81. The negative side of James's ambivalence towards linguistic assimilation, however, becomes apparent in 'The Question of Our Speech', a text to which Posnock does not refer.

36 See Margolis, *Henry James and the Problem of Audience*, pp. 81–2.

37 See Regenia Gagnier, *Idylls of the Marketplace: Oscar Wilde and the Victorian Public* (Aldershot: Scolar Press, 1987), pp. 103–35.
38 Adorno and Horkheimer, *Dialectic of Enlightenment*, p. 135.
39 See n. 2 above.
40 Quoted by Edel in James, *The Complete Plays*, p. 49.
41 In a letter to William, James later referred to *Guy Domville* as his 'sacrificed little play' (*L* III 514).
42 See, for example, the comments by George Bernard Shaw, quoted by Edel in James, *The Complete Plays*, p. 479.
43 Edel, 'Editor's Foreword' to *Guy Domville* in James, *The Complete Plays*, p. 474.
44 See Habermas, *Structural Transformation*, pp. 236–50.
45 Gustave Le Bon, *The Crowd: A Study of the Popular Mind* (London: Ernest Benn, 1947), pp. 35–6, 39, 124, 53.
46 See Huyssen, *After the Great Divide*, pp. 52–3.
47 Le Bon, *The Crowd*, p. 150. For James's references to interviewing as a symptomatic practice of modern culture, see *NB* 82, 148.
48 On the later development of Le Bon's political thought, see Robert A. Nye, *The Origins of Crowd Pyschology: Gustave Le Bon and the Crisis of Mass Democracy in the Third Republic* (London and Beverly Hills, Calif.: Sage Publications, 1975), pp. 83–113.
49 Le Bon, *The Crowd*, p. 52.
50 John Carey, *The Intellectuals and the Masses: Pride and Prejudice among the Literary Intelligentsia, 1880–1939* (London and Boston: Faber and Faber, 1992), p. 21.
51 Friedrich Nietzsche, *The Gay Science*, tr. Walter Kaufmann (New York: Vintage Books, 1974), pp. 325–6.
52 On the cuts imposed upon James's plays, see Edel, *The Treacherous Years*, pp. 20–1.
53 See Henrik Ibsen, *An Enemy of the People* in *The Oxford Ibsen*, vol. VI, tr. and ed. James Walter McFarlane (London: Oxford University Press, 1960), pp. 19–126; and Henry James, *The Scenic Art: Notes on Acting and the Drama 1872–1901*, ed. Allan Wade (London: Rupert Hart-Davis, 1949), p. 255. On contemporary drama as a medium for the 'psychology of the masses', see Max Nordau's comments on Ibsen and Gerhart Hauptmann in *Degeneration* (1895) (Lincoln, Nebr. and London: University of Nebraska Press, 1993), pp. 356, 372, 398, 526, 531.
54 For this criticism of the play, see Edel, 'Editor's Foreword' to *Guy Domville* in James, *The Complete Plays*, pp. 480–1.
55 For Edel's reading of the play, see 'Henry James: The Dramatic Years' in James, *The Complete Plays*, pp. 59–60.
56 Henry James, *Guy Domville* in *The Complete Plays*, pp. 489, 486, 490.
57 Ralph Waldo Emerson, 'Success' in *Society and Solitude: The Complete Works of Ralph Waldo Emerson*, 12 vols., with a biographical introduction and notes by Edward Waldo Emerson (Boston and New York: Houghton, Mifflin, 1912), vol. VII, p. 308.

58 Friedrich Nietzsche, *Nietzsche contra Wagner: Out of the Files of a Psychologist* in *The Portable Nietzsche*, ed. and tr. Walter Kaufmann (Harmondsworth: Penguin, 1976), p. 665.
59 For James's use of this dictum in relation to 'The Next Time', see *NB* 180, 200; and in connection with the theatre, see *L* III 509, 510.
60 See Keating, *The Haunted Study*, pp. 439–41.
61 E.A. Bennett, *Fame and Fiction: An Enquiry into Certain Popularities* (London: Grant Richards, 1901), pp. 123, 5–6, 23, 9.
62 See Carey, *The Intellectuals and the Masses*, p. 152.
63 Henry James, 'Edmond Rostand' in *The Scenic Art*, pp. 303, 304.
64 Henry James, *A Small Boy and Others* (London: Macmillan, 1913), p. 361.
65 For examples, see Anesko, *'Friction with the Market'*, p. 25; and Jacobson, *Henry James and the Mass Market*, pp. 92–9. The myth of James's retreat into a 'monastic cell of letters' was fostered, primarily, by Edel. See 'Henry James: The Dramatic Years' in James, *The Complete Plays*, p. 60.

3 'THE INSURMOUNTABLE DESIRE TO *KNOW*': PRIVACY, BIOGRAPHY, AND 'THE ASPERN PAPERS'

1 For James's critical reservations about Flaubert, see his review of the *Correspondence de Gustave Flaubert* (1893) and his 'Introduction to *Madame Bovary*' (1902) in *LC* II, pp. 295–346. The tale that I have in mind, here, is 'The Death of the Lion' (1894), whose Flaubertian narrator is implicitly ironized, as I argue later in this chapter.
2 On the formation of the literary market and its facilitation of a new public rhetoric of private subjectivity, see Habermas, *Structural Transformation*, pp. 49–51; for a similar analysis of the construction of female subjectivity in eighteenth-century periodicals, see Kathryn Shevelow, *Women and Print Culture: The Construction of Femininity in the Early Periodical* (London and New York: Routledge, 1989), pp. 58–92.
3 For a recent account of the Enlightenment valorization of 'curiosity', as well as its subsequent utilitarian reduction to a stigmatized form of idle speculation, see Posnock, *The Trial of Curiosity*, pp. 37–9, 43–5. Posnock's attempt to read James's later career in terms of an affirmative, anti-utilitarian practice of curiosity is fascinating, although it also fails to acknowledge James's persistent criticism of certain cultural forms of the 'desire to know'.
4 For example, see Samuel Taylor Coleridge's similar remarks upon 'the cravings of worthless curiosity' in 'A Prefatory Observation on Modern Biography' (1810), reprinted in *Biography as an Art: Selected Criticism 1560–1960*, ed. James L. Clifford (London: Oxford University Press, 1962), pp. 57–9.
5 See Habermas, *Structural Transformation*, pp. 83–5, 100–2.
6 'The Interview', *The New Princeton Review*, 3, 1887, pp. 127, 130.
7 Ibid., p. 130.

8 Samuel D. Warren and Louis D. Brandeis, 'The Right to Privacy', *Harvard Law Review*, IV (5), 1890, p. 196.

9 Ibid., pp. 197–200, 205. For a slightly different interpretation of Warren and Brandeis's definition of the 'right to privacy' and its bearing upon James's fiction, see Thomas, 'The Construction of Privacy', pp. 721–9, 737–8.

10 M.O.W. Oliphant, 'The Ethics of Biography', *The Contemporary Review*, 44, 1883, p. 84.

11 Ibid., p. 91.

12 These quotations are taken from a letter which James wrote to his literary executor and nephew, Harry James, in April 1914. The extracts are quoted in Ian Hamilton, *Keepers of the Flame: Literary Estates and the Rise of Biography* (London: Hutchinson, 1992), p. 220. For another recent discussion of James's attempt to exert control over the posthumous use of his 'literary remains', see Michael Millgate, *Testamentary Acts: Browning, Tennyson, James, Hardy* (Oxford: Clarendon Press, 1992), pp. 73–109.

13 See Altick, *Lives and Letters*, p. 34; and also Marcus, *Auto/biographical Discourses*, pp. 56–64.

14 Altick, *Lives and Letters*, p. 193.

15 Michel Foucault, *The History of Sexuality* vol. I: *An Introduction*, tr. Robert Hurley (Harmondsworth: Penguin, 1990), pp. 11–12.

16 Ibid., p. 45.

17 See Altick, *Lives and Letters*, pp. 151, 329. For a similar account of the shift from Victorian to 'modern' biographical practices, see Robert Skidelsky, 'Only Connect: Biography and Truth' in *The Troubled Face of Biography*, ed. Eric Homberger and John Charmley (Houndmills: Macmillan, 1988), pp. 1–16.

18 Lytton Strachey, *Eminent Victorians: Cardinal Manning, Florence Nightingale, Dr Arnold, General Gordon* (London: Chatto and Windus, 1918), p. ix.

19 'About Autobiographies', *Chambers' Journal of Popular Literature, Science and Arts*, 5th series, 8 (383), 2 May 1891, p. 335.

20 Here, I would disagree with Adam Bresnick's argument that Vawdrey exists in a state of 'being-for-others', but only through 'sheer specularity with himself'. See Bresnick, 'The Artist that was Used Up: Henry James's "Private Life"', *The Henry James Review*, 14 (1), Winter 1993, p. 94.

21 See Susanne Kappeler, *Writing and Reading in Henry James* (London and Basingstoke: Macmillan, 1980), pp. 34, 58.

22 Ibid., pp. 28–9.

23 See Eve Kosofsky Sedgwick, *Epistemology of the Closet* (Berkeley and Los Angeles: University of California Press, 1990), pp. 195–212.

24 For the narrator's speculation about Gwendolen's possession of Vereker's 'secret', see 'The Figure in the Carpet', *CT* IX, pp. 305–6.

25 Sedgwick, *Epistemology of the Closet*, p. 73.

26 For the possible connection between James's concern with biographical enquiry and his response to the 'scandalous' revelations of the Wilde trial, see Hamilton, *Keepers of the Flame*, pp. 214–15.
27 Sigmund Freud, 'Leonardo da Vinci and a Memory of his Childhood' in *Art and Literature*, The Pelican Freud Library vol. XIV, tr. James Strachey (Harmondsworth: Penguin, 1985), pp. 223, 229.
28 Ibid., p. 225.
29 J. Hillis Miller, 'History, Narrative and Responsibility: Speech Acts in Henry James's "The Aspern Papers"', *Textual Practice*, 9 (2), Summer 1995, pp. 259, 261.
30 Friedrich Nietzsche, *The Will to Power*, tr. Walter Kaufmann and R.J. Hollingdale (New York: Vintage Books, 1968), p. 301. For an interesting account of the broader relationship between James and Nietzsche, see Stephen Donadio, *Nietzsche, Henry James, and the Artistic Will* (New York: Oxford University Press, 1978).
31 For a discussion of Nietzsche's critique of the Kantian distinction between 'phenomenon' and 'noumenon' which underpins the idea of an unknowable object of knowledge, see Ruediger Hermann Grimm, *Nietzsche's Theory of Knowledge* (Berlin and New York: Walter de Gruyter, 1977), pp. 56–60.
32 William James, 'The Will to Believe' in *The Will to Believe and Other Essays in Popular Philosophy* and *Human Immortality: Two Supposed Objections to the Doctrine* (New York: Dover Publications, 1956), p. 21.
33 William James, 'Remarks on Spencer's Definition of Mind as Correspondence' in *Collected Essays and Reviews* (London: Longmans, Green, 1920), p. 66.
34 On this point, see Nietzsche, *The Will to Power*, pp. 267–72.
35 Ibid., p. 314.
36 See Paul B. Armstrong, *The Phenomenology of Henry James* (Chapel Hill, NC and London: University of North Carolina Press, 1983), pp. 40, 52–3.
37 For a useful account of Silsbee's quest, see Robert Gittings and Jo Manton, *Claire Clairmont and The Shelleys 1798–1879* (Oxford and New York: Oxford University Press, 1992), pp. 235–7.
38 Henry James, *The Sacred Fount*, ed. John Lyon (Harmondsworth: Penguin, 1994), p. 40.
39 See Hamilton, *Keepers of the Flame*, pp. 207–13.
40 See, for example, 'She and He: Recent Documents' (1897) and 'George Sand: The New Life' (1902) in *LC* II, pp. 736–55, 755–75.
41 See Gary Scharnhorst, 'James, "The Aspern Papers", and the Ethics of Literary Biography', *Modern Fiction Studies*, 36 (2), Summer 1990, pp. 211–17. For James's own reflections upon his role as biographer in this study, see *Hawthorne* in *LC* I, pp. 349–50.
42 Both Hamilton and Scharnhorst, for example, discuss James's attitude towards biography from a straightforwardly biographical perspective:

the critical aspect of James's thought is not permitted to affect their underlying assumptions.

43 Edward Dowden, 'The Interpretation of Literature', *The Contemporary Review*, 46, May 1886, pp. 701–2.

44 According to Gittings and Manton, Dowden was a self-declared 'fanatical worshipper' of Shelley, although, in his essay, he actually argues against an undue veneration of 'great authors'. See *Claire Clairmont and The Shelleys*, p. 241; and Dowden, 'The Interpretation of Literature', p. 710. On contemporary biographical interest in the Romantics, see Altick, *Lives and Letters*, pp. 177–9, 238.

45 Dowden, 'The Interpretation of Literature', p. 717.

46 See Tzvetan Todorov, 'The Secret of Narrative' in *The Poetics of Prose*, tr. Richard Howard (Ithaca, NY: Cornell University Press, 1992), p. 169.

47 James discussed Flaubert's notion of artistic impersonality in his 1893 review of the *Correspondence de Gustave Flaubert*, where he also noted the ironic disjunction between Flaubert's aesthetic theory and the publication of the letters in which that theory was expounded. It is here that James raised 'the whole question of the rights and duties, the decencies and discretions of the insurmountable desire to *know*' (*LC* II 295–7).

48 See Todorov, 'The Secret of Narrative', pp. 145, 171.

49 For a more extended account of the formation of the New Journalism, see chapter 4.

50 See Altick, *Lives and Letters*, pp. 116–18.

51 Edmund Yates, 'Mark Twain at Hartford' in *Celebrities at Home*, 3 vols., ed. Edmund Yates (London: Office of The World, 1877–9), vol. III, p. 135.

52 Yates's article on Mary Braddon (from which the phrase 'literary workshop' is taken) offers a good example of the way in which he constructs this spatial iconography of privacy. See Yates, 'Miss M.E. Braddon (Mrs Maxwell) at Richmond' in *Celebrities at Home*, vol. I, pp. 319–20.

53 For the periodical publication of this series, see 'English Celebrities at Home', *The World: A Journal for Men and Women*, 5, 23 August 1876, pp. 171–3 and thereafter.

54 On the development of the interview as a journalistic technique, see Nils Gunnar Nilsson, 'The Origin of the Interview', *Journalism Quarterly* (Minneapolis), Winter 1971, pp. 707–13. For examples of the 'author at home' interview, see *The Idler Magazine: An Illustrated Monthly*, 1, 1892 and thereafter; and *The Strand Magazine: An Illustrated Monthly*, 2, 1891 and thereafter.

55 The practice of visiting the 'shrines' of famous authors was fostered and recorded in a host of volumes (some of which consisted of articles reprinted from magazines) published from the mid nineteenth century onwards. The generic proportions reached by this literature are indicated by such formulaic titles as H.B. Baildon *et al.*, *Homes and Haunts*

of Famous Authors (London: Wells Gardner, Darton & Co., 1906); Theodore F. Wolfe, *A Literary Pilgrimage among the Haunts of Some Famous British Authors* (Philadelphia: J.B. Lippincott, 1895); and, by the same author, *Literary Haunts and Homes: American Authors* (Philadelphia: J.B. Lippincott, 1898). The prototypical 'literary pilgrimage' probably centred around Shakespeare's birthplace, which became a site for tourists from as early as the eighteenth century (see Altick, *Lives and Letters*, pp. 115–16). It is this Shakespearean legend, of course, which James satirized in his tale 'The Birthplace' (1903) (see *CT* XI, pp. 403–65).

56 For an example of this strategy, see Yates, 'Mr Tennyson at Haslemere' in *Celebrities at Home*, vol. I, p. 25.

4 THE POWER OF THE PRESS: FROM SCANDAL TO HUNGER

1 Throughout this chapter I will be referring to the original 1888 text of *The Reverberator*, which is significantly different from the revised New York edition. See Henry James, *The Reverberator* (New York: Grove Press, 1957).

2 For examples of this earlier criticism, see Ilse Dusoir Lind, 'The Inadequate Vulgarity of Henry James', *Publications of the Modern Language Association of America*, 66, 1951, pp. 886–910; and Abigail Ann Hamblen, 'Henry James and the Press: A Study of Protest', *The Western Humanities Review*, 11 (2), 1957, pp. 169–75.

3 See Habegger, *Gender, Fantasy, and Realism*, pp. 93–5.

4 See Matthew Arnold, 'Up to Easter' in *Complete Prose*, vol. IX, p. 202.

5 T.P. O'Connor, 'The New Journalism', *The New Review*, 1 (5), 1889, pp. 423, 428–9.

6 For a fascinating account of the debates surrounding the questions of journalistic anonymity and signature from the 1860s onwards, see Laurel Brake, *Subjugated Knowledges: Journalism, Gender and Literature* (Houndmills: Macmillan, 1994), pp. 19–26, 86–91.

7 Tighe Hopkins, 'Anonymity?' [I], *The New Review*, 1 (6), 1889, p. 527.

8 W.T. Stead, 'The Future of Journalism', *The Contemporary Review*, 50, 1886, p. 663.

9 See Williams, *The Long Revolution*, pp. 199–206; Alan J. Lee, *The Origins of the Popular Press in England 1855–1914* (London: Croom Helm, 1980), pp. 79–93, 216–21; and Dicken-Garcia, *Journalistic Standards*, pp. 60–2.

10 On the demise of the politically radical New Journalism, see John Goodbody, 'The *Star*: Its Role in the Rise of the New Journalism' in *Papers for the Millions: The New Journalism in Britain, 1850s to 1914*, ed. Joel H. Wiener (Westport, Conn.: Greenwood Press, 1988), pp. 158–60.

11 W.D. Howells, *A Modern Instance* (Bloomington, Ind. and London: Indiana University Press, 1977), p. 194.

12 Ibid., p. 328.

13 For a discussion of Stead's political campaigns, see Lucy Brown, *Victorian News and Newspapers* (Oxford: Clarendon Press, 1985), pp. 187–93.

14 Howells, *A Modern Instance*, p. 197.

15 Hopkins, 'Anonymity?', p. 530. It is also worth noting that two of James's texts were published in *The New Review* in the same year that the articles by Hopkins and O'Connor appeared: his dialogue 'After the Play' in June 1889 and the first instalment of 'The Solution' in December.

16 Although the term 'New Journalism' was used primarily within a British context, it was often taken to refer to a form of 'personal journalism' which was American in origin; roughly speaking, the development of journalistic discourse in both countries can be seen as parallel. For discussions of this American practice of 'personal journalism', see Dicken-Garcia, *Journalistic Standards*, pp. 200–1; and Michael Schudson, *Discovering the News: A Social History of American Newspapers* (New York: Basic Books, 1978), pp. 88–106.

17 See Adorno, *In Search of Wagner*, pp. 30–1.

18 Here, I am referring to Baudrillard's analysis of the similar rhetorical mode of advertising. See 'Mass Media Culture' in Jean Baudrillard, *Revenge of the Crystal: Selected Writings on the Modern Object and its Destiny, 1968–1983*, ed. and tr. Paul Foss and Julian Pefanis (London and Concord, Mass.: Pluto Press, 1990), p. 94.

19 See Strychacz, *Modernism, Mass Culture, and Professionalism*, pp. 55–7.

20 Ibid., pp. 57–60.

21 Stead, 'The Future of Journalism', p. 664.

22 Margolis argues that James diluted his original conception of a novel which would explore the modern phenomenon of publicity because of the recent critical and commercial failure of a similar project in *The Bostonians*. See *Henry James and the Problem of Audience*, p. 4.

23 Ibid., pp. 4–5.

24 As I show in the previous chapter, to suggest that privacy is often synonymous with a notion of autonomy is not, of course, to argue that James unquestioningly accepted this notion.

25 This is an alignment which is operative, for example, in *The American* (1876–7), where the aristocratic entrenchment of the Bellegardes resembles the collective identity of the Proberts, and where Christopher Newman plays the paradigmatic 'self-made' individual. See Henry James, *The American*, ed. with an introduction by William Spengemann (Harmondsworth: Penguin, 1986).

26 For different reasons, Strychacz has also noted the way in which the apparent opposition between the Proberts and the Dossons (or between 'privacy' and 'publicity') fails to hold true. See *Modernism, Mass Culture, and Professionalism*, pp. 50–2.

27 See *The Oxford English Dictionary*, 20 vols., 2nd edn (Oxford: Clarendon Press, 1989), vol. XIII, pp. 817–18. James also used this word in

expressing his sense of outrage at American press coverage of the Spanish–American war in 1898. In perhaps his strongest statement of hostility towards the press, he informed his brother William that he could 'see nothing but the madness, the passion, the hideous clumsiness of rage, or mechanical reverberation; and I echo with all my heart your denouncement of the foul criminality of the screeching newspapers. They have long since become, for me, the danger that overtops all others' (*L* IV 72).

28 See Dicken-Garcia, *Journalistic Standards*, pp. 53–5.

29 See Frank Luther Mott, *American Journalism: A History: 1690–1960* (New York: Macmillan, 1962), pp 498–9.

30 On the establishment of the news agencies, see James Melvin Lee, *History of American Journalism*, 2nd edn (New York: Garden City, 1923), pp. 384–6, 415–17; and Alan J. Lee, *The Origins of the Popular Press*, pp. 91, 123, 152–5, 226–9.

31 See Henry James, *The Portrait of a Lady*, ed. Robert D. Bamberg (New York and London: W.W. Norton, 1975), pp. 23–5.

32 Emerson, 'Works and Days' in *Society and Solitude*, p. 163.

33 See Daniel J. Boorstin, *The Americans: The Democratic Experience* (New York: Vintage Books, 1974), pp. 89–90. Where Boorstin's analysis is inadequate is in his rather puzzling claim that the construction of 'consumption communities' is somehow 'nonideological'.

34 See Wicke, *Advertising Fictions*, p. 97.

35 Whereas Habermas suggests that it was within both of these sites that the 'bourgeois public sphere' first crystallized, Sennett describes an ostensibly similar shift in 'public culture' by locating, within the coffee-house, a space in which class (if not gender) distinctions were 'temporarily suspended' from social intercourse. See Habermas, *Structural Transformation*, pp. 31–43; and Sennett, *The Fall of Public Man*, pp. 80–3.

36 I say that this tendency is by no means simple for, in the case of Habermas at least, the very function of the *salon* or coffee-house was that it allowed its inhabitants to discuss public knowledge that was accessible precisely because of its dissemination within newspapers and other forms of print culture.

37 Edmund Yates, the editor of *The World*, for example, recalled having been accused of practising 'the worst principles of American journalism', and hence of being 'un-English'. See *Edmund Yates: His Recollections and Experiences*, 2 vols. (London: Richard Bentley, 1884), vol. II, pp. 333–4.

38 Adorno and Horkheimer, *Dialectic of Enlightenment*, pp. 162–3.

39 This collection also includes 'The Birthplace', another story of modern publicity. See Henry James, *The Better Sort* (London: Methuen, 1903).

40 David Howard, 'Henry James and "The Papers"' in *Henry James: Fiction as History*, ed. Ian F.A. Bell (London: Vision, 1984), p. 58.

41 See Leo Braudy, *The Frenzy of Renown: Fame and its History* (New York and Oxford: Oxford University Press, 1986), pp. 139–40, 162–3, 386–7.

42 See Howard, 'Henry James and "The Papers"', pp. 57–8.
43 See Peter Conn, *The Divided Mind: Ideology and Imagination in America, 1898–1917* (Cambridge: Cambridge University Press, 1983), pp. 21–2.
44 To be more precise, James is alluding to the mud-diving contest in book II of *The Dunciad*. See *The Poems of Alexander Pope*, ed. John Butt (London: Methuen, 1985), pp. 391–7.
45 James's preposterously named celebrity also echoes Edgar Allan Poe's Brevet Brigadier General John A.B.C. Smith in 'The Man that was Used Up' (1839). Like Beadel-Muffet, Poe's 'character' only appears in public; in private he is literally disembodied, a mere bundle of disjointed limbs. The parallel between Poe's fable of a man who needs to be assembled for political performance and James's tale of a celebrity who is entirely constructed within the medium of the Papers is evident enough. See Edgar Allan Poe, *Poetry and Tales* (New York: Library of America, 1984), pp. 307–16.
46 On the corporatization of the newspaper industry, see n. 9 above.
47 See Sennett, *The Fall of Public Man*, pp. 211–14.
48 Susan Sontag, *On Photography* (Harmondsworth: Penguin, 1977), p. 178.
49 Maud's fantasy is perhaps not as unlikely as it might seem. In his article 'Government by Journalism' (1886), W.T. Stead had already outlined a project for merging the press with the authority of the state. Since the communicative resources of the press far outstripped the representative capacity of Parliament, it was the former, Stead claimed, which came closest to expressing public opinion. One of the more disturbing conclusions of this argument was that the state should make use of the press as an instrument of government. See W.T. Stead, 'Government by Journalism', *The Contemporary Review*, 49, 1886, p. 660.
50 See Benjamin, *Charles Baudelaire*, p. 43.
51 In Britain, for example, the centralization of the telegraphic system via the Post Office was seen specifically as an attempt to prevent private interests from controlling the telecommunications network. Commenting on this danger, one observer remarked in 1899 that 'It looks as if it might soon be thought necessary to nationalize the ether.' More disturbingly, though, what James's tale evokes is a centralized network of communications, controlled by agencies which are no longer clearly demarcated as those of state or press. See Asa Briggs, *Victorian Things* (Harmondsworth: Penguin, 1990), p. 395.

5 THE SECRET OF THE SPECTACLE: ADVERTISING *THE AMBASSADORS*

1 See Jean Méral, *Paris in American Literature*, tr. Laurette Long (Chapel Hill, NC and London: University of North Carolina Press, 1989), pp. 16–40.
2 F.O. Matthiessen attributes this remark to Thomas Appleton in his

chapter '*The Ambassadors*', reprinted in *Twentieth Century Interpretations of 'The Ambassadors': A Collection of Critical Essays*, ed. Albert E. Stone (Englewood Cliffs, NJ: Prentice Hall, 1969), p. 43. Wilde's quotation of the epigram occurs in a section of dialogue which is transferred almost wholesale from novel to play. See Oscar Wilde, *The Picture of Dorian Gray* in *Plays, Prose Writings and Poems*, ed. Isobel Murray (London: Everyman, 1990), p. 94; and *A Woman of No Importance* in *Two Society Comedies*, ed. Ian Small (London: Ernest Benn, 1983), p. 25.

3 Reprinted in Stone, *Twentieth Century Interpretations*, p. 46.

4 Ibid., p. 9.

5 See Wicke, *Advertising Fictions*, pp. 102–12. Wicke is one of the few critics to have discussed the significance of advertising in *The Ambassadors*, and I have found her reading of the novel extremely suggestive. As I shall argue, however, Wicke tends to circumscribe the phenomenon of advertising within a narrowly American cultural context, and thus preserves Strether's idealized vision of European cultural authenticity.

6 Ibid., pp. 109–10.

7 In Maud Ellmann's deconstructionist reading of the novel, for example, 'Paris "is" nothing, for it names an energy within the text which dissipates identities and definitions', in contrast to the 'semantic, as well as moral, absolutism' of Woollett. See Ellmann, '"The Intimate Difference": Power and Representation in *The Ambassadors*' in *Henry James: Fiction as History*, ed. Ian F.A. Bell (London: Vision, 1984), p. 101. Ross Posnock offers a similar, but more nuanced, account of 'the disintegration of . . . [Strether's] old identity based on authority and control' in Paris. See Posnock, *The Trial of Curiosity*, p. 227.

8 See *The Complete Notebooks of Henry James*, ed. with introductions and notes by Leon Edel and Lyall H. Powers (New York and Oxford: Oxford University Press, 1987), pp. 547, 550.

9 As Marx points out, 'From the mere look of a piece of money, we cannot tell what breed of commodity has been transformed into it. In their money-form all commodities look alike.' See *Capital*, p. 204.

10 See Ellmann, '"The Intimate Difference"', pp. 98–113.

11 The phrase is taken from Franklin's *Advice to a Young Tradesman* (1748) and is quoted in Max Weber, *The Protestant Ethic and the Spirit of Capitalism* (1904–5), tr. Talcott Parsons (London and New York: Routledge, 1992), p. 48.

12 Veblen, *Theory of the Leisure Class*, p. 43.

13 Terry Eagleton, *Criticism and Ideology: A Study in Marxist Literary Theory* (London and New York: Verso, 1992), p. 142.

14 Wicke, *Advertising Fictions*, pp. 104–5.

15 Marx, *Capital*, pp. 279–80.

16 Michael Schudson has shown how this ambiguity clouds the attempt to dismiss advertising as a consciously and effectively manipulative practice. Since a belief in the 'magical' powers of advertising is fostered by

advertisers themselves, the critique of advertising as a form of 'mystification' or 'false consciousness' is in danger of repeating the very assumptions which it claims to dispel. As Schudson points out, the primary aim of the advertising agencies of the late nineteenth century 'was to sell the idea of advertising to business'. Their insistence upon the efficacy of advertising as a form of persuasion was thus couched in the performative mode of advertising itself, and cannot be read as a disinterested appraisal of its effects. See Schudson, *Advertising, The Uneasy Persuasion: Its Dubious Impact on American Society* (London: Routledge, 1993), pp. 168–76.

17 For examples, see Thomas Smith, *Successful Advertising: Its Secrets Explained* (London), 7th edn 1885, pp. 5–10; 8th edn 1886; 9th edn 1887 [Thomas Smith and J.H. Osborne]; and 21st edn 1899 [Smith's Advertising Agency].

18 William Stead, Jr, *The Art of Advertising: Its Theory and Practice Fully Described* (London: T.B. Browne, 1899), p. 147.

19 Ibid., p. 61.

20 Wicke argues that Strether's experience of Paris involves a 'superannuated mode of cultural recognition', increasingly out of step with the new visual forms of advertising. By contrast, I argue that Paris may be read as the primary textual site of a modern 'way of seeing'. See *Advertising Fictions*, pp. 104–5, 110.

21 See William Greenslade, 'The Power of Advertising: Chad Newsome and the Meaning of Paris in *The Ambassadors*', *ELH*, 49 (1), Spring 1982, pp. 100–8.

22 Quoted in Edel, *The Treacherous Years*, p. 262. I am also grateful to William Greenslade whose quotation of part of this extract alerted me to the existence of the letter. See 'The Power of Advertising', p. 99.

23 Paul Greenhalgh, *Ephemeral Vistas: The 'Expositions Universelles', Great Exhibitions and World's Fairs, 1851–1939* (Manchester: Manchester University Press, 1988), p. 47.

24 G. Moynet, 'Le Palais Lumineux Ponsin' in *L'Exposition de Paris*, 3 vols. (Paris: Montgredien, 1900), vol. I, p. 124. This catalogue contains descriptions and illustrations of the various attractions. For the Palais de l'Electricité, see vol. I, pp. 94–5, 99–102, 302–3; for the Palais des Illusions, see vol. III, Plate no. 12.

25 See Susan Buck-Morss, *The Dialectics of Seeing: Walter Benjamin and the Arcades Project* (Cambridge, Mass. and London: The MIT Press, 1991), pp. 83–6. The quotation is taken from Patrick Geddes, 'The Closing Exhibition – Paris 1900' which is quoted in Greenhalgh, *Ephemeral Vistas*, p. 1.

26 Thomas Richards, for example, has argued that the Great Exhibition of 1851 – the first international trade fair, held in the Crystal Palace in London – 'inaugurated a way of seeing that marked indelibly the cultural and commercial life of Victorian England and fashioned a

mythology of consumerism that has endured to this day'. See *The Commodity Culture of Victorian England: Advertising and Spectacle, 1851–1914* (Stanford: Stanford University Press, 1990), p. 18. The great precursor of this line of cultural analysis is Walter Benjamin, whose unfinished *Passagen-Werk* (Arcades Project) placed Paris at the epicentre of nineteenth-century urban consumer culture. As Buck-Morss has observed, 'Benjamin described the spectacle of Paris as a "phantasmagoria" – a magic-lantern show of optical illusions, rapidly changing size and blending into one another' (*Dialectics of Seeing*, p. 81). For Benjamin's own discussion of this 'phantasmagoria', see 'Grandville or the World Exhibitions' in *Charles Baudelaire*, pp. 164–6.

27 On James's impressionism, see Charles R. Anderson, *Person, Place, and Thing in Henry James's Novels* (Durham, NC: Duke University Press, 1977), pp. 239–41; for his use of the language of Paterian aestheticism, see Jonathan Freedman, *Professions of Taste: Henry James, British Aestheticism, and Commodity Culture* (Stanford, Calif.: Stanford University Press, 1990), p. 197.

28 See Moynet, 'Le Palais Lumineux Ponsin', p. 126.

29 Ibid., p. 124.

30 The relationship between satisfaction and desire in consumer culture is examined extensively in the work of Jean Baudrillard. In *Le Système des objets*, Baudrillard argues that the desire of the consumer is subject to proliferation precisely because it is predicated upon lack rather than need (*Système*, p. 283). In a later work, however, he suggests that exchange value 'is equivalent to a *phantasmic organization*, in which desire is fulfilled and lack resolved; in which desire is achieved and performed and in which the symbolic dimension and all difference are abolished'. Thus, the persistence of lack in the desire of the subject is not merely a functional inversion of the realization of exchange value, but instead offers an irreducible challenge to the system of value itself. See *For a Critique of the Political Economy of the Sign*, tr. Charles Levin (St Louis: Telos Press, 1981), p. 206. I explore this more radical reading of Strether's resistance to consumption later in this chapter.

31 See Freedman, *Professions of Taste*, p. 199.

32 For this argument, see Buck-Morss, *Dialectics of Seeing*, pp. 85–6.

33 See Bowlby, *Just Looking*, pp. 32–3.

34 See Marx, 'The Fetishism of the Commodity and its Secret' in *Capital*, pp. 163–77.

35 See Theodore Dreiser, *Sister Carrie*, ed. Neda M. Westlake, John C. Berkey, Alice M. Winters and James L.W. West III (Harmondsworth: Penguin, 1986), pp. 15–29.

36 For an historical account of these developments, see Charles Singer *et al.*, eds., *History of Technology* vol. v: *The Late Nineteenth Century c. 1850 to c. 1900* (Oxford: Oxford University Press, 1958), pp. 671–82.

37 A. Growoll, *The Profession of Bookselling: A Handbook of Practical Hints for the*

Apprentice and Bookseller, 2 vols. (New York: Office of The Publishers' Weekly, 1893–5), vol. 1, p. 33.

38 See Wicke, *Advertising Fictions*, p. 107.

39 See Wolfgang Fritz Haug, *Commodity Aesthetics, Ideology and Culture* (New York and Bagnolet: International General, 1987), pp. 115–16. The colour of these books also adds weight to Jonathan Freedman's argument that *The Ambassadors* conducts a covert dialogue with the figure of Oscar Wilde. In this respect, Strether, like Dorian Gray, is seduced by the allure of a 'yellow book', with all its attendant connotations. See Freedman, *Professions of Taste*, pp. 192–201; and for a more general survey of this connection with aestheticism, Eben Bass, 'Lemon-Colored Volumes and Henry James', *Studies in Short Fiction*, 1, 1963–4, pp. 113–22.

40 For Kant's distinction between sensory gratification and the 'disinterested' faculty of aesthetic judgement (or between the *agreeable* and the *beautiful*), see *The Critique of Judgement*, pp. 42–50. For a sociological critique of Kant's 'principle of pure taste', see Bourdieu, *Distinction*, pp. 485–500.

41 Posnock, *The Trial of Curiosity*, p. 245. Like Ellmann, Posnock celebrates the vagrancy of Strether's Parisian experience as a form of wastage, which resists the purposive rationality of industrial society. But as I have suggested, Strether's apparently idle curiosity is itself implicated in an 'aristocratic' expenditure of time and money, which cannot be exempted from all economies of value. For Baudrillard's account of the radical alterity (or 'lack') which threatens the achievement of desire, see n. 30 above. This account is evidently influenced by the pyschoanalytic formulations of Jacques Lacan: see, in particular, 'The Subversion of the Subject and the Dialectic of Desire in the Freudian Unconscious' in *Ecrits: A Selection*, tr. Alan Sheridan (London: Routledge, 1993), pp. 292–325.

42 Wicke, *Advertising Fictions*, p. 108.

43 Stéphane Mallarmé, 'The Book: A Spiritual Instrument' in *Selected Poetry and Prose*, ed. Mary Ann Caws (New York: New Directions, 1982), p. 83. See also 'Le Livre, instrument spirituel' in *Oeuvres de Mallarmé*, ed. Yves-Alain Favre (Paris: Garnier, 1985), pp. 294–8.

44 See Jacques Derrida, *Dissemination*, tr. Barbara Johnson (London: The Athlone Press, 1993), pp. 209–16, 258–60.

45 Mallarmé, *Selected Poetry*, pp. 81–2.

46 Mallarmé's text begins with the famous assertion that 'all earthly existence must ultimately be contained in a book' ('tout, au monde, existe pour aboutir à un livre'). See *Selected Poetry*, p. 80; and *Oeuvres*, p. 294.

47 See William R. Goetz, *Henry James and the Darkest Abyss of Romance* (Baton Rouge, La.: Louisiana State University Press, 1986), p. 186.

48 For Jacques Derrida, of course, the indeterminacy of this boundary is a constitutive function of the figure of the frame (or *parergon*). See *The*

Truth in Painting, tr. Geoff Bennington and Ian McLeod (Chicago and London: University of Chicago Press, 1987), p. 45.

49 See Todorov, *The Poetics of Prose*, pp. 169–70.

50 Henry James, *The Painter's Eye: Notes and Essays on the Pictorial Arts*, ed. John L. Sweeney with a foreword by Susan M. Griffin (Madison, Wis.: University of Wisconsin Press, 1989), p. 109.

51 Agnew, 'The Consuming Vision', p. 94.

52 See Henry James, *The Golden Bowl*, ed. Gore Vidal (Harmondsworth: Penguin, 1985), p. 43.

53 See Adorno and Horkheimer, *Dialectic of Enlightenment*, pp. 135–6; and also Theodor W. Adorno, 'The Culture Industry Reconsidered' in *Critical Theory and Society: A Reader*, ed. Stephen Eric Bronner and Douglas MacKay Kellner (New York and London: Routledge, 1989), p. 128. Guy Debord offers a similar vision of the universalizing trajectory of modern capitalist culture. According to Debord, 'The spectacle is the moment when the commodity has attained the *total occupation* of social life. Not only is the relation to the commodity visible but it is all one sees: the world one sees is its world.' See *Society of the Spectacle*, part II, 42.

POSTSCRIPT

1 See Introduction, n. 15.

2 For an example of the tendency to read James's comments upon the topography of American institutions as evidence of his basic 'aristocratic' conservatism, see the 'Introduction' by John F. Sears in Henry James, *The American Scene*, ed. John F. Sears (Harmondsworth: Penguin, 1994), pp. xvi–xvii.

3 See Herbert Marcuse, 'The Obsolescence of the Freudian Concept of Man' in *Critical Theory and Society: A Reader*, ed. Stephen Eric Bronner and Douglas MacKay Kellner (New York and London: Routledge, 1989), p. 238.

4 See David Riesman with Nathan Glazer and Reuel Denney, *The Lonely Crowd: A Study of the Changing American Character* (New Haven and London: Yale University Press, 1989), pp. 14–17, 19–24.

5 James's 'other-directed' self is evident, most notably, in his response to the 'alien' figure of the Jew. On this point, see Posnock, *The Trial of Curiosity*, pp. 276–81.

6 Ibid., pp. 260–2.

7 For two differing accounts of James's response to the bureaucratic administration of American culture (including that of the 'hotel-spirit'), see Mark Seltzer, *Henry James and the Art of Power* (Ithaca, NY and London: Cornell University Press, 1984), pp. 96–145; and Posnock, *The Trial of Curiosity*, pp. 250–4, 262–76.

8 See Habermas, *Structural Transformation*, p. 200.

9 See Seltzer, *Henry James and the Art of Power*, pp. 112–14.

10 See Posnock, *The Trial of Curiosity*, p. 264.
11 Seltzer offers a similar argument, for example, in his reading of the complicity between civic society and economic and administrative power in the chapters on Philadelphia and Washington, although I do not share his sense of James's evasion of this complicity. See *Henry James and the Art of Power*, pp. 116–35.
12 On the response to James's lecture tour, see Edel, *Henry James: A Life*, pp. 601–3; for an invaluable bibliography of articles published on James in the American press, see Linda J. Taylor, *Henry James, 1866–1916: A Reference Guide* (Boston: G.K. Hall, 1982).
13 Florence Brooks, 'Henry James in the Serene Sixties', *New York Herald*, 2 October 1904 (magazine supplement), p. 3.
14 Quoted in Taylor, *Henry James, 1866–1916*, p. 475.
15 On 14 September 1904, two weeks after his arrival in America, James wrote to his literary agent James Pinker, complaining that he had suffered 'an assault of interviewers and escaped them all for the time – all that is save one who passed on here from New York three days ago, and whom I couldn't cast forth (it was a young woman with an introduction from Scribners!) after a journey of 250 miles'. The interviewer whom James failed to 'escape' was Florence Brooks. See *L* IV, p. 322.
16 See Sidney Brooks, 'Mr. Henry James at Home', *Harper's Weekly*, 48 (2494), 8 October 1904, pp. 1548–9.
17 For further details on the 'author at home' genre, see chapter 1, n. 32 and chapter 3, n. 54.
18 Sidney Brooks, 'Henry James at Home', p. 1548.
19 Florence Brooks, 'Henry James in the Serene Sixties', p. 3.
20 See Braudy, *The Frenzy of Renown*, pp. 401–8, 417–45, 523–6.
21 Max Beerbohm, 'Felix Argallo and Walter Ledgett' in *Seven Men and Two Others* (Oxford: Oxford University Press, 1980), p. 169. Also quoted in Braudy, *The Frenzy of Renown*, p. 524.
22 Florence Brooks, 'Henry James in the Serene Sixties', p. 3.
23 Witter Bynner, 'A Word or Two with Henry James', *The Critic and Literary World* (New York), 46 (2), 1905, p. 148.
24 See Witter Bynner, 'On Henry James's Centennial' (1943) in *The Works of Witter Bynner: Prose Pieces*, ed. James Kraft (New York: Farrar, Straus, Giroux, 1978), pp. 14–15.
25 Ibid., p. 16.

Bibliography

'About Autobiographies', *Chambers' Journal of Popular Literature, Science and Arts*, 5th series, 8 (383), 2 May 1891, pp. 333–5.

Adorno, Theodor W., 'The Culture Industry Reconsidered' in *Critical Theory and Society: A Reader*, ed. Stephen Eric Bronner and Douglas MacKay Kellner (New York and London: Routledge, 1989), pp. 128–35.

In Search of Wagner, tr. Rodney Livingstone (London: NLB, 1981).

Adorno, Theodor W. and Max Horkheimer, *Dialectic of Enlightenment*, tr. John Cumming, 2nd edn (London and New York: Verso, 1986).

'Advertisement as a Gentle Art', editorial, *The National Review*, 26 (155), 1896, pp. 650–6.

Agnew, Jean-Christophe, 'The Consuming Vision of Henry James' in *The Culture of Consumption: Critical Essays in American History, 1880–1980*, ed. Richard Wightman Fox and T.J. Jackson Lears (New York: Pantheon, 1983), pp. 65–100.

Altick, Richard D., *The English Common Reader: A Social History of the Mass Reading Public, 1800–1900* (Chicago: University of Chicago Press, 1957).

Lives and Letters: A History of Literary Biography in England and America (New York: Alfred A. Knopf, 1966).

Anderson, Charles R., *Person, Place, and Thing in Henry James's Novels* (Durham, NC: Duke University Press, 1977).

Anesko, Michael, *'Friction with the Market': Henry James and the Profession of Authorship* (New York and Oxford: Oxford University Press, 1986).

Armstrong, Paul B., *The Phenomenology of Henry James* (Chapel Hill, NC and London: University of North Carolina Press, 1983).

Arnold, Matthew, *The Complete Prose Works of Matthew Arnold*, 11 vols., ed. R.H. Super (Ann Arbor: University of Michigan Press, 1960–77).

Letters of Matthew Arnold 1848–1888, 2 vols., collected and arranged by George W.E. Russell (London and New York: Macmillan, 1895).

Baildon, H.B. *et al.*, *Homes and Haunts of Famous Authors* (London: Wells Gardner, Darton & Co., 1906).

Barthes, Roland, *Mythologies*, tr. Annette Lavers (London: Vintage, 1993).

Bass, Eben, 'Lemon-Colored Volumes and Henry James', *Studies in Short Fiction*, 1, 1963–4, pp. 113–22.

Baudrillard, Jean, *For a Critique of the Political Economy of the Sign*, tr. Charles Levin (St Louis: Telos Press, 1981).

'Mass Media Culture', in *Revenge of the Crystal: Selected Writings on the Modern Object and its Destiny, 1968–1983*, ed. and tr. Paul Foss and Julian Pefanis (London and Concord, Mass.: Pluto Press, 1990), pp. 63–97.

Revenge of the Crystal: Selected Writings on the Modern Object and its Destiny, 1968–1983, ed. and tr. Paul Foss and Julian Pefanis (London and Concord, Mass.: Pluto Press, 1990).

Le Système des objets (Paris: Gallimard, 1968).

Beerbohm Max, 'Felix Argallo and Walter Ledgett' in *Seven Men and Two Others* (Oxford: Oxford University Press, 1980), pp. 187–232.

Seven Men and Two Others (Oxford: Oxford University Press, 1980).

Bell, Ian F.A., *Henry James and the Past: Readings into Time* (Houndmills: Macmillan, 1991).

Bell, Ian F.A., ed., *Henry James: Fiction as History* (London: Vision, 1984).

Benjamin, Walter, *Charles Baudelaire: A Lyric Poet in The Era of High Capitalism*, tr. Harry Zohn (London and New York: Verso, 1989).

Illuminations, tr. Harry Zohn (Bungay: Fontana, 1982).

'The Work of Art in the Age of Mechanical Reproduction' in *Illuminations*, tr. Harry Zohn (Bungay: Fontana, 1982), pp. 219–53.

Benn, S.I. and G.F. Gaus, eds., *Public and Private in Social Life* (London and Canberra: Croom Helm, 1983).

Bennett, E.A., *Fame and Fiction: An Enquiry into Certain Popularities* (London: Grant Richards, 1901).

Bercovitch, Sacvan, ed., *Reconstructing American Literary History* (Cambridge, Mass. and London: Harvard University Press, 1986).

Besant, Walter, *Autobiography of Sir Walter Besant* (London: Hutchinson, 1902).

'How Can a Love and Appreciation of Art be Best Developed among the Masses of the People?' in Rev. W. Tuckwell, Charles Godfrey Leland and Walter Besant, *Art and Hand Work for the People: Being Three Papers Read Before the Social Science Congress, September 1884* (Manchester: J.E. Cornish, 1885).

Bloch, Ernst *et al.*, *Aesthetics and Politics*, tr. and ed. Rodney Taylor (London: NLB, 1977).

Bolton, Charles Knowles, *The Reign of The Poster: Being Comments and Criticism* (Boston: Winthrop B. Jones, 1895).

Boorstin, Daniel J., *The Americans: The Democratic Experience* (New York: Vintage Books, 1974).

Borus, Daniel H., *Writing Realism: Howells, James, and Norris in the Mass Market* (Chapel Hill, NC and London: University of North Carolina Press, 1989).

Bourdieu, Pierre, *Distinction: A Social Critique of The Judgement of Taste*, tr. Richard Nice (London: Routledge, 1989).

Bowlby, Rachel, *Just Looking: Consumer Culture in Dreiser, Gissing and Zola* (New York and London: Methuen, 1985).

Brake, Laurel, *Subjugated Knowledges: Journalism, Gender and Literature in the Nineteenth Century* (Houndmills: Macmillan, 1994).

Braudy, Leo, *The Frenzy of Renown: Fame and its History* (New York and Oxford: Oxford University Press, 1986).

Bresnick, Adam, 'The Artist that was Used Up: Henry James's "Private Life"', *The Henry James Review*, 14 (1), Winter 1993, pp. 87–98.

Briggs, Asa, *Victorian Things* (Harmondsworth: Penguin, 1990).

Bronner, Stephen Eric and Douglas MacKay Kellner, eds., *Critical Theory and Society: A Reader* (New York and London: Routledge, 1989).

Brooks, Florence, 'Henry James in the Serene Sixties', *New York Herald* (magazine supplement), 2 October 1904, p. 3.

Brooks, Sidney, 'Mr. Henry James at Home', *Harpers' Weekly*, 48 (2494), 8 October 1904, pp. 1548–9.

Brown, Lucy, *Victorian News and Newspapers* (Oxford: Clarendon Press, 1985).

Buchanan, Robert, *A Look Round Literature* (London: Ward and Downey, 1887).

Buck-Morss, Susan, *The Dialectics of Seeing: Walter Benjamin and the Arcades Project* (Cambridge, Mass. and London: The MIT Press, 1991).

Bynner, Witter, 'A Word or Two with Henry James', *The Critic and Literary World* (New York), 46 (2), 1905, pp. 146–8.

'On Henry James's Centennial' (1943) in *The Works of Witter Bynner: Prose Pieces*, ed. James Kraft (New York: Farrar, Straus, Giroux, 1978), pp. 11–16.

The Works of Witter Bynner: Prose Pieces, ed. James Kraft (New York: Farrar, Straus, Giroux, 1978).

Calhoun, Craig, ed., *Habermas and the Public Sphere* (Cambridge, Mass. and London: MIT Press, 1992).

Carey, John, *The Intellectuals and the Masses: Pride and Prejudice among the Literary Intelligentsia, 1880–1939* (London and Boston: Faber and Faber, 1992).

Carpignano, Paulo, Robin Andersen, Stanley Aronowitz and William Difazio, 'Chatter in the Age of Electronic Reproduction: Talk Television and the "Public Mind"' in *The Phantom Public Sphere*, ed. Bruce Robbins (Minneapolis and London: University of Minnesota Press, 1993), pp. 93–120.

Clifford, James L., ed., *Biography as an Art: Selected Criticism 1560–1960* (London: Oxford University Press, 1962).

Coleridge, Samuel Taylor, 'A Prefatory Observation on Modern Biography' (1810) in *Biography as an Art: Selected Criticism 1560–1960* (London: Oxford University Press, 1962), pp. 57–9.

Conn, Peter, *The Divided Mind: Ideology and Imagination in America, 1898–1917* (Cambridge: Cambridge University Press, 1983).

Corbett, Mary Jean, *Representing Femininity: Middle-Class Subjectivity in Victorian and Edwardian Women's Autobiographies* (New York and Oxford: Oxford University Press, 1992).

Crawford, F. Marion, *The Novel: What it Is* (London and New York: Macmillan, 1893).
Cross, Nigel, *The Common Writer: Life in Nineteenth-Century Grub Street* (Cambridge: Cambridge University Press, 1985).
Debord, Guy, *Society of the Spectacle* (Detroit: Black and Red, 1983).
Derrida, Jacques, *Dissemination*, tr. Barbara Johnson (London: The Athlone Press, 1993).
The Truth in Painting, tr. Geoff Bennington and Ian McLeod (Chicago and London: University of Chicago Press, 1987).
Dicken-Garcia, Hazel, *Journalistic Standards in Nineteenth-Century America* (Madison, Wisc: University of Wisconsin Press, 1989).
Donadio, Stephen, *Nietzsche, Henry James, and the Artistic Will* (New York: Oxford University Press, 1978).
Douglas, Ann, *The Feminization of American Culture* (New York: Alfred A. Knopf, 1979).
Dowden, Edward, 'The Interpretation of Literature', *The Contemporary Review*, 49, May 1886, pp. 701–19.
Dreiser, Theodore, *Sister Carrie*, ed. Neda M. Westlake, John C. Berkey, Alice M. Winters and James L.W. West III (Harmondsworth: Penguin, 1986).
Eagleton, Terry, *Criticism and Ideology: A Study in Marxist Literary Theory* (London and New York: Verso, 1992).
Edel, Leon, 'Editor's Foreword' to Henry James, *Guy Domville* in Henry James, *The Complete Plays of Henry James*, ed. Leon Edel (London: Rupert Hart Davis, 1949), pp. 465–83.
Henry James: A Life (London: Collins, 1987).
'Henry James: The Dramatic Years', in Henry James, *The Complete Plays of Henry James*, ed. Leon Edel (London: Rupert Hart Davis, 1949).
Henry James: The Treacherous Years 1895–1901 (London: Rupert Hart-Davis, 1969).
Ellmann, Maud, '"The Intimate Difference": Power and Representation in *The Ambassadors*' in *Henry James: Fiction as History*, ed. Ian F.A. Bell (London: Vision, 1984), pp. 98–113.
Emerson, Ralph Waldo, *Society and Solitude: The Complete Works of Ralph Waldo Emerson*, 12 vols. with a biographical introduction and notes by Edward Waldo Emerson (Boston and New York: Houghton Mifflin, 1912), vol. VII.
'English Celebrities at Home', *The World: A Journal for Men and Women*, 5, 23 August 1876, pp. 171–3.
Evans, Richardson, *The Age of Disfigurement* (London and Sydney: Remington & Co., 1893).
Felski, Rita, *Beyond Feminist Aesthetics: Feminist Literature and Social Change* (London: Hutchinson Radius, 1989).
Fisher, Philip, 'Appearing and Disappearing in Public: Social Space in

Late-Nineteenth-Century Literature and Culture' in *Reconstructing American Literary History*, ed. Sacvan Bercovitch (Cambridge, Mass. and London: Harvard University Press, 1986), pp. 155–88.

Foucault, Michel, *The History of Sexuality* vol. I: *An Introduction*, tr. Robert Hurley (Harmondsworth: Penguin, 1990).

Fox, Richard Wightman and T.J. Jackson Lears, eds., *The Culture of Consumption: Critical Essays in American History, 1880–1980* (New York: Pantheon, 1983).

Fraser, Nancy, 'Rethinking the Public Sphere: A Contribution to the Critique of Actually Existing Democracy' in *The Phantom Public Sphere*, ed. Bruce Robbins (Minneapolis and London: University of Minnesota Press, 1993), pp. 1–32.

Freedman, Jonathan, *Professions of Taste: Henry James, British Aestheticism, and Commodity Culture* (Stanford, Calif.: Stanford University Press, 1990).

Freud, Sigmund, *Art and Literature*, The Pelican Freud Library vol. XIV, tr. James Strachey (Harmondsworth: Penguin, 1985).

'Leonardo da Vinci and a Memory of his Childhood' in *Art and Literature*, The Pelican Freud Library vol. XIV, tr. James Strachey (Harmondsworth: Penguin, 1985), pp. 145–231.

Gagnier, Regenia, *Idylls of the Marketplace: Oscar Wilde and the Victorian Public* (Aldershot: Scolar Press, 1987).

Gittings, Robert and Jo Manton, *Claire Clairmont and The Shelleys 1798–1879* (Oxford and New York: Oxford University Press, 1992).

Godden, Richard, 'Some Slight Shifts in the Manner of the Novel of Manners' in *Henry James: Fiction as History*, ed. Ian F.A. Bell (London: Vision, 1984), pp. 156–83.

Goetz, William R., *Henry James and the Darkest Abyss of Romance* (Baton Rouge, La.: Louisiana State University Press, 1986).

Goodbody, John, 'The *Star*: Its Role in the Rise of the New Journalism' in *Papers for the Millions: The New Journalism in Britain, 1850s to 1914*, ed. Joel H. Wiener (Westport, Conn.: Greenwood Press, 1988), pp. 143–63.

Greenhalgh, Paul, *Ephemeral Vistas: The 'Expositions Universelles', Great Exhibitions and World's Fairs, 1851–1939* (Manchester: Manchester University Press, 1988).

Greenslade, William, 'The Power of Advertising: Chad Newsome and the Meaning of Paris in *The Ambassadors*', *ELH*, 49 (1), Spring 1982, pp. 99–122.

Grimm, Ruediger Hermann, *Nietzsche's Theory of Knowledge* (Berlin and New York: Walter de Gruyter, 1977).

Growoll, A., *The Profession of Bookselling: A Handbook of Practical Hints for the Apprentice and Bookseller*, 2 vols. (New York: Office of The Publishers' Weekly, 1893–5).

Habegger, Alfred, *Gender, Fantasy, and Realism in American Literature* (New York: Columbia University Press, 1982).

Henry James and the 'Woman Business' (Cambridge: Cambridge University Press, 1989).

Habermas, Jürgen, *The Structural Transformation of the Public Sphere: An Inquiry into a Category of Bourgeois Society*, tr. Thomas Burger with the assistance of Frederick Lawrence (Cambridge: Polity Press, 1992).

Halsey, Francis Whiting, *Our Literary Deluge and Some of its Deeper Waters* (London: Grant Richards, 1902).

Hamblen, Abigail Ann, 'Henry James and the Press: A Study of Protest', *The Western Humanities Review*, 11 (2), 1957, pp. 169–75.

Hamilton, Ian, *Keepers of the Flame: Literary Estates and the Rise of Biography* (London: Hutchinson, 1992).

Harrison, Frederic, *The Choice of Books and Other Literary Pieces* (London: Macmillan, 1886).

Haug, Wolfgang Fritz, *Commodity Aesthetics, Ideology and Culture* (New York and Bagnolet: International General, 1987).

Homberger, Eric and John Charmley, eds., *The Troubled Face of Biography* (Houndmills: Macmillan, 1988).

Hopkins, Tighe, 'Anonymity?' [I], *The New Review*, I (6), 1889, pp. 513–31.

Howard, David, 'Henry James and "The Papers"' in *Henry James: Fiction as History*, ed. Ian F.A. Bell (London: Vision, 1984), pp. 49–64.

Howells, W.D., *A Modern Instance* (Bloomington, Ind. and London: Indiana University Press, 1977).

Huyssen, Andreas, *After the Great Divide: Modernism, Mass Culture, and Postmodernism* (Houndmills: Macmillan, 1988).

Ibsen, Henrik, *The Oxford Ibsen*, vol. VI, tr. and ed. James Walter McFarlane (London: Oxford University Press, 1960).

The Idler Magazine: An Illustrated Monthly, I, 1892.

'The Interview', *The New Princeton Review*, 3, 1887, pp. 127–31.

Jacobson, Marcia, *Henry James and the Mass Market* (Alabama: University of Alabama Press, 1983).

James, Henry, *The Ambassadors*, ed. S.P. Rosenbaum, 2nd edn (New York and London: Norton, 1994).

The American, ed. with an introduction by William Spengemann (Harmondsworth: Penguin, 1986).

The American Scene (London: Granville, 1987).

The Better Sort (London: Methuen, 1903).

The Bostonians, ed. Charles R. Anderson (Harmondsworth: Penguin, 1986).

The Complete Notebooks of Henry James, ed. with introductions and notes by Leon Edel and Lyall H. Powers (New York and Oxford: Oxford University Press, 1987).

The Complete Plays of Henry James, ed. Leon Edel (London: Rupert Hart Davis, 1949).

The Complete Tales of Henry James, 12 vols., ed. Leon Edel (London: Rupert Hart-Davis, 1962–4).

French Writers and American Women, ed. Peter Buitenhuis (Branford, Conn.: Compass, 1960).

The Golden Bowl, ed. Gore Vidal (Harmondsworth: Penguin, 1985).

Henry James Letters, 4 vols., ed. Leon Edel (Cambridge, Mass.: Harvard University Press, 1974–84).

Literary Criticism vol. I: *Essays on Literature, American Writers, English Writers* (New York: Library of America, 1984).

Literary Criticism vol. II: *French Writers, Other European Writers, the Prefaces to the New York Edition* (New York: Library of America, 1984).

The Notebooks of Henry James, ed. F.O. Matthiessen and Kenneth B. Murdock (New York: Oxford University Press, 1961).

Notes of a Son and Brother (London: Macmillan, 1914).

The Painter's Eye: Notes and Essays on the Pictorial Arts, ed. John L. Sweeney with a foreword by Susan M. Griffin (Madison, Wis.: University of Wisconsin Press, 1989).

The Portrait of a Lady, ed. Robert D. Bamberg (New York and London: W.W. Norton, 1975).

The Princess Casamassima, ed. Derek Brewer (Harmondsworth: Penguin, 1986).

The Question of Our Speech, The Lesson of Balzac: Two Lectures (Boston and New York: Houghton, Mifflin, 1905).

The Reverberator (New York: Grove Press, 1957).

The Sacred Fount, ed. John Lyon (Harmondsworth: Penguin, 1994).

The Scenic Art: Notes on Acting and the Drama 1872–1901, ed. Allan Wade (London: Rupert Hart-Davis, 1949).

'The Science of Criticism', *The New Review*, 4 (24), 1891, pp. 398–402.

A Small Boy and Others (London: Macmillan, 1913).

The Tragic Muse (Harmondsworth: Penguin, 1988).

James, William, *Collected Essays and Reviews* (London: Longmans, Green, 1920).

'Remarks on Spencer's Definition of Mind as Correspondence' in *Collected Essays and Reviews* (London: Longmans, Green, 1920), pp. 43–68.

The Will to Believe and Other Essays in Popular Philosophy and *Human Immortality: Two Supposed Objections to the Doctrine* (New York: Dover Publications, 1956).

Jameson, Fredric, *The Political Unconscious: Narrative as a Socially Symbolic Act* (London and New York: Routledge, 1989).

'Reification and Utopia in Mass Culture', *Social Text: Theory, Culture, Ideology*, 1, 1979, pp. 130–48.

Kant, Immanuel, *The Critique of Judgement*, tr. James Meredith Creed (Oxford: Clarendon Press, 1992).

Kappeler, Susanne, *Writing and Reading in Henry James* (London and Basingstoke: Macmillan, 1980).

Keating, Peter, *The Haunted Study: A Social History of the English Novel 1875–1914* (London: Fontana, 1991).

Lacan, Jacques, *Ecrits: A Selection*, tr. Alan Sheridan (London: Routledge, 1993).

Leavis, F.R., 'Mass Civilization and Minority Culture' in *Education and the University: A Sketch for an 'English School'* (Cambridge: Cambridge University Press, 1979), pp. 143–71.

Leavis, Q.D., *Fiction and the Reading Public* (London: Chatto and Windus, 1978).

Le Bon, Gustave, *The Crowd: A Study of the Popular Mind* (London: Ernest Benn, 1947).

Lee, Alan J., *The Origins of the Popular Press in England 1855–1914* (London: Croom Helm, 1980).

Lee, James Melvin, *History of American Journalism*, 2nd edn (New York: Garden City, 1923).

L'Exposition de Paris, 3 vols. (Paris: Montgredien, 1900).

Lind, Ilse Dusoir, 'The Inadequate Vulgarity of Henry James', *Publications of the Modern Language Association of America*, 66, 1951, pp. 886–910.

Mallarmé, Stéphane, *Oeuvres de Mallarmé*, ed. Yves-Alain Favre (Paris: Garnier, 1985).

Selected Poetry and Prose, ed. Mary Ann Caws (New York: New Directions, 1982).

Marcus, Laura, *Auto/biographical Discourses: Theory, Criticism, Practice* (Manchester and New York: Manchester University Press, 1994).

Marcuse, Herbert, 'The Obsolescence of the Freudian Concept of Man' in *Critical Theory and Society: A Reader*, ed. Stephen Eric Bronner and Douglas MacKay Kellner (New York and London: Routledge, 1989), pp. 233–46.

Margolis, Anne T., *Henry James and the Problem of Audience: An International Act* (Ann Arbor: UMI Research Press, 1985).

Marx, Karl, *Capital: A Critique of Political Economy*, vol. 1, tr. Ben Fowkes (Harmondsworth: Penguin, 1990).

Méral, Jean, *Paris in American Literature*, tr. Laurette Long (Chapel Hill, NC and London: University of North Carolina Press, 1989).

Miller, J. Hillis, 'History, Narrative and Responsibility: Speech Acts in Henry James's "The Aspern Papers" ', *Textual Practice*, 9 (2), Summer 1995, pp. 243–67.

Millgate, Michael, *Testamentary Acts: Browning, Tennyson, James, Hardy* (Oxford: Clarendon Press, 1992).

Mott, Frank Luther, *American Journalism: A History: 1690–1960* (New York: Macmillan, 1962).

Moynet, G., 'Le Palais Lumineux Ponsin' in *L'Exposition de Paris*, 3 vols. (Paris: Montgredien, 1900), vol. 1, pp. 124–6.

Nietzsche, Friedrich, *The Gay Science*, tr. Walter Kaufmann (New York: Vintage Books, 1974).

The Portable Nietzsche, ed. and tr. Walter Kaufmann (Harmondsworth: Penguin, 1976).

The Will to Power, tr. Walter Kaufmann and R.J. Hollingdale (New York: Vintage Books, 1968).

Nilsson, Nils Gunnar, 'The Origin of the Interview', *Journalism Quarterly* (Minneapolis), Winter 1971, pp. 707–13.

Nordau, Max, *Degeneration* (1895) (Lincoln, Nebr. and London: University of Nebraska Press, 1993).

Nye, Robert A., *The Origins of Crowd Pyschology: Gustave Le Bon and the Crisis of Mass Democracy in the Third Republic* (London and Beverly Hills, Calif.: Sage Publications, 1975).

O'Connor, T.P., 'The New Journalism', *The New Review*, 1 (5), 1889, pp. 423–34.

Oliphant, M.O.W., 'The Ethics of Biography', *The Contemporary Review*, 44, 1883, pp. 76–93.

The Oxford English Dictionary, 20 vols., 2nd edn (Oxford: Clarendon Press, 1989).

Pateman, Carole, 'Feminist Critiques of the Public/Private Dichotomy' in *Public and Private in Social Life*, ed. S.I. Benn and G.F. Gaus (London and Canberra: Croom Helm, 1983), pp. 281–303.

Poe, Edgar Allan, *Poetry and Tales* (New York: Library of America, 1984).

Pope, Alexander, *The Poems of Alexander Pope*, ed. John Butt (London: Methuen, 1985).

Posnock, Ross, *The Trial of Curiosity: Henry James, William James, and the Challenge of Modernity* (New York and Oxford: Oxford University Press, 1991).

Richards, Thomas, *The Commodity Culture of Victorian England: Advertising and Spectacle, 1851–1914* (Stanford, Calif.: Stanford University Press, 1990).

Riesman, David with Nathan Glazer and Reuel Denney, *The Lonely Crowd: A Study of the Changing American Character* (New Haven and London: Yale University Press, 1989).

Robbins, Bruce, ed., *The Phantom Public Sphere* (Minneapolis and London: University of Minnesota Press, 1993).

Robins, Elizabeth, *Theatre and Friendship* (London and Toronto: Jonathan Cape, 1934).

Scharnhorst, Gary, 'James, "The Aspern Papers", and the Ethics of Literary Biography', *Modern Fiction Studies*, 36 (2), Summer 1990, pp. 211–17.

Schudson, Michael, *Advertising, The Uneasy Persuasion: Its Dubious Impact on American Society* (London: Routledge, 1993).

Discovering the News: A Social History of American Newspapers (New York: Basic Books, 1978).

Sears, John F., 'Introduction' to Henry James, *The American Scene*, ed. John F. Sears (Harmondsworth: Penguin, 1994), pp. vii–xxii.

Sedgwick, Eve Kosofsky, *Epistemology of the Closet* (Berkeley and Los Angeles: University of California Press, 1990).

Seltzer, Mark, *Henry James and the Art of Power* (Ithaca, NY and London: Cornell University Press, 1984).

Sennett, Richard, *The Fall of Public Man* (London and Boston: Faber and Faber, 1993).
Shevelow, Kathryn, *Women and Print Culture: The Construction of Femininity in the Early Periodical* (London and New York: Routledge, 1989).
Singer, Charles *et al.*, *History of Technology* vol. v: *The Late Nineteenth Century c. 1850 to c. 1900* (Oxford: Oxford University Press, 1958).
Skidelsky, Robert, 'Only Connect: Biography and Truth' in *The Troubled Face of Biography*, ed. Eric Homberger and John Charmley (Houndmills: Macmillan, 1988), pp. 1–16.
Smith, Thomas, *Successful Advertising: Its Secrets Explained* (London), 7th edn 1885; 8th edn 1886; 9th edn 1887 [Thomas Smith and J.H. Osborne]; and 21st edn 1899 [Smith's Advertising Agency].
Sontag, Susan, *On Photography* (Harmondsworth: Penguin, 1977).
Stead, William, Jr, *The Art of Advertising: Its Theory and Practice Fully Described* (London: T.B. Browne, 1899).
Stead, W.T., 'The Future of Journalism', *The Contemporary Review*, 50, 1886, pp. 663–79.
'Government by Journalism', *The Contemporary Review*, 49, 1886, pp. 653–74.
Stone, Albert E., ed., *Twentieth Century Interpretations of 'The Ambassadors': A Collection of Critical Essays* (Englewood Cliffs, NJ: Prentice Hall, 1969).
Strachey, Lytton, *Eminent Victorians: Cardinal Manning, Florence Nightingale, Dr Arnold, General Gordon* (London: Chatto and Windus, 1918).
The Strand Magazine: An Illustrated Monthly, 2, 1891.
Strychacz, Thomas, *Modernism, Mass Culture, and Professionalism* (Cambridge: Cambridge University Press, 1993).
Taylor, Linda J., *Henry James, 1866–1916: A Reference Guide* (Boston: G.K. Hall, 1982).
Thomas, Brook, 'The Construction of Privacy In and Around *The Bostonians*', *American Literature*, 64 (4), December 1992, pp. 719–47.
Tocqueville, Alexis de, *Democracy in America*, 2 vols., tr. Henry Reeve (New York: Alfred A. Knopf, 1945).
Todorov, Tzvetan, *The Poetics of Prose*, tr. Richard Howard (Ithaca, NY: Cornell University Press, 1992).
'The Secret of Narrative' in *The Poetics of Prose*, tr. Richard Howard (Ithaca, NY: Cornell University Press, 1992), pp. 143–78.
Tuchman, Gaye with Nina E. Fortin, *Edging Women Out: Victorian Novelists, Publishers, and Social Change* (London: Routledge, 1989).
Veblen, Thorstein, *The Theory of the Leisure Class: An Economic Study of Institutions* (New York: Random House, 1934).
Warner, Michael, *The Letters of the Republic: Publication and the Public Sphere in Eighteenth-Century America* (Cambridge, Mass. and London: Harvard University Press, 1990).
'The Mass Public and the Mass Subject' in *The Phantom Public Sphere*, ed.

Bruce Robbins (Minneapolis and London: University of Minnesota Press, 1993), pp. 234–56.

Warren, Samuel D. and Louis D. Brandeis, 'The Right to Privacy', *Harvard Law Review*, 4 (5), 1890, pp. 193–220.

Weber, Max, *On Charisma and Institutional Building: Selected Papers*, ed. S.N. Eisenstadt (Chicago and London: University of Chicago Press, 1968).

The Protestant Ethic and the Spirit of Capitalism, tr. Talcott Parsons (London and New York: Routledge, 1992).

Wicke, Jennifer, *Advertising Fictions: Literature, Advertisement, and Social Reading* (New York: Columbia University Press, 1988).

Wiener, Joel H., ed., *Papers for the Millions: The New Journalism in Britain, 1850s to 1914* (Westport, Conn.: Greenwood Press, 1988).

Wilde, Oscar, *Plays, Prose Writings and Poems*, ed. Isobel Murray (London: Everyman, 1990).

Two Society Comedies, ed. Ian Small and Russell Jackson (London: Ernest Benn, 1983).

Williams, Raymond, *The Long Revolution* (London: The Hogarth Press, 1992).

Wolfe, Theodore F., *A Literary Pilgrimage among the Haunts of Some Famous British Authors* (Philadelphia: J.B. Lippincott, 1895).

Literary Haunts and Homes: American Authors (Philadelphia: J.B. Lippincott, 1898).

Yates, Edmund, *Edmund Yates: His Recollections and Experiences*, 2 vols. (London: Richard Bentley, 1884).

Yates, Edmund, ed., *Celebrities at Home*, 3 vols. (London: Office of *The World*, 1877–9).

Zola, Emile, *Nana*, tr. George Holden (Harmondsworth: Penguin, 1987).

Index